D0202739

FERGUSON

CAREER COACH

MANAGING YOUR CAREER IN

Law Enforcement

The Ferguson Career Coach Series

FERGUSON

CAREER COACH

MANAGING YOUR CAREER IN

Law Enforcement

Shelly Field

Ferguson
An imprint of Infobase Publishing

Ferguson Career Coach: Managing Your Career in Law Enforcement

Ferguson
An imprint of Infobase Publishing, Inc.
132 West 31st Street
New York NY 10001

Library of Congress Cataloging-in-Publication Data

Field, Shelly.
  Ferguson career coach : managing your career in law enforcement / Shelly Field. — 1st ed.
    p. cm. — (The Ferguson career coach series)
  Includes bibliographical references and index.
  ISBN-13: 978-0-8160-5360-5 (alk. paper)
  ISBN-10: 0-8160-5360-X (alk. paper)
  1. Law enforcement—Vocational guidance—United States. 2. Police—Vocational
guidance—United States. I. Title.
  HV8143.F48 2008
  363.2023'73—dc22   2008018312

Ferguson books are available at special discounts when purchased in bulk quantities for businesses, associations, institutions, or sales promotions. Please call our Special Sales Department in New York at (212) 967-8800 or (800) 322-8755.

You can find Ferguson on the World Wide Web at http://www.fergpubco.com

Text design by Kerry Casey
Cover design by Takeshi Takahashi

Printed in the United States of America

VB Hermitage 10 9 8 7 6 5 4 3 2 1

This book is printed on acid-free paper and contains 30 percent postconsumer recycled content.

Disclaimer: The examples and practices described in this book are based on the author's experience as a professional career coach. No guarantee of success for individuals who follow them is stated or implied. Readers should bear in mind that techniques described might be inappropriate in some professional settings, and that changes in industry trends, practices, and technology may affect the activities discussed here. The author and publisher bear no responsibility for the outcome of any reader's use of the information and advice provided herein.

CONTENTS

1

INTRODUCING YOUR CAREER COACH

The importance of law enforcement in our society is clear. Without it, there would be mayhem and chaos. Do you want a career in this exciting field? Then read on.

Everyone wants to feel that they are safe and secure; that their family is out of harm's way; and that they are protected. Everyone wants to feel that justice is served. Everyone wants to feel that if there is a situation where the law has been broken, someone will catch the bad guys.

Some leave this job to others. Some go after the job themselves.

A career in law enforcement can be exciting, challenging, and fulfilling. A career in law enforcement can help you make a positive impact on an individual, and a community. And most importantly, a career in law enforcement just might be the career you have been dreaming about.

When you think of law enforcement, what professions come to mind? If you're like most people, police officers are generally the first. While police officers are the most prominent profession in the field of law enforcement, the industry encompasses a wide variety of other career options.

Law enforcement is a very diverse field. There are hundreds of job possibilities in a variety of areas. What do you want to do? What is your dream?

Is your dream to be a police officer? Do you want to walk the beat? Do you want to be a detective? What about an investigator? Do you want to be a juvenile officer? How about a state trooper? What about a federal agent? How about a probation officer?

Is it your dream to be a SWAT officer? The chief of police? What about a deputy sheriff? Is it your dream to work with the United States Secret Service...perhaps guarding the president?

Do you want a career as a border patrol agent? How about a special agent with the Drug Enforcement Administration? What about working as a special agent with the Environmental Protection Agency? Is it your dream to work with the FBI? The CIA? What about with Immigration and Customs? Do you want to work with the law enforcement branch of the IRS? What about a career as a Deputy U.S. Marshal?

Do you want a career as a state highway patrol officer? A crime scene investigator? Is it your dream to solve homicides? What about solving sex crimes? How about investigating fraud? Is it your dream instead to have a career in crime prevention?

Are you dreaming of a career as a private investigator? A security manager? What about a career as a private security guard for a movie star or a major recording artist?

Is it your dream to work as a court bailiff? A corrections officer? What about a probation officer? How about an attorney? What about a judge?

Do you want to work as a court reporter? What about a journalist reporting on what has happened in court cases? How about an artist sketching the action in court?

What about a career working with an anti-terrorist team? What about protecting our country? What about teaching new recruits the skills necessary to become a great officer?

One of the wonderful things about a choosing a career in law enforcement is that there are so many varied opportunities. While many choose to work hands-on in various segments of law enforcement, there are also other opportunities in the peripheral areas.

Depending on the area of law enforcement you choose to work, there are opportunities for software engineers, computer science specialists, and information systems specialists. There are also opportunities in the business and administration segments of the industry as well as support services. There are opportunities for accountants, public relations people, marketing specialists, attorneys, paralegals, journalists, educators, and more.

There are so many opportunities that, for some, it is hard to choose. Where will you fit? What will be your contribution? No matter which segment of the industry you choose, a career in law enforcement can be exciting and rewarding. Every day will be different. Every day will be full of new challenges and new experiences. Are you ready?

The dream is yours. You just have to identify exactly what it is.

Do you have a strong desire to help others? Do you want to be a role model? Do you want to make a difference? Do you have a strong belief in the legal system? Do you want to work to make it better?

Do you have great communication skills? Do you have good management skills? Are you a strong leader? Are you good dealing with the public? If so, you've chosen the right field. No matter what segment of law enforcement you choose to work, you will be in the position to make a difference in the lives of others.

Some parts of the industry are easier to enter. Some are more competitive. Can you make it? Can you succeed?

I'm betting you can and if you let me, I want to help you get where you want to be. Whether you've just decided that you want to work in some aspect of law enforcement, it's been your dream for some time, or you already work in the industry and you want to move up the career ladder, this book is for you.

Whether you want a career protecting your community or our nation, this book is for you. Whether you want a career working hands-on in law enforcement, in the business, administration, or support segments of the industry, in the peripherals or anywhere in between, this book can be your guide to success.

I have been where you are. I know what it's like to have a dream. I know what it is like to want to have the career of your dreams so badly you can taste it. I know what it is like to want to experience success.

It doesn't matter if your dream is exactly like my dream or my dream is like yours. It doesn't even really matter exactly what you want to do. What matters is that if you have a dream—whatever it is—know you can find a way to attain it.

While I would love to tell you that working in law enforcement was my dream, it was not. When I was starting my career, I had another dream and I was not about to give it up. Although it wasn't related to law enforcement, I'm going to share it with you for a number of reasons.

Why? To begin with, I want to illustrate to you that dreams can come true. I want to show you how perseverance in your career (or in anything else, for that matter) can help you achieve your dreams and goals. Furthermore, you also might find it interesting to see how sometimes things you do in your career are stepping stones to the career of your dreams.

I've done a lot of things in my life in pursuing *my own* dreams. Some worked out...and some didn't. What I can say, however, is that I never will have to look back at my life and say, "I wish I had done this or that," because when I wanted to try something, I always did. My hope is that you will be able to do the same thing.

Do I work in law enforcement now? While I am involved in many things, part of my career *has* touched the peripherals of law enforcement. Earlier in my career, while working on the road with recording groups and sports personalities, it was often my job to help oversee security issues for my clients. I similarly have been in charge of overseeing the security for a number of traveling museum exhibits.

As a career expert, through seminars, workshops, and classes, I now often teach people how to find, enter, and succeed in their *perfect* career, one of which is law enforcement.

As a stress management specialist, I also have helped those in various aspects of law enforcement learn how to deal with stress, how to

manage stress, and to reduce stress in their work and life. I teach people how to use humor to feel better and how to find ways to laugh.

These segments of my career came after I had done a lot of other things, and lived a lot of dreams. They might not have otherwise occurred. This type of thing might happen to you as well.

It's important to remember that dreams can change, but as long as you keep moving toward your goals, you're on the right road.

With that in mind, here's my story. For as long as I can remember, I wanted to be in the music industry, probably more than anything else in the world. I struggled to get in. Could I find anyone to help? No. Did I know anyone in the business? No. Did I live in one of the music capitals? No. The only thing I had going for me was a burning desire to be in the industry and the knowledge that I wasn't going to quit until it happened.

At the time I was trying to enter the industry, I wished there was a book to give me advice on how to move ahead, to guide me toward my goals, and to give me insider tips. Unfortunately there wasn't. I wished that I had a mentor or a coach or someone who really knew what I should be doing and could tell me what it was. Unfortunately, I didn't have that either.

Did anyone ever help me? It wasn't that no one wanted to help, but most of the people in my network just didn't have a clue about the music industry. Did they know that the music industry was a multibillion-dollar business? Did they know that it offered countless opportunities? It really didn't matter, because no one I knew could give me an edge on getting in anyway.

A couple of times I did run into some music industry professionals who did try to help. In one instance, a few months after I had started job hunting, I finally landed an interview at a large booking agency. I arrived for my appointment and sat waiting for the owner of the agency to meet with me. I sat and sat and sat.

A recording artist who was a client of the agency walked over to me after his meeting with the agent and asked how long I had been there. "Close to three hours," I replied. My appointment was for 1 p.m. and it was almost 4 p.m. "What are you here for?" he asked. "I want to be in the music industry," was my answer. "I want to be a tour manager."

"Someday," he said, "you'll make it and this joker [the agency owner] will want something from you and you can make *him* wait. Mark my words; it will happen." He then stuck his head inside the agency owner's door and said, "This woman has been sitting out here for hours; bring her in already." As I walked into the office, I had a glimmer of hope. It was short lived, but it was hope just the same.

The agency owner was very nice. During our meeting he told me something to the effect of, if he ever needed someone with my skills and talents, he would be glad to give me a call and I should keep plugging away. In other words, thanks for coming in. I talked to you; now please leave. Don't call me; I'll call you.

He then explained in a hushed voice, "Anyway, you know how it is. Most managers don't want *girls* on the road with their acts." Not only was I being rejected because of my skills and talents, but now it was because I was a *girl*. (Because my name is Shelly, evidently many people incorrectly assumed I was male instead of female when their secretaries were setting up appointments. The good news is that this got me into a lot of places I probably wouldn't have had a chance to get into otherwise. The bad news: Once I got there, they realized I was not a man.)

> ### ★ Tip from the Top
>
> During that interview I learned two important lessons. One, use what you have to get your foot in the door. If someone thought I was a man because of my name, well, my idea was not to correct them *until* I got in the door. At least that way I could have a chance at selling myself.
>
> The second lesson is choose your battles wisely. Had I complained about sexual discrimination at that point, I might have won the battle, but I would have lost the war.

I smiled, thanked the agent for meeting with me, and left wondering if I would ever get a job doing what I wanted. Was it sexual discrimination? Probably it was, but in reality the agent was just telling me the way it was at that time. He actually believed he was being nice. Was it worth complaining about? I didn't think so. I was new to the industry and I wasn't about to make waves *before* I even got in. The problem was, I just couldn't find a way to get in.

On another occasion, I met a road manager at a concert and told him about how I wanted to be a tour manager. He told me he knew how hard it was to get into the industry so he was going to help me. "Call me on Monday," he told me Saturday. I did. "I'm working on it," he said. "Call me Wednesday." On Wednesday he said, "Call me Friday." This went on for a couple of weeks before I realized that while he was trying to be nice, he really wasn't going to do anything for me.

I decided that if I were ever lucky enough to break into the music industry, I would help as many people as I possibly could who ever wanted a job doing *anything* to fulfill their dream. I wasn't sure when I'd make it, but I knew I would get there eventually.

While like many others I dreamed about standing on a stage in front of thousands of adoring fans, singing my number-one song, in reality, I knew that was not where my real talent was. I knew, however, that I did have the talent to make it in the business end of the industry.

I did all the traditional things to try to get a job. I sent my resume, I searched out employment agencies that specialized in the music industry, I made cold calls, and I read the classifieds.

And guess what? I still couldn't land a job. Imagine that? A college degree and a burning desire still couldn't get me the job I wanted. I had some offers, but the problem was that they weren't offers to work in the music industry. I had offers for jobs as a social worker, a newspaper reporter, a teacher, and a number of other positions I have since forgotten. Were any of these jobs I wanted? No! I wanted to work in the music business, period. End of story.

Like many of you might experience when you share your dreams, I had people telling me why *my* dreams were a bad idea. I had people tell me that I was pipe dreaming. "The music industry," I was told "is for *the other people.* You know, the *lucky ones.*" I was also told consistently how difficult the music industry was to get into and, once in, how difficult it was to succeed. In essence, I was being told not to get my hopes up.

Want to hear the good news? I eventually did get into the music industry. I had to "think outside of the box" to get there, but the important thing was I found a way to get in. Want to hear some more good news? If I could find a way to break into the industry of my dreams and create a wonderful career, you can find a way to break into the industry of your dreams and create a wonderful career too! As a matter of fact, not only can you get in, but you can succeed.

Coming full circle, remember when I said that if I got into the music business, I would help every single person who ever wanted a job doing anything?

Well, you want to work in some aspect of law enforcement and I want to help you get there. I want to help you succeed. And I want to help you live your dreams.

⭐ Tip from the Coach

As big as the world is, it really is small. Always leave a good impression. Remember what the recording artist at the agency told me? A number of years after I broke into the industry, his words actually did come true. At the time I was working on a project booking the talent for a big music festival overseas, and the booking agent heard about it. He put in a call to me to see if I'd consider using his talent for the show. "Hi, Shelly, it's Dave. It's been a long time," said the voice mail. "I heard you were booking a new show and wanted to talk to you about having some of my acts appear on the show. Give me a call." As soon as I heard his name, the words of that recording artist came flooding back into my mind. This was a true "mark my words" moment.

I was busy, so I couldn't call him right away. He kept calling back. He really wanted his acts on the show. I finally took his call and told him we'd get back to him. He must have called 25 times in a two-day period to see if we'd made up our mind. He finally said, "How long do you expect me to wait?"

I then reminded him of the day I sat in his office and waited and waited for him to see me. He, of course, didn't even remember the moment, but to his credit, he apologized profusely and promised never to have me wait again. I accepted his apology and told him he'd only have to wait… a little bit longer.

> ### ⭐ Tip from the Coach
> In addition to not leaving a bad impression, try not to burn bridges. The bridges you burn today might just be the bridges you need to cross tomorrow.

I am a career expert and have written numerous books on a wide array of career-oriented subjects. I give seminars, presentations, and workshops around the country on entering and succeeding in the career of your dreams. I'm a personal coach and stress management specialist to people in various walks of life, including celebrities, corporate executives, and people just like you who want a great career and a great life. Unfortunately, as much as I wish I could, I can't be there in person for each and every one of you.

So with that in mind, through the pages of this book, I'm going to be your personal coach, your cheerleader, and your inside source to not only finding your dream career but getting in and succeeding as well.

A Personal Coach—What's That?

The actual job title of "personal coach" is relatively new, but coaches are not. Athletes and others in the sports industry have always used coaches to help improve their game and their performance. Over the past few years, coaches have sprung up in many other fields as well.

There are those who coach people toward better fitness or nutrition, vocal coaches to help people improve their voices, acting coaches to help people with acting skills, and etiquette coaches to help people learn how to act in every situation. There are parenting coaches to help people parent better, retirement coaches to help people be successful in retirement, and time management coaches to help people better manage their time.

There are stress management coaches to help people better manage their stress; executive business coaches to help catapult people to the top; life coaches to help people attain a happier, more satisfying life; and career coaches to help people create a great career. Personal coaches often help people become more successful and satisfied in a combination of areas.

"I don't understand," you might be saying. "Exactly what does a coach do and what can he or she do for me?" Well, there are a number of things.

Basically a coach can help you find your way to success faster. He or she can help motivate you, help you find what really makes you happy, get you on track, and help you focus your energies on what you really want to do. Unlike some family members or friends, coaches aren't judgmental. You, therefore, have the ability to freely explore ideas with your coach without fear of them being rejected. Instead of accepting your self-imposed limitations, coaches encourage you to reach your full potential and improve your performance.

Coaches are objective, and one of the important things they can do for you is point out things that you might not see yourself. Most of all, coaches help *you* find the best in you and then shows *you* ways to bring it out. This in turn will make you more successful.

As your coach, what do I hope to do for you? I want to help you find your passion and then help you go after it. If a career in some segment of law enforcement is what you want, I want to help you get in and I want you to be successful.

Is your dream to work in law enforcement in a small community or a large city? Do you want to be a community police officer or break up a big cartel? Do you want a career with the FBI or the Department of Homeland Security? Do you want to be a special agent with the Department of ATF (Alcohol, Tobacco, Firearms, and Explosives) or a police officer with the Capitol police?

Do you want to be the communications director for a large city police department or would you rather be a criminologist? Do you want to work in the field or in a police crime lab?

Do you want to be a corrections officer or a youth officer?

Is it your passion, instead, to work in a less formal setting? Maybe you want to be a body guard for a major movie star. Maybe you want to design security systems for homes or businesses? Do you want to teach people how they can better protect themselves and their homes? If you think outside of the box, the possibilities are endless!

"What if I want to work in another segment of the industry?" you ask. "What if I want to work in the business or administration segment of law enforcement? What if I want to work in support services?

What if I want a career as a lobbyist or a marketing specialist? What if I want to be a beat reporter or a journalist reporting on criminal activity or court cases for a major newspaper? What if I want to be a legal analyst for a television or radio station? What then?"

If you want to be in the business or administrative end of the industry, support services, communications, or any area in between, I'm going to help you find ways to get there. Then we'll work on finding ways to catapult you to the top. If you're already in, we'll work on ways to help you climb the career ladder to your dream position.

Whatever your dream is, we'll work together to find a way to help you get in and achieve your dreams.

Look at me as your personal cheerleader and this book as your guide. I want you to succeed and will do as much as possible to make that happen. No matter what anyone tells you, it is possible not only to get the job of your dreams but to succeed at levels higher than you dare to dream. Thousands of people have done so and now one of them can be you!

Have you ever noticed that some people just seem to attract success? They seem to get all the breaks, are always in the right place at the right time, and have what you want? It's not that you're jealous, but you just want to get a piece of the pie too.

"They're so lucky," you say.

Well, here's the deal. You can be that lucky too. Want to know why? While a little bit of luck is always helpful, it's not just chance. Some people work to attract success. They work to get what they want. They follow a plan, keep a positive attitude, and know that they're worthy of the prize. Others just wait for success to come. The problem is that when all you do is wait, success may just pass you by.

The good news here is that you can be one of the lucky ones who attract success, if you take the right steps. This book will give you some of the keys to control your destiny; it will hand you the keys to success in your career and your life.

Through the pages of this book, you'll find the answers to many of your questions about a career in law enforcement. You'll get the inside scoop on how the industry works, key employment issues, and finding opportunities.

You'll find insider tips, tricks, and techniques that have worked for others who have succeeded in the industry. You'll discover secrets to help get you get in the door and up the ladder of success, as well as the lowdown on things others wish they had known when they were first beginning their quest for success.

If you haven't attended any of my career seminars, my workshops on climbing the career ladder and succeeding in your dream career, my stress management seminars, or any of the other presentations I offer, you will get the benefit of being there. If you have attended one, here is the book you've been asking for!

Change Your Thinking, Change Your Life

Sometimes, the first step in getting what you want is just changing the way you think. Did you know that if you think you don't deserve something, you usually don't get it? Did you know that if you think you aren't good enough, neither will anyone else? Did you know that if you think you deserve something, you have a much better chance of getting it? Or, if you think you are good enough, your confidence will shine through?

When you have confidence in yourself, you start to find ways to get what you want and guess what? You succeed!

And while changing your thinking can change your life, this book is not just about a positive attitude. It's a book of actions you can take.

While a positive attitude is always helpful in order to succeed in whatever part of the industry you're interested in pursuing, you need to take positive actions, too.

If all it took for you to be successful was for me to tell you what you needed to do or even me doing it for you, I would. I love what I do and my career and truly want to help everyone live their dream too.

Here's the reality of the situation. I can only offer advice, suggestions, and tell you what you need to do. You have to do the rest. Talking about what you can do or should do is fine, but without your taking action, it's difficult to get where you want to go.

This is your chance to finally get what you want. You've already taken one positive step toward getting your dream career simply by picking up this book. As you read through the various sections, you'll find other actions to take that will help get you closer to the great career you deserve.

One of the things we'll talk about is creating your own personal action plan. This is a plan that can help you focus on exactly what you want and then show you the actions needed to get what you want.

Your personal action plan is a checklist of sorts. Done correctly, it can be one of the main keys to your career success. It will put you in the driver's seat and give you an edge over others who haven't prepared a plan themselves.

We'll also discuss putting together a number of different kinds of journals to help you be more successful in your career and life. For example, one of the problems many people experience when they're trying to get a new job, move up the career ladder, or accomplish a goal is that they often start feeling like they aren't accomplishing anything. A career journal is a handy tool to help you track exactly what you've done to accomplish your goals. Once that is in place, you know what else needs to be done.

Is This the Right Career for Me?

Unsure about exactly which part of law enforcement you want to become involved in? As you read through this book, you'll get some ideas.

"But what if I'm already working at a job in another industry," you ask? "Is it too late? Am

I stuck there forever? Is it too late to go after a career in law enforcement?"

Here's the deal. It is never too late to change careers, and going after something you're passionate about can drastically improve the quality of your life. While, of course, there are age limitations in various careers in law enforcement, you generally can always find a creative way to live out your dreams.

Thousands of people stay in jobs because it's easier than going after what they want. You don't have to be one of them.

We all know people who are in jobs or careers that they don't love. They get up every day waiting for the workweek to be over. They go through the day waiting for it to be over. They waste their lives waiting and waiting. Is this the life you want to lead? I'm guessing you don't.

You now have the opportunity to get what you want. Are you ready to go after it? I'm hoping you are.

As we've discussed, there are countless opportunities in law enforcement. In addition to the traditional ones most people think of, there is an array of others for you to explore. No matter what your skills or talents, you can almost always find a way to parlay them into some aspect of a career in law enforcement, if you think creatively.

Don't be afraid to put your dreams together.

"Like what?" you ask.

Let's say you want to work in some aspect of law enforcement and you also want to work

---

Words from the Wise

Always carry business or networking cards with your phone number and other contact information. Make it easy for people to find you when an opportunity presents itself.

---

in either the sports or entertainment industry. Perhaps you have been working as a police officer or as the director of security for a retail chain. You might look for your dream job as the director of security for a major recording act. You might create a position as director of security for a champion prizefighter. You might become the personal bodyguard for a movie star.

"Really?" you ask.

Yes! Most major recording groups, sports stars, movie stars, and television personalities utilize the services of either bodyguards or private security. You might have to get creative to find a position like this, but it can be done.

This is just one idea. If you get creative and think outside of the box, you'll be able to find lots of ways to put your dreams together.

A Job versus a Career: What's the Difference?

What do you want in life? Would you rather just have a job or do you want a career? What's the difference? A job is just that. It's something you do to earn a living. It's a means to an end. A career, on the other hand, is a series of related jobs. It's a progressive path of achievement, a long-term journey. A career is something you build using your skills, talents, and passions.

You might have many jobs in your career. You might even follow more than one career path. The question is what do you want?

Tip from the Coach

Don't procrastinate. Every day you wait to get the career you are passionate about is another day you're not living your dream. Start today!

If all you want is to go to work, day after day, week after week just to get paid, a job is all you need, and there is nothing wrong with that. On the other hand, if you would like to fill your life with excitement and passion while getting paid, you are a prime candidate for a great career.

How can you get that? Start planning now to get what you want. Define your goals and then start working toward them.

Not everyone starts off with a dream job. If you just sit and wait for your dream job to come to you, you could be sitting forever. What you can do, however, is take what you have and make it work for you until you get what you want. What does that mean?

It means that you can make whatever you do better, at least for the time being. The trick in this whole process is finding ways to give the job you have some meaning. Find a way to get some passion from what you're doing. If you get that mind-set, you'll never have a bad job. Focus on your ultimate career goal and then look at each job as a benchmark along the way to getting what you want.

How to Use This Book to Help You Succeed in Law Enforcement

Ideally, I would love for you to read this book from beginning to end, but I know from experience that's probably not the way it's going to happen. You might browse the contents and look for something that can help you *now*, you might see a subject that catches your eye, or you might be looking for an area of the book that solves a particular problem or challenge you have.

For this reason, as you read the book, you might see what appears to be some duplication of information. In this manner, I can be assured that when I suggest something that may be helpful to you in a certain area, you will get all the information you need even if you didn't read a prior section.

You might have heard the saying that knowledge is power. This is true. The more you know about the law enforcement industry and how it works, the better your chances are of succeeding. This book is full of information to help you learn everything you need to know about the industry and how it works. I'm betting that you will refer back to information in this book long after you've attained success.

As you read through the various sections, you'll find a variety of suggestions and ideas to help you succeed. Keep in mind that every idea and suggestion might not work in every situation and for every person. The idea is to keep trying things until one of them works. Use the book as a springboard to get you started. Just because something is not written here doesn't mean that it's not a good idea. Brainstorm to find solutions to barriers you might encounter in your career, even if you have to brainstorm with yourself.

My job is to lead you on your journey to success in the law enforcement industry. Along the way you'll find exercises, tasks, and assignments that will help get you where you want to be faster. No one is going to be standing over your shoulder to make you do these tasks. You alone can make the decision on the amount of time and work you want to put into your career. While no one can guarantee you success, what you should know is that the more you put into your career, the better your chances of having the success you probably are dreaming about.

Are you worth the time and effort? I think you are! Is a career in law enforcement worth it? I believe it is! If you have the passion and desire to work in this industry, it can be one of the best fields in the world in which to work. Aside from the opportunity to make a living and fulfill your dreams, you have the opportunity to impact the lives of others.

No matter what level you're currently at in your career and whatever capacity, this book is for you. You might not need every section or every page, but I can guarantee that there are parts of this book that can help you.

Whether you're just starting to think about a career in law enforcement or have been in the industry for a while; whether you're going through college or police training; whether you're a rookie or an up-and-coming chief of police; whether you're in the business segment of the industry, support services, or a peripheral area; this book can help you experience more success in your career and help you have a happier, more satisfying, stress-free life.

A Sampling of What This Book Covers

This informative guide to success in law enforcement is written in a friendly, easy-to-read style. Let it be your everyday guide to success. Want to know how a specific segment of the law enforcement industry works? Want to learn how to focus on what you really want to do? Check out the book!

Want to learn how to plan and prepare for your dream career? Do you want to focus in on job search strategies geared especially for the law enforcement industry? How about tips for making those important industry contacts? Need some ideas on how to network? How about ways to create the ideal resume or cover letter specifically geared toward law enforcement? Check out the book!

Do you need to know how to develop your action plan? Do you want to get your portfolio together? Want to know what business or networking cards can do for you and your career? Check out the book!

Want to learn how to get your foot in the door? How about checking out tried-and-true methods to get people to call you back? Do you want to learn the best way to market yourself and why it's so important? Do you want to learn how to succeed n the workplace, deal with workplace politics, keep an eye out for opportunities, and climb the career ladder? You know what you have to do: Check out the book!

Do you want to know a bit about the application process? What about exams you might have to take? Want to know how to make yourself stand out in a positive way at an interview? Check out the book!

Want to know how to succeed in your chosen field? How to move up the ladder? You got it. You need to read this book.

Do you need important contact information so you can move your career forward? Check out the listings of important organization, unions, and associations. Want some Web sites to get you started looking for a great career? Check out the book's appendix.

While this book won't teach you how to catch a criminal, make an arrest, or run a police department, it will help you to find ways to garner success wherever your passion lies.

Anyone can apply for a job and hope they get it. Many people do just that. But I'm guessing that you do not just want a job. You want a career you can be passionate about. You want a career you love. You want a career that gives you joy! Take charge of your career now and you can have all that and more.

If your dream is not only working in law enforcement but having a successful career, this book can help turn your dream into a reality. Have fun reading it. Know that if your heart is in it, you can achieve anything.

Now let's get started.

2

FOCUSING ON A GREAT CAREER IN LAW ENFORCEMENT

Focusing on What You Really Want to Do

Unless you're independently wealthy or just won the mega million dollar lottery, you, like most people, have to work. Just in case you're wondering, life is not supposed to be miserable. Neither is your job.

Life is supposed to have a purpose. That purpose is not sleeping, getting up, going to a job that you don't particularly care about, coming home, making dinner, and watching TV, only to do it all over again the next day.

In order to be happy and fulfilled, you need to enjoy life. You need to do things that give you pleasure. As a good part of your life is spent working, the trick then is to find a career that you love and that you're passionate about—the career of your dreams.

This is not something everyone does. Many people just fall into a career without thinking about what it will entail ahead of time. Some-one may need a job, hear of an opening, answer an ad, and then go for it without thinking about the consequences of working at something for which they really have no passion. Once hired,

it's either difficult to give up the money, just too hard to start job hunting again, or they don't know what else to do, so they stay. They wind up with a career that is okay but one they're not really passionate about.

Then there are the other people. The ones who have jobs they love, the lucky people. You've seen them. They're the people who have the jobs and life you wish you had.

Have you noticed that the people who love their jobs are usually successful not only in their career but in other aspects of their life too? They almost seem to have an aura around them of success, happiness, and prosperity. Do you want to be one of them? Well you can!

Finding a career that you want and love is challenging but it is possible. You are in a better

---

⭐ **Tip from the Coach**

Okay is just that: It's okay. Just so you know, you don't *want* just okay; you don't *want* to settle; you want *great*! That's what you deserve and that's what you should go after.

---

position than most people. If you're reading this book, you've probably at least have zeroed in on a career path. You likely decided that you are passionate about some segment of law enforcement. Now all you have to do is determine exactly what you want to do within the industry.

What's *your* dream career? What do you *really* want to do? This is an important question you need to ask yourself? Once you know the answer, you can work toward achieving your goal.

If someone asked you right now what you really wanted to do, could you answer the question? Okay, one, two, three: "What do you want to do with your life?"

If you're saying, "Uh, um, well . . . What I really want to do is . . . well it's hard to explain," then it's time to focus in on the subject. Sometimes the easiest way to figure out what you want to do is to focus in on what you don't want.

Most people can easily answer what they don't want to do. "I don't want to be a doctor. I don't want to be a nurse. I don't want to work in a factory. I don't want to work in a store. I don't want to sell. I don't want to be a teacher. I don't want to work with numbers. I don't want to work in a job where I have to travel." And the list goes on. The problem is that just saying what you don't like or don't want to do doesn't necessarily get you what you want to do. You can, however, use this information to your advantage.

It may seem simple, but sometimes just looking at a list of what you don't like will help you see more clearly what you do like.

Sit down with a sheet of paper or fill in the "Things I Dislike Doing/Things I Don't Want to Do" worksheet and make a list of work-related things you don't like to do. Remember that this list is really just for you. While you can show it to someone if you want, no one else really has to see it, so try to be honest with yourself.

Here's an example to get your started. When you make your list, add things *you* don't like or you don't want to do.

- I hate the idea of being cooped up in an office all day.
- I don't want to do anything too dangerous.
- I don't want to be bored in my job.
- I don't want to do the same thing every day.
- I hate the idea of having to work with numbers.
- I don't want to work in a big city.
- I don't want to have to do a lot of reports.
- I don't want to have to go to work early in the morning.
- I don't want to have to work evenings.
- I don't want to have to travel for my job.
- I don't want a job where I have to work on a computer a lot of the time.
- I don't want to have to speak in front of large groups of people.
- I don't want to work in a large city police department.
- I don't want to have to commute for an hour each way every day.
- I don't want to work in sales.
- I don't like doing the same thing day after day.
- I don't like being in charge.
- I don't like taking risks.
- I don't like working under constant pressure.
- I don't like being under constant deadlines.

◎ I don't like not having challenges.

◎ I don't like having a boss working right on top of me.

◎ I don't like someone telling me what to do every minute of the day.

◎ I don't like working where I don't make a difference.

◎ I don't like working for someone.

◎ I don't like working where I'm not appreciated.

◎ I don't like working in situations where I don't interact with a lot of people.

◎ I don't like working in stressful situations.

Things I Dislike Doing/Things I Don't Want to Do

_____

_____

_____

_____

_____

_____

_____

_____

_____

_____

_____

We now know what you don't like. Use this list as a beginning to see what you do like. If you look closely, you'll find that many of the things you enjoy are the opposite of the things you don't want to do.

Here are some examples to get you started. You might make another list, as well as using the "Things I Enjoy Doing/Things I Want to Do" worksheet. Remember that the reason you're writing everything down is so you can look at it, remember it, and focus in on getting exactly what you want.

◎ I hate the idea of being cooped up in an office all day.
  ▫ But I really would love to move around as part of my job. I think I would love being in a patrol car or walking the beat and seeing different people every day.
◎ I don't want to do anything too physically dangerous.
  ▫ But I want to work in law enforcement in some manner. I love working with computers and I'm good at it. I think I would like working in computer security.
◎ I don't want to be bored in my job.
  ▫ I want to be challenged. I want to do something new every day.
◎ I don't want to do the same thing every day.
  ▫ That is why I am really excited about training to be a police officer.
◎ I don't want to work in a big city.
  ▫ I want to work in a local or regional police or sheriff's department.
◎ I don't want to have to go to work early in the morning.
  ▫ From what I've heard, many police departments have rotating shifts.

Even if I work early in the morning for a while, I know I'll eventually be working day and evening shifts.
◎ I don't want to have to commute for an hour each way every day.
  ▫ I noticed that a lot of the jobs in police departments require you to live right in the community. If I can't find a job close to where I live, I'm going to consider moving.
◎ I don't like being in charge.
  ▫ As a police officer, I will be in charge a lot of the time. Perhaps this isn't the job for me.
◎ I don't like working under constant pressure.
  ▫ But I realize that we all make a lot of our own pressure. I think I'm going to take a class or seminar on dealing with stress and pressure.
◎ I don't like not having challenges.
  ▫ I've heard that every day in police work you have new challenges. I can't wait to go through training and get a job.
◎ I don't like someone telling me what to do every minute of the day.
  ▫ Perhaps instead of looking for a job, I would be better off becoming a consultant or having my own business of some sort. I know you still have clients telling you what to do, but I think I would be happier. I'm going to have to look into some possibilities.
◎ I don't like working where I don't make a difference.
  ▫ I really want to make a difference. And I really want to make a difference working in law enforcement. My dream job will be working in a large

city police department as a detective in the special victims unit. I know I *will* be making a difference.

◎ I hate the idea of having to work with numbers.

  ▫ But I really like working with people. As a police officer I don't have to work with numbers on a constant basis.

◎ I don't want to have to do a lot of reports. The thought of it bothers me.

  ▫ I don't want to do reports because I'm not confident in my writing skills. Perhaps if I take some writing classes I'll begin to feel more confident.

◎ I don't want to work in a large city police department.

  ▫ But I would really like working in a smaller community police department. I want to get to know the people in the community.

◎ I don't like working with adult alcoholics and drug addicts who should know better.

  ▫ But I really want to be a youth officer.

As you can see, once you've determined what you don't like doing, it's much easier to get ideas on what you'd like to do. It's kind of like brainstorming with yourself.

You probably know some people who don't like their job. There are tons of people in this world who don't like what they do or are dissatisfied with their career. Here's the good news. You don't have to be one of them.

⭐ The Inside Scoop

A number of years ago I hired a number of off-duty police officers to do some private security work for a client of mine. During this time, I got to know an officer who often told me how much he loved his work. The officer worked for a rural police department. One day when he came into work, he heard that an agency was looking for volunteers to work undercover to break up a major drug cartel. The young man jumped at the chance and after some additional training was on his way to his new undercover assignment. He loved his new job and ended up part of a team that eventually successfully broke up the cartel, resulting in a number of very important arrests. Unfortunately, somewhere down the line, his cover was blown and he went back to his job at the rural police department. Somewhere during this time he experienced a bad back injury on the job. In a lot of pain, the man went on medical leave. The doctors told him he would never be able to do police work again and urged him to retire, but the man didn't want to. He loved his job. He offered to sign an affidavit stating that if he further injured himself while on the job, he would not take action against the police department, but they refused. They instead suggested that he retire and asked him if he wanted to be retrained in another area.

He told me that he really wanted to go back to work because he loved what he did. He loved making a difference and he loved being a police officer. He also guaranteed me that he *would* find a way to get back to work.

He continued to do rehab and despite doctors telling him his back would never be better, he experienced enough improvement to do what he had promised. He was able to go back to the work he loved. The man continued to work, retiring when he had twenty years of service under his belt.

He then went back to school and became a school guidance counselor, helping young people find careers they will love.

Things I Enjoy Doing/Things I Want to Do

_____

_____

_____

_____

_____

_____

_____

_____

_____

_____

_____

_____

_____

_____

_____

You and you alone are in charge of your career. Not your mother, father, sister, brother, girlfriend, boyfriend, spouse, or best friend. Others can care, others can help, and others can offer you advice, but in essence, you need to be in control. What this means is that the path you take for your career is largely determined by the choices you make.

The fastest way to get the career you want is by making the choice to take action now and go after it! You *can* have a career you love and you *can* have it in the area of law enforcement you want. And when you're doing something that you love, you'll be on the road not only to a great career but a satisfied and fulfilled life.

The next section will discuss how to develop your career plan. This plan will be your road map to success. It will be full of actions you can take not only to get the career in law enforcement you want but to succeed in it as well. Before you get too involved in the plan, however, you need to zero in on exactly what you want your career to be.

At this point you might be in a number of different employment situations. You might still be in school planning your career, just out of school beginning your career, or in a job that you don't really care for. You might just have come out of a stint in the military or you might even already be in a career in law en-

---

Tip from the Coach

Try to associate with positive people who like what they do. Otherwise, the negativity of others may begin to rub off on you.

Tip from the Coach

If you give up your dream because you think it's too late to start, the success you are wishing for might never come your way.

---

forcement and want to move up the career ladder or change directions within the industry.

Perhaps you always wanted to work in some segment of law enforcement or maybe you've done some research on various career areas and decided law enforcement is for you. With so many options to choose from, do you know what your dream career is?

There are hundreds of exciting career choices in law enforcement and the peripheral areas no matter where your passion lies. So let's take some time to focus in for a bit on exactly what you want to do.

What's Your Dream?

I'm betting that you already have an idea of what your dream job is and I'm sure that you have an idea of what it should be like. I'm also betting that you don't have that job yet or, if you do, you're not at the level you want to be. So what can we do to make that dream a reality?

One of the challenges many people often have in getting their dream job is that they just don't think they deserve it. They feel that dream jobs are something many people talk about and wish they had but just don't. Many people think that dream jobs are for the lucky ones.

Well, I'm here to tell you that you are the lucky one. You *can* get your dream job, a job you'll love, and it can be in law enforcement.

If I had a magic wand and could get you any job you wanted, what would it be? Would it be a police officer? What about a state trooper or highway patrol officer? How about a sheriff or deputy? Would you be a detective or investigator?

How about an agent with the FBI or CIA? Would you have a career in the law enforcement area of the Forest Service? What about the Department of Defense? How about the PFPA (Pentagon Force Protection Agency)?

Is your dream to work in the Department of Homeland Security? How about the law enforcement area of the National Park Service? Is it your dream instead to work in the National Institutes of Health Police Branch? What about the ATF (Alcohol, Tobacco, Firearms, and Explosives)? How about the DEA (Drug Enforcement Agency)? Do you want to work with the fire police?

Do you want a career with the U.S. Marshal Service? What about a career as an animal control officer or supervisor? Do you want to work with the state gaming board? What about a career as a gaming surveillance officer? How about as a gaming investigator?

Is it your dream to be a forensic scientist? What about a sketch artist? How about a coroner or medical examiner? Do you think you would like to be a polygraph examiner?

Do you want a career as a private investigator? What about a probation officer or parole officer? Is it your dream to be a prosecutor or defense attorney? Do you want to be an investigator with a law enforcement agency? How about an attorney or paralegal? What about a judge or bailiff?

Do you want a career as a corrections officer? What about a warden? Is it your dream

> ### Tip from the Coach
> What are your dreams? Are you ready to turn them into reality? You increase your chances of success if you have a deep belief in yourself, your vision, and your ideas.

instead to be a journalist? What about a courtroom sketch artist?

Do you want to work in the business segment of the industry? How about one of the administrative areas? Do you want to work in technology? How about consulting or sales?

Is it your dream to work in communications? Security, surveillance, or another area of law enforcement? Your dream job can be a reality, if you prepare.

Not sure what you want to do? Then read on!

Determining what you really want to do is not always easy. Take some time to think about it. Throughout this process, try to be as honest with yourself as possible. Otherwise you stand the chance of not going after the career you really want.

Let's get started with another writing exercise. While you might think these are a pain now, if you follow through, you will find it easier to attain your dream.

Get a pad of paper and a pen and find a place where you can get comfortable. Maybe it's your living room chair. Perhaps it's your couch or even your bed. Now all you have to do is sit down and daydream for a bit about what you wish you could be and what you wish you were doing.

"Why daydream?" you ask.

When you daydream, your thinking becomes freer. You stop thinking about what you *can't* do and start thinking about what you *can* do. What is your dream? What is your passion? What do you really want to do? Admit it now or forever hold your peace!

Many people are embarrassed to admit when they want something because if they don't get it they fear looking stupid. They worry that people are going to talk badly about them or call them a failure. Is this what you worry about?

Do you really want to be a police officer but you're afraid you'll fail? Is your dream to be a detective, but you're not sure you'll make it? Do you want a career with the FBI but aren't sure anyone else will think you're good enough to get in? Do you want your own call-in radio show focusing on some aspect of law enforcement but you're worried everyone will think it's a stupid idea?

First of all, don't ever let fear of failure stop you from going after something you want. While no one can guarantee you success, what I can guarantee you is that if you don't go after what you want, it is going to be very difficult to get it.

One thing you never want to do is get to the end of your life and say with regret, "I wish I had done this or I wish I had done that." Will you get each and every thing you want? While I would like to give you a definitive "Yes," that probably wouldn't be true.

The truth of the matter is that you might not succeed at everything. But, and this is a major

---

Tip from the Coach

If there is something that you want to do or something that you want to try in your career or your life, my advice is go for it. No matter what the risk, no matter how scared you are, no matter what. Your life and career will benefit more than you can imagine, and you'll never look back with regrets. Even if it doesn't work out, you'll feel successful because you tried.

---

but, even if you fail, when you try to do something, it usually is a stepping-stone to something else. And that something else can be the turning point in your career.

"How so?" you ask. "What do you mean?"

There are often things that you do in your life and your career that, while at the time, you can't see the importance, end up impacting your career in a positive way.

At one point in my life, I wanted to become a comedienne and do stand-up comedy. The reason I bring it up here is to illustrate the point that while I certainly didn't turn into a mega star stand-up comedienne, performing comedy was a major stepping-stone for me to do other things I wanted to accomplish in my career. Had I not done stand-up, I probably would never have ended up teaching stress management, becoming a motivational speaker, doing corporate training, or even coming up with ideas about doing something in those areas.

Had I been too scared to try it or not wanted to take the risk for fear I would fail, I would have missed out on important opportunities that helped shape my career. I also would have always looked back and said, "I wish I had."

And while your dreams are probably totally different from mine, what you need to take

---

Words from the Wise

The only thing we have to fear is fear itself.

–Franklin Delano Roosevelt

from the story is the concept that taking risks and pursuing your dreams can lead to wonderful things.

Let's get started. Think about things that make you happy. Think about things that make you smile. Continue to indulge your passions as you daydream. As ideas come to you, jot them down on your pad. Remember, nothing is foolish, so write down all the ideas you have for what you want to do. You're going to fine-tune them later.

Here's an example to get you started.

◎ I want to be a detective. As a matter of fact, I want to be a detective for a major city police department. I want to specialize in homicides and solve every one.

◎ I want to be a police officer. It's my dream to be a youth officer. I can make a real difference in that type of job.

◎ I want to be the chief of police for a large metropolitan police department.

◎ I want to be a bounty hunter.

◎ I want to be a sought-out private investigator with a large roster of clients.

◎ I want to be a state trooper. I want to work in my home state of New York. As a matter of fact, I want to become a captain of my troop.

◎ I want to be a warden of a large prison and help find ways to decrease the recidivism of inmates. I want to develop a pilot program that works.

◎ I want a career in the Secret Service. I really want to protect the president and his family.

◎ I want to become a SWAT officer.

◎ I want to be a hostage negotiator.

> ### ⭐ The Inside Scoop
> When you write down your ideas, you are giving them power. Once they are written down on paper, it makes it easier to go over them, look at them rationally, and fine-tune them.

◎ I want to protect our country. I want to be a border patrol officer. As a matter of fact, I want to be a border patrol supervisor.

◎ I want to coordinate in-service programs for law enforcement agencies.

◎ I want to develop security systems for computer information systems.

◎ I want to be a judge.

◎ I want to be a sought-out forensic scientist.

◎ I want to be a community relations director for a large police department.

◎ I want to be the director of security for a major touring recording act.

◎ I want to be the personal body guard for major television and movies stars.

◎ I want to be director of surveillance for a large casino.

◎ I want to be director of security for a large casino.

◎ I want to teach recruits how to be the best officers possible.

Do you need some help focusing on what you really want to do in law enforcement? In order to choose just the right career, you should pinpoint your interests and what you really love doing. What are your skills? What are your personality traits? What are your interests? Fill in the following worksheet to help you zero in even more.

Focusing on the Job of Your Dreams

Finish the following sentences to help you pinpoint your interests and find the job of your dreams.

In my free time I enjoy

_____

In my free time I enjoy going

_____

My hobbies are

_____

Activities I enjoy include

_____

When I volunteer the types of projects I enjoy most are

_____

When I was younger I always dreamed of being a

_____

My skills are

_____

My talents are

_____

My passions are

_____

My best personality traits include

_____

I am great at

_____

My current job is

_____

Prior types of jobs have been

_____

The subjects I liked best in school were

_____

If I didn't have to worry about any obstacles, the three jobs I would want would be

_____

What do I love about each of these three jobs?

_____

_____

_____

What steps can I take to get each of those jobs?

_____

_____

_____

What Is Stopping You from Getting What You Want?

Now that you have some ideas written down about what you want to do, go down the list. What has stopped you from attaining your goal?

Is it that you told people what you wanted to do and they told you that you couldn't do it? Did they tell you it was too difficult and your chances of making it were slim?

Is it that people told you it was too dangerous to become involved in law enforcement and perhaps you should find a safer occupation?

Is it that you don't have the confidence in yourself to get what you want? Or is it that you need more education or training?

Is it that you are concerned that you won't do well in the testing process? Or is it that you aren't in the best physical shape of your life right now?

Perhaps it's because you aren't in the geographic location most conducive to your dream career. Or you need to be fluent in a foreign language and you're not. If you can identify the obstacle, you usually can find a way to overcome it, but you need to identify the problem first.

Do you know exactly what you want to do but can't find an opening? Have you, for example,

---

⭐ **Tip from the Coach**

Start training yourself to practice finding ways to turn *can'ts* in your life into *cans*.

taken the civil service exam for police officers and done well, but there aren't any current openings? Are there current openings in the police department, but you had your heart set on a career with the state police?

Sometimes while you know what type of job you want, you just can't find a job like that which is available. Don't give up. Keep looking. Remember, you may have to think outside of the box to get what you want, but if you're creative, you can succeed. Try to find ways to get your foot in the door and then once it is in, don't let it out until you get what you want.

Have you taken the test for a promotion, but didn't do as well as you hoped? The good news is, you can take it again. Don't let one disappointment stop you from going after your dreams. Keep plugging away and you will get what you want.

Tip from the Top

If you are having trouble with the testing process, look for a seminar that can help you improve your scores or go to the bookstore and pick up one or more examination preparation books. These are helpful whether you are just beginning your career or working toward a promotion.

Have you found the perfect job and interviewed for it, but then the job wasn't offered to you? While at the time you probably felt awful about this, there is some good news. Generally, when one door closes, another one opens.

Hard to believe? It may be, but if you think about it, you'll see it's true. Things generally work out for the best. If you lost what you

The Inside Scoop

A man called one day to ask for some advice. At the time he was working as a police officer and loved it. The problem was that he had been hired with money the municipality had been awarded from a grant, and the grant money had dried up. He had looked for another job and hadn't yet found one.

"What do you think you want to do?" I asked. "Do you have any prospects?"

"I don't know," he replied. "I just can't find a job. I'm driving to Vegas for a couple days to clear my head," he continued. "I love it there."

"I bet you can find a job in one of the casinos," I told him. "Why don't you stop by their human resources department and see what they have available in security or surveillance. Do you think you would like that?"

"I never even thought of that," he said. "But, it's really not like being a cop."

"No one is telling you that you have to take the job," I said. "You're just checking out possibilities."

The man did look into jobs at a couple of casinos in Las Vegas. While he was offered a job in security, he didn't take it. A couple months after that, however, he did hear about an opening that intrigued him in the surveillance department. He interviewed, got the job, and took it. He quickly moved up to a supervisory position.

The next time I heard form him, he told me how lucky he was that the grant money had dried up from his original job. "I loved working as a community police officer," he said, "but I really love my new job too. Had that not happened, I wouldn't have been prepared for doing this and I probably wouldn't have even looked for something else."

thought was the job of your dreams, a better one is out there waiting for you. You just have to find it!

Perhaps you're just missing the skills necessary for the type of job you're seeking. This is a relatively easy thing to fix. Once you know the skills that are necessary for a specific job, if you don't have them, take steps to get them. Take classes, go to workshops, attend seminars, or become an apprentice or intern.

"But I'm missing the education necessary for the job I want," you say. "The ad I read said I needed a minimum of a bachelor's degree. What can I do?"

Here's the deal. In certain cases, educational requirements may be negotiable. Just because an ad states that a job has a specific educational requirement doesn't mean you should just pass it by if your education doesn't meet the requirement. First of all, advertisements for jobs generally contain the highest hopes of the people placing the ads, not necessarily the reality of what they will settle for. Secondly, some organizations will accept experience in lieu of education. Lastly, if you're a good candidate in other respects, many organizations will hire you while you're finishing the required education.

Is a lack of experience what's stopping you from your dream career? If you are going through police training, you will receive supervised experience in patrol, traffic control, use of firearms, self-defense, first aid, and emergency response. Some individuals who are interested in a career in law enforcement also get experience while in the military.

Take every opportunity that presents itself to get the experience you need. Depending on what you want to do and where you live, you might also need to get creative, but you can definitely find a way to do it. Volunteer when you can to get any additional experience under your belt.

The Inside Scoop

If you have graduated high school but have not reached the minimum age requirement necessary to become a police officer, you might look into a program offered in some of the larger police departments in the country. In this program, the police department hires individuals to work as police cadets or trainees. During this time period, which generally lasts from one to two years, individuals perform clerical work and attend classes. When they reach the minimum age requirement, they are appointed to the regular police force.

Depending on what you want to do and where you live, you might need to get creative, but you can definitely find a way to do it.

Is one of the obstacles you're facing that you just aren't in the geographic location of the opportunities you're looking for? Do you, for example, want to work in a large, metropolitan police department, yet you don't live anywhere near a large city?

There's no question that living in an area that doesn't have the opportunities you're looking for makes your job search more difficult. If this obstacle is holding you back, put some time into developing a solution and find a way to move forward. If you're not prepared to move and don't want to give up your career dreams, you might want to start your career working in a smaller police department, closer to where you live. After a year or two, perhaps you might be ready to move on.

Is what's holding you back that you don't have any contacts? Here's the deal. You have to find ways to make contacts. If you are just starting your career, make sure when you are going to school or going through training that you get to know people, both your instructors and your classmates. If you're further along in your career, don't stop your education. Continue taking classes, seminars, and workshops in subject areas related to the segment of law enforcement in which you're interested.

As I just mentioned, volunteer when you can. Even if you aren't directly volunteering in the area in which you want a career, it doesn't matter. You will begin to make contacts. You'll get known in the community and people will begin to know who you are.

Make cold calls. Network, network, and network some more. Put yourself in situations where you can meet people in various aspects of law enforcement and sooner or later you will meet them.

Is your physical fitness level what is holding you back? If you are pursuing a career working hands-on in law enforcement, you need to be in good physical shape. If you are not currently in good shape, don't despair. Start today. Find ways to eat better and exercise until you are in good shape. Join a gym; find a trainer. Don't give up. This is an obstacle you can overcome.

What else is standing between you and success? "The only thing between me and success," you say "is a big break." Getting your big break may take time. Keep plugging away. Most of all, don't give up. Your break will come when you least expect it.

Are you just frightened about going after what you want? Are you not sure you have the talent or the skills. Are you not sure you can make it? If you start doubting yourself, other people might do the same. As we just discussed, do not let fear stop you from doing what you want.

Most importantly, don't let anyone chip away at your dream and whatever you do, don't let anyone burst your bubble. What does that mean?

> ⭐ **Tip from the Coach**
> While you're working on your daydreaming exercise, don't get caught up in thinking that any of your ideas are foolish or stupid. Let your imagination run freely. If these negative ideas come into your head, consciously push them way.

You know how it is when you get excited about doing something and you're so excited that you just can't keep it to yourself. You might share your ideas of what you want to do with your family and friends. And while you want them to be excited too, they start trying to destroy your dream by pointing out all the possible problems you might encounter.

It's not that they're trying *not* to be supportive, but for some people it seems to be their nature to try to shoot other people's dreams down.

Why? There are a number of reasons. Let's look at a few scenarios.

Scenario 1—Sometimes people are just negative. "You don't want to get involved in law enforcement," they might say to you. "It's not like it was years ago. It's dangerous. It's a horrible career choice. Trust me; you don't want to get involved."

"Well," you tell them. "I do. I think being a law enforcement officer can be very rewarding. I want to help people in the community feel safer and be safer. I want a job where I can make a difference. I'm excited."

Their response?

"You could get shot—or killed. You have to deal with all kinds of nuts. You'll hate it. Find some other way to make a difference."

Scenario 2—Sometimes people are jealous. They might hate their job and be jealous that you are working toward finding a great career. They might have similar dreams to yours and be jealous that you have a plan and they don't. Some might just be jealous that you might make it before them.

Scenario 3—Sometimes people are just scared of change. In many cases friends and family are concerned about your well-being and are just scared of change. "You have a job," your girlfriend may say. "Why do you want to change careers? Why don't you think about it for a while?"

Scenario 4—Sometimes people just think you're pipe dreaming. "You're a pipe dreamer," your family may say. "What you need is a dose of reality. You are never going to be able to make it through police training and pass the exams you have to take. The odds are not good for you to succeed. Give up before you fail."

Scenario 5—Sometimes people really think that it's not realistic to think you can make a living doing something you love. "Nobody likes their job," a family member may tell you. "Work is just something you have to do. Find an easier job. Work your 40 hours a week and suffer like the rest of us."

Whatever the scenario, there you sit, starting to question yourself. Well, stop! Do not let anyone burst your bubble. No matter what anyone says, at least *you* are trying to get the career you want. At least *you* are following your dream.

While I can't promise you that you will definitely achieve every one of your dreams, I can promise you that if you don't go after your dream, it will be very difficult to achieve.

What I want you to do is not listen to anyone who is negative about your dreams. Just tune them out and keep working toward what you want. No one can stop you from doing what you want, except you!

> ⭐ **Tip from the Coach**
> Almost everything you can wish for in life, including your career, starts with a dream. Go after yours!

What Gives You Joy? What Makes You Happy?

Let's zero in further on what you want to do. Let's talk about what gives you joy. Let's talk about what makes you happy. Did you ever notice that when you're doing something that you love, you smile? It's probably subconscious, but you're smiling. You're happy inside. And it's not only that you're happy; you make others around you happy.

Let's think about it for a few minutes. What makes you happy? What gives you joy? Is it helping others? Is it teaching others? Is it writing? Is it helping to know that the streets are safer? Is it organizing things? Is it developing things? Is it developing a solution to a problem? Is it a combination?

Does the thought of reuniting a young child with her parents make you smile? What about stopping a robbery in progress? When you close your eyes, can you see yourself successfully solving a homicide?

Can you almost hear yourself giving a perpetrator his or her Miranda rights? Are you smiling as you think about seeing the words *chief of police* and your name on a sign outside of your new office? Can you almost see the article in the paper calling you a hero when, without thinking, you saved a woman's life?

Are you smiling as you think about riding down the highway in your state police car? Can you almost imagine your heart beating as you convince a gunman to put down his weapon? Then maybe that's your dream—that is what would make you happy.

Can you see yourself as a corrections officer in a prison? Can you see yourself doing something different every day? Can you see yourself working hands-on with inmates? What about doing intake when new inmates come in? Is it important to you that convicted criminals who are incarcerated still are treated in a humane manner? Then maybe a career in corrections is for you.

Can you imagine yourself working with inmates in a capacity outside of being a corrections officer? Can you see yourself, for example, working with programs involving inmates in vocational or technical training? Do you want to find ways to cut the rate of recidivism?

Are you smiling as you think about handling the security for a large concert? Can you feel your heart beating as you imagine yourself quickly stepping in front of the president of the United States when you saw he was in danger?

Can you hear yourself speaking to the media about an event that transpired in the police department? When you see a police spokesperson giving a press conference, do you wish it were you behind the microphone?

Can you see yourself driving down the highway in a high-speed chase in an attempt to catch someone who had just kidnapped a child? Can you feel your heart beating? Can you imagine how you'll feel when the chase ends successfully?

Are you smiling as you think about all the wonderful possibilities that might unfold in your career in law enforcement? Then you have chosen the right field.

Keep dreaming. Keep asking yourself what makes you happy. What gives you joy? Are you having a hard time figuring it out? Many of us do. Here's an idea to help get your juices flowing.

Take out your pad and a pen again. Make a list of any jobs or volunteer activities you've done, things you do in your "off time," and hobbies. If you're still in school, you might add extracurricular activities in which you've participated.

Note what aspects of each you like and what you didn't like. This will help you see what type of job you're going to enjoy.

What are your special talents, skills, and personality traits? What gives you joy and makes you happy?

Do you truly enjoy helping others? Are you the one who always protected the underdog in school? Are you a leader? Do you have good communications skills? A career working hands-on in law enforcement in some capacity might be just turn into your dream career.

Is your special talent negotiating? Have you always been good at motivating others? Are you inspiring? Do people feel comfortable talking to you? Perhaps a career in hostage negotiation might be for you.

Are you artistic? Is your special talent sketching? Can you see yourself sitting in a courtroom, sketching the people sitting on the witness stand? What about the judge? Can you imagine bring-

---

⭐ Tip from the Coach

Whether I'm giving a radio interview, a seminar, or consulting with someone on career-oriented subjects, people always want to know what the hottest careers are and the best careers to pursue? The answer is that the hottest careers are those where you use your talents and skills with passion.

ing the action of the courtroom to life through your pictures? Then perhaps a career as a courtroom sketch artist might be for you.

Are you artistic but want another career possibility in law enforcement? Do you have great communications skills? Can you transfer a witness's explanation of what someone looked like and sketch it on paper? Then a career as a police sketch artist might be for you.

Are your talents and passions in computers and information technology? Do you wish you could weave those talents together with a career in law enforcement? There are tons of possibilities from which you can choose. Do you want to keep information that people or companies put into a computer safe and secure? A career in some facet of computer security might be for you. What about using your computer knowledge to seek out child predators before they can get close to a child? How rewarding would that be? What about a career using computer technology to seek out terrorist cells? There are so many options for you to choose from.

Do you have a special talent for dealing with younger people? Perhaps a career as a youth officer would be for you? Maybe you can find a way to parlay your special skills and talents into working to help young people stay out of gangs. Maybe you can help create a program to help young people find a safe way out of gangs. Perhaps you might craft a career helping runaways off the street and find a way home.

Are your talents in writing? Do you love to craft words? Perhaps you want a career as a grant writer for law enforcement agencies. Maybe you want to be a communications director for a large police department. There are dozens of other ways you can turn these talents into a wonderful career on the periphery of law enforcement, from a career as a journalist spe-

cializing in reporting stories about cases in the courts to writing books about notable criminal cases. The choice is yours.

Are you the one who is always volunteering to do the publicity for a charity or community organization? Do you deal well with the media? Do you enjoy developing press releases? What about acting as a spokesperson? If you love doing that, you probably would really love working in the media relations department of a large police department or other state or federal law enforcement agency. Many of these agencies similarly have public relations or community relations departments.

Are your special skills in administration? You need only decide what area of law enforcement administration you want to pursue. Do you want to work in a police department, local jail, state, or federal prisons? Do you want to work for a governing agency? A law enforcement association? The choice is yours.

Are your skills in teaching? Can you find ways to explain information so others can understand and absorb it? If so, perhaps you want to teach new recruits. Maybe you want to teach others how to increase their scores on tests and exams they often need to work in law enforcement. You might want to teach others how to protect themselves. You might even want to teach those working in law enforcement how to management their stress better. There are a plethora of possibilities.

> ## ⭐ Words from the Wise
> The first requisite for success is the ability to apply your physical and mental energies to one problem incessantly without growing weary.
>
> –Thomas Edison

The choice is yours. What you have to do is use your special skills, talents, and passions to create your career. What is going to give you joy? What are your aspirations?

What Are Your Talents?

It's very important in this process to define your talents. Sometimes we're so good at something that we just don't even think twice about it. The problem with this is that often we don't see the value in our talents. What does this mean? It means that we may overlook the possibilities associated with our talents.

It is also important to know that you can have more than one talent. Just because you are a talented writer does not mean that you can't be a great leader. Just because you're a talented writer doesn't mean you can't be a great speaker. Just because you are great working with numbers doesn't mean you're not good at organizing. Just because you're creative doesn't mean you can't make people laugh. Just because you are a great negotiator does not mean that you can't be a great problem solver.

Most of us have more than one talent. The trick is making sure you know what *your* talents are and then using them to your advantage.

Do you know what your talents are? Can you identify them? This is another time you're going to have to sit down with a pad and start writing. Write down everything that you're good at. Write down all of your talents, not just the ones you think are related to the area of law enforcement in which you're interested.

This is not the time to be modest. Remember. that this list is for you, so be honest with yourself.

Can you finish this sentence? "I am a talented _____." You might be a talented negotiator, problem solver, motivator, teacher, administrator, writer, publicist, care giver, photographer, salesperson, and so on.

Now finish the sentence, "I am talented in _____." You might be talented in organizing, supervising, cooking, or baking. You might be talented at negotiating, teaching, making people feel better about themselves, listening, writing, persuasion, painting, drawing, decorating, or public speaking. Whatever your talents, there is usually a way you can use them to help your career.

How? Let's say your ultimate goal is to be the chief of police for a large city police department. Your talents among others are problem solving, motivation, and leadership. You also are very persuasive, creative, and a great negotiator. In addition, you are a gourmet cook. While being a good problem solver and having the ability to motivate and lead others are talents that can help you become a good chief of police, having the talent to persuade others and the talent to negotiate in a variety of situations can be priceless.

What can being a talented gourmet cook do for your career in law enforcement? In depends. If you think outside of the box, your talent might help you get involved with the community, it might garner some publicity, and it might just help your career.

I know a sheriff, for example, who is a gourmet chef. He has frequently volunteered to cook his gourmet specialties at a "Men Who Cook" fund-raiser sponsored by the local hospital. This has helped get his face out into the community in a positive manner and in a capacity other than law enforcement. It helps people in the community get to know him. It also helps him create a positive image in the community. So positive, in fact, that for a number of years, a few police officers from the local police department also took part in the fund-raiser. Generally, when these types of events occur, there is media coverage. The end result is that the individual may get a mention in the paper or some type of publicity. This brings his or her name to the attention of the public in a positive manner.

While gourmet cooking may not be your special talent, I'm sure you have your own. Use every talent you have to catapult you to the top. Don't discount those you feel are not "job" related. Whether your extra talents get you in the door, help you stand out, or enable you to climb the career ladder, they will be a useful tool in your career.

Getting What You Want

How do you get what you want? How do you turn your dream into reality? One of the most important things you need to do is have faith in yourself and your dream. It is essential that you believe that you can make it happen in order for something to actually take place.

As we've discussed, you need to focus on exactly what you really want. Otherwise, you're going to be going in a million different directions. Remember that things may not always come as fast as you want. No matter how it appears, most people are not overnight successes.

Generally, in life, you have to "pay your dues." What's that mean? On the most basic level, it means you probably have to start small to get

to the big time. Before you get to ride in the limo, you're going to have to drive a lot of Chevys. (There's nothing wrong with a Chevy; it's just not the same as having a chauffeured limo.)

Depending on your situation, it might mean working in smaller police departments before finding a position in a larger department. It might mean being assigned less desirable shifts instead of the more desirable time slots. It might mean getting less desirable assignments. It might mean walking the beat before you get to ride in the police cruiser. It might mean working as a coordinator before you become a director.

Paying your dues means you may have to pound on a lot of doors before the right one opens. It means you may have to take jobs that are not your perfect choice to get experience so you can move up the career ladder and get the job of your dreams. You may have to do a lot of the grunt work and stay in the background while others get the credit. While all this is going on, you have to be patient with the knowledge that everything you do is getting you closer to your goal.

If you look at every experience as a stepping-stone to get you to the next level of your career, it's a lot easier to get through the difficult things or trying times you may have to go through.

Setting Goals

Throughout this whole process, it's essential to set goals. Why? If you don't have goals, it's hard to know where you want to end up. It's hard to know where you're going. If you don't know where you're going, it's very difficult to get there.

It sometimes is easier to look at *goals* as the place you arrive in at the end of a trip. You can also look at *actions* as the trips you take to get to your destinations.

What's the best way to set goals? To start with, be as specific as you can. Instead of your goal being "I want to work in law enforcement," it might be "I want a career as a police officer in a mid-sized department." Or, "I want a career as a sergeant with the state police." Instead of your goal being, "I think I want to work in security in some manner," it might be, "I want to be in charge of the personal security of celebrities in the music and sports industries."

Instead of your goal being "I want to be an artist," it might be "I want to be a sketch artist covering notable trials for a major New York City television station." Instead of your goal being "I want to be an administrator in law enforcement," it might be "I want to be the warden of a large, federal prison."

Instead of "I want to be advance my career in law enforcement," your goal might be, "I want to become a homicide detective in a large police department in the Midwest." Instead of your goal being "I want to work in federal law enforcement," it might be, "I want to be an agent with the FBI."

Try to make sure your goals are clear and concise. You'll find it easier to focus in on your goals if you write them down. Writing down your goals will help you see them more clearly. Writing down your goals will also give them power, and power is what can make it happen.

Tip from the Top

Successful people continue setting goals throughout their career. That ensures that their career doesn't get stagnant and they always feel passion for what they do.

Tip from the Coach

Goals are not written in stone. Just because you have something written down does not mean that you can't change it. As you change, your goals might change as well. This is normal.

Take out your pad or notebook and get started. As you think of new ideas and goals, jot them down. Some people find it easier to work toward one main goal. Others find it easier to develop a series of goals leading up to their main goal.

To help you do this exercise, first develop a number of long-term goals. Where do you think you want to be in your career in the next year? How about the next two years, three years, five years, and even 10 years?

Need some help? Here is an example of the goals for someone who just applied to and was accepted in the police academy.

First-year goals
◎ I want to a complete my bachelor's degree in criminal justice.
◎ I want to become fluent in Spanish.

Second-year goals
◎ I want to submit an application to the Any City Police Department.
◎ I want to take the written police exam and do well.
◎ I want to take the physical agility test.
◎ I want to go through the police academy.

Third-year goals
◎ I want to become a police officer.

Long-term goals
◎ I want to be promoted first to a detective and eventually become the captain of detectives.

◎ I want to be recognized as a competent, talented, and innovative law enforcement officer by my peers.

Once you've zeroed in on your main goals, you can develop short-range goals you might want or need to accomplish to reach your long-range goals. Feel free to add details. Don't concern yourself with situations changing. You can always adjust your goals.

When focusing in on your goals, remember that there are general work-related goals and specific work-related goals. What's the difference? Specific goals are just that. See the following examples:

◎ General goal: I want to get a promotion.
  ▫ Specific goal: I want to become the detective captain.
◎ General goal: I want to work in some segment of law enforcement.
  ▫ Specific goal: I want a career as an FBI agent.
◎ General goal: I want to be a detective.
  ▫ Specific goal: I want to be detective in the vice and narcotics division of a major police department.
◎ General goal: I want to work in some sort of communications job in some area of law enforcement.
  ▫ Specific goal: I want a career as the director of media relations in a large city police department.

Visualization Can Help Make It Happen

Visualization is a powerful tool that can help you succeed in all aspects of your career and your life. Visualization is "seeing" or "visualizing" a situation the way you want it. It's setting up a picture in your mind of the way you would like a situation to unfold.

How do you do it? It's simple. Close your eyes and visualize what you want. Visualize the situation that you long for. Think about each step you need to take to get where you want to go in your career and then see the end result in your mind. Want to see how it's done?

What do you want to be? How do you want your career to unfold? What is your dream?

The options in law enforcement are endless. The decision is yours. Whatever your dream career is, visualization can help you get there!

How so? Visualize filling in your application. Visualize taking the written exam and doing well. Visualize taking the physical test. Now visualize yourself going through the police academy.

Think about how excited you are. Imagine all you are going to learn. Visualize sitting in class. Now visualize getting supervised experience. Keep thinking about each step of the process. Now imagine yourself graduating. Imagine how proud your family is. Imagine how proud you are of yourself.

You are now an officer. Can you see yourself in your new uniform? Can you see yourself walking into the police department on your first day? Now imagine your first assignment. Can you hear someone saying, "Thank you, officer."

You've finished your first day as an officer. You feel tired but ecstatic. Wow! You can hardly believe you are living your dream.

Now visualize yourself waking up the next day and putting on your uniform. See yourself going in to work. See yourself getting into the patrol car with your partner. You get a call. You turn on the siren and you are off. You pull up to the address. Visualize seeing the victim. She is really glad to see you. Your heart is pounding in a good way as you run after a perpetrator. You and your partner catch him, read him his rights, and put him in the car. You are doing what you prepared for and trained to do. What a feeling.

It's a good day and it's only one of many. You are a police officer and you are doing your job. Got the picture? That's visualization!

Are you getting the idea? You need to visualize your life and your career the way you want it to be. Visualize yourself as you would like others to see you.

No matter what you want to do, you can visualize it to help make it happen. Visualize the career you want. Visualize the career you deserve. See yourself going for the interview, getting the job, and then sitting at your desk. Visualize speaking to coworkers, going to meetings, and doing your work.

The more details you can put into your visualization, the better. Add the colors of things that are around you; the fragrance of the flowers as you walk into the police department; the aroma of the coffee in your mug; the appearance of the uniform you are wearing; even the bright blue sky outside. Details will help bring your visualization to life.

Whatever your dreams, concentrate on them, think about them, and then visualize them. Here's the great news. If you can visualize it, you can make it happen! No one really knows why, but it does seem to work and it works well. Perhaps it's positive energy. Perhaps you're just concentrating more on what you want.

The Inside Scoop

Visualization works for more than your career. Use it to help you make all your dreams come true in all facets of your life.

Tip from the Coach

Make a commitment to your dream and stick to it. Without this commitment, your dream will turn into a bubble that will fly away and burst in mid air.

One of the tricks in visualizing to get what you want is actually visualizing all the actions you need to take to achieve your goal. If you don't know what these actions are or should be, an easy exercise that might help you is called reverse visualization. In essence, you're going to play the scenes in reverse.

Start by visualizing at the point in your life where you want to be and then go back to the point where you are currently. So what this means is if your dream is to be a chief of police in a large city police department, that's where you're going to start. If you currently are in college finishing up your bachelors, that's you're going to end up in this specific visualization exercise.

In the same vein, if your dream is to be a border patrol supervisor, that is where you're going to start. If you are just finishing your training, that is where you're going to end up.

Let me show you how it works. Let's go back to the scenario where your dream is to become a police officer. As we just did a moment ago, start visualizing that you have what you want. You have a great job as a police officer. Now visualize the police department you work in, its location, what the building looks like from the outside. Visualize what it looks like once you walk in the door. Visualize the setup of the rooms, the desks, the offices, the holding cells. Add every detail you can.

Now visualize the people in that building. Imagine saying, "Good morning," as you walk in the door. Can you smell the coffee brewing? Imagine yourself grabbing a cup.

Now, take one step back. Right before you got to that point in your career, what did you do? There were probably a number of things. Let's make a list of how events might have unfolded in reverse.

◎ You became a full-fledged police officer.
◎ You went through a probationary period.
◎ You graduated from the police academy with flying colors—yay! You made it!
◎ You went through a training program at the police academy.
◎ You had a background check done on you.
◎ You went through a medical examination and then a psychological evaluation.
◎ You were called back and took the fitness test and a drug screening test.
◎ You took the police exam.
◎ You decided that you wanted to fulfill your dream of becoming a police officer. You filled in an application. (This is the point where you are now.)

Here's a different example of the same reverse visualization exercise you might do if you were interested in pursuing a career as a probation officer. Think about where you are working. Think about your job title. Visualize that you *are* a probation officer.

Add in your office environment, the office décor. Now add your coworkers. Next, put yourself in the picture. Remember to visualize what you're wearing, your accessories, even the color of your suit.

Visualize yourself speaking to your clients. Create a picture in your mind of yourself asking questions. Now imagine yourself filling in reports.

Now go backwards. Visualize yourself driving to work your first day. Keep visualizing. Now you're thinking about getting dressed that morning. Keep going. Remember hearing the alarm buzzing and how you just couldn't wait to get up to go to work.

Keep visualizing in reverse. Hear your cell phone ringing and remember the feeling you had when the voice at the other end told you that you got the job. Going back, visualize the feeling that you had waiting for that call. Visualize the thank-you note you wrote to the human resources director of the company that hired you. See the letter in your mind. Now, remember leaving the interview. Visualize in detail what you wore, what the experience was like, the questions you were asked, and the feelings you had at that moment. Remember how much you hoped you would be hired.

Visualize filling out the application and developing and sending in your resume with your perfectly tailored cover letter. Now visualize seeing the job advertised and the excited feeling you had.

Recall all the preparation you did to find that job. The skills you updated. The people you

Words from the Wise

Law enforcement officers are never 'off duty.' They are dedicated public servants who are sworn to protect public safety at any time and place that the peace is threatened. They need all the help that they can get.

—U.S. Senator Barbara Boxer

> ### ⭐ Words from the Wise
> I have learned this at least by my experiment: that if one advances confidently in the direction of his dreams, and endeavors to live the life which he has imagined, he will meet with a success unexpected in common hours.
>
> —Henry David Thoreau

spoke to. The networking. Visualize the internship you went through.

You are now back at the position in the visualization process where you currently are in your career. You now have an idea of the steps needed to get where you want to go. This might not be the exact way your situation unfolds, but hopefully it can get you started on the visualization process.

Paint a picture in your mind of what you want to achieve detail by detail. Whether you're using a reverse visualization or a traditional visualization technique, this powerful tool can help you get what you want. Give it a try. You'll be glad you did.

3

Plan for Success in Law Enforcement

Take Control and Be Your Own Career Manager

You might have heard the old adage that if you want something done right, you need to do it yourself. While this might not always hold true for everything, there's a shred of accuracy in relation to your career.

It's important to realize that no one cares about your career as much as you do. Not your mother, your father, your sister, or your brother. Not your best friend, girlfriend, boyfriend, or spouse. Not your colleagues, your supervisors, or even your mentor. It's not that these people don't care at all, because in most situations, they probably not only care but want you to be successful. But no one really cares as much as you do.

If you want more control over success in your career, a key strategy to incorporate is becoming your own career manager. What does this mean? It means that you won't be leaving your career to chance. You won't be leaving your career in someone else's hands. You will be in the driver's seat! *You* will have control and *you* can make your dream career happen!

Will it take a lot of work? Yes, being your own career manager can be a job in itself. The payoff, however, will be worth it.

If you look at successful people in almost any industry, you will notice that most have a tremendous dedication to their careers. Of course, they may have friends, colleagues, professionals, and others who advise them, but when it comes to the final decision making, they are the ones who take the ultimate responsibility for their careers.

Now that you've decided to be your own career manager, you have some work to do. Next on the list is putting together an action plan. Let's get started!

What Is an Action Plan?

Let's look at success a little closer. What's the one thing successful people, successful businesses, and successful events all have in common? Is it money? Luck? Talent? While money, luck, and talent all certainly are part of the mix, generally the common thread most share is a well-developed plan for success. Whatever your goal, be it short range or long range, if you have a plan to achieve it, you have a better chance of succeeding. With that in mind, let's discuss how you can create your own plan for success.

What can you do with your plan? The possibilities are endless.

People utilize all types of plans to help ensure success. Everyone has his or her own version of what is best. To some, just going over what

> **Voice of Experience**
> Once you get the knack of creating action plans, you can use them for everything in your life, not just your career. You'll find that everything goes smoother with a plan in place.

they're going to do and how they're going to do it in their mind is enough. Some, especially those working on a new business, create formal business plans. Some people develop action plans. That's what we're going to talk about now.

What exactly is an action plan? In a nutshell, an action plan is a written plan detailing all the actions you need to take to accomplish your ultimate goal. In this case, that goal is success in your chosen career.

Frequently, during seminars, while going over the section on action plans, there are always some people who ask if they really need them.

"Why do I need a plan?" someone often asks. "All I want is a job."

The answer is simple. You don't just want a job. You want to craft a great career. An action plan can help you do that.

How an Action Plan Can Help You Succeed

Success is never easy, but you can stack the deck in your favor by creating your own personal action plan. Why is this so critical? To begin with, there are many different things you might want to accomplish to succeed in your career. If you go about them in a haphazard manner, however, your efforts might not be as effective as they could be. An action plan helps define the direction to go and the steps needed to get the job done. It helps increase your efficiency in your quest for success.

Another reason to develop an action plan is that sometimes actually seeing your plan in writing helps you to see a major shortcoming or simply makes you notice something minor that may be missing. At that point, you can add the actions you need to take and the situation will be easily rectified.

With an action plan, you know exactly what you're going to be doing to reach your goals. It helps you focus so that everything you need to do is more organized.

Many of us have had the experience of looking in a closet where everything is just jumbled up.

If you need a jacket or a pair of pants from the closet, you can probably find it, but it may be frustrating and take you a long time. If you organize your closet, however, when you need that jacket or pair of pants, you can reach for them and find them in a second with no problem.

One of the main reasons you develop a plan is to have something organized to follow and when you have something to follow, things are easier to accomplish and far less frustrating. In essence, what you're creating with your action plan is a method of finding and succeeding in your dream career no matter what segment of law enforcement you are interested in pursuing.

When you put that plan into writing, you're going to have something to follow and something to refer to, making it easier to track your progress.

"Okay," you say. "How do I know what goes into the plan? How do I do this?"

Well, that depends a lot on what you want to do and what type of action plan you're putting together. Basically your action plan is going to be composed of a lot of the little, detailed steps you're going to have to accomplish to reach your goal.

Some people make very specific and lengthy action plans. Others develop general ones. You might create a separate action plan for each job you pursue, a plan for your next goal, or even a plan that details everything you're going to need to do from the point where you find yourself now up

> ### Tip from the Coach
> When you break large projects up into smaller tasks, they seem more manageable. It's kind of like spring cleaning. If you look at cleaning the entire house at one time, it can seem impossible. Yet, if you break the job up into cleaning one or two rooms at a time, it seems easier to accomplish. When you look at the ultimate task of finding the perfect career and then becoming successful, it, too, can seem like a huge undertaking. Breaking up the tasks you need to accomplish will help you reach your goal more effectively.

to the career of your dreams. As long as you have some type of plan to follow, the choice is yours.

Your Personal Action Plan for Success in Law Enforcement

Now that you've decided to be your own career manager, it's up to *you* to develop your personal action plan for success in your career in law enforcement. Are you ready to get started?

A great deal of your action plan will depend on what area of the industry you're interested in and exactly what you want to do. Let's start with some basics.

Take a notebook, sit down, and start thinking about your career and the direction you want it to go. Begin by doing some research.

What do you want to find out? Almost any information can be useful in your career. Let's look at some of the things that might help you.

Your Market

One of the first things to research is your market. What does that mean? Basically it means that you need to determine what jobs and employment situations are available and where they are located. Who will your potential employers be? If you are interested in working for yourself or

having your own business, who will your clients be? Where will they be located?

While jobs in law enforcement can be located throughout the country, in some situations you might have to relocate to find the perfect job. Where are the best opportunities for the area you're interested in pursuing? With a bit of research, you can start to find the answers.

Remember that the clearer you are in your goals, the easier it will be to reach them, so it's important when identifying your goals to clarify them as much as possible.

Let's say you've decided you want to be a municipal police officer. Do you want to work in a small community? A rural area? The suburbs? A large metropolitan city?

Do you want to work as patrol officer? A detective? Do you want to work as a juvenile officer? An officer with the canine patrol? If you do some research, you'll find a variety of options?

Do you want to be a state police officer? A highway patrol officer? What part of the country do you want to want to work in?

Do you want to be an investigator with the DA's office? How about an investigator for animal welfare? What about a forensic scientist? How about a private investigator?

Is it your goal to work in federal law enforcement? Do you want a career as a border patrol agent? A federal police officer? What about a DEA special agent? What about a career in the FBI? Do you think you would like working in the FBI? Would you be interested in working as an inspector general auditor? What about an intelligence officer? Are you interested in a career as a U.S. Park Ranger? How about a career in the Secret Service?

Are you interested in a career as a corrections officer? Do you want to work in a state prison? A federal facility? Where are these facilities located?

Maybe you're interested in a career in administration. What type of situation interests you? Where are job openings? Where are the opportunities?

Maybe you're interested in teaching new recruits. Maybe you're interested in teaching people to defend themselves. Perhaps you want to teach people how to make their homes more secure. Maybe you want to be a vocational instruction officer in a correctional facility. Where can you find these opportunities? These are your markets.

If you want to work in the business or corporate end of law enforcement, you might consider a position, for example, as a corporate security consultant. Who will your potential clients be? Who will your employers be? What industry within the corporate world are you interested in? The choice is yours.

Do you want a career in sales? Do you think you would like to sell equipment needed by police or other law enforcement departments? What about equipment or supplies used in prisons or correctional facilities? If you love sales, your options are unlimited.

Do you love writing and want to work in some aspect of law enforcement? You have so many options! What about writing textbooks? What about writing other educational materials for those working in law enforcement? What about writing test-prep books?

How about a position as a publications director for a large enforcement agency or association? What about a job as a copywriter or writer for a Web site, newspaper, or periodical geared toward some area of law enforcement? Would any of these be possibilities for you? If so, where specifically might your markets be located?

Why do you have to research your market now? Why do you need this information at all? Because information is power! The more you think about your potential options and markets now, the more opportunities you may find down the line.

What Do You Need to Do to Get What You Want?

Next, research what you need to do to get the career you want. Do you need additional skills? Training? Education? Experience? Do you need to move to a different location? Make new contacts? Get an internship? Do you need to get certified? Licensed? Do you need to take exams? What do you need?

Do you need to get your bachelor's degree? What about your graduate degree? Do you need your doctorate? Would additional continuing education help you get where you want to go?

Do you need to join a union? Would joining a trade association help you? Do you need to find new ways to network? Do you need more contacts?

Do you need to take a class or seminar to help increase your testing scores? Do you need to get a book to help you ace the exam you must pass to get that promotion you want?

Tip from the Top

With a bit of creativity, you can weave your passions together in your career. If you want to be around the music industry, for example, and you want to work in the peripherals of law enforcement, you might locate a position on the road as the head of security with major touring recording artists. If you wish you could be around the glitz and glamour of Hollywood, you might want to search out a position as a personal bodyguard or security advisor for a major Hollywood film or television star. If you are interested in working around the gaming industry, you might weave together your love for both law enforcement and gaming with a career in casino surveillance or security. If you enjoy teaching vocational subjects and you want to work in a correctional facility, you might love a career teaching vocational subjects to prisoners. Get creative. Think outside of the box and you might just find the career of your dreams.

What you need to determine is what is standing in between you and the career you want. What obstacles do you face?

If you are already working in law enforcement in some capacity, you need to determine what is standing between you and the success you are looking for. How can you climb the career ladder of success and perhaps even skip a few rungs to get where you want to go?

Take some time thinking about this. If you can determine exactly what skills, qualifications, training, education, licensing, certification, or experience you're missing or what you need to do, you're halfway there.

It often helps to look at exactly what is standing between you and what you want on paper. What barriers do you face? Here's a sample to give you an idea.

What Stands Between Me and What I Want?	Possible Solution
I need my degree.	I'm going to finish college.
I am not old enough to become a police officer.	I am going to prepare the best I can now and get ready. Perhaps there is an opportunity as an intern or a job I can find in administration until I can become an officer.
I can't find an opening as a police officer.	I'm going to go on the Web and check out Web sites and newspapers to see if there are opportunities available in other locations. Maybe there are some jobs I haven't seen yet.
I don't know how to find a job as a body guard for a recording artist.	I'm going to cold call and send out letters to see if there are jobs available or I can create my own job. I'm going to check out the Web and browse to find some possibilities. Perhaps I'll put a small ad in *Billboard*.
I need to be bilingual.	I'm going to look into an immersion course to see if I can learn another language quickly.
I need to be in better physical condition.	I need to lose some weight and I need to improve my endurance and strength. I'm going to start by going on a sensible diet. I then am going to get into the gym, talk to a trainer, and get into good physical condition.
I need to find a way to advance my career but can't get a promotion, because I'm not doing well on the written exam.	I'm going to get some test-prep books and find a way to do better the next time.
Although I have my CPA, I really wanted to be an FBI agent and now can't figure out how to get started.	First, I'm going to the FBI Web site and then I'm going to contact the FBI to see what I can do and how I can become an agent. With my accounting skills, I'm sure I can be of use to the agency.

What Stands Between Me and What I Want?	Possible Solution

Use this form to help you clarify each situation and the possible solution to what you feel is standing between you and the career success you want.

How Can You Differentiate Yourself?

No matter what area you want to be involved in law enforcement, I can almost guarantee that there are other people who want the same type of job.

There are thousands of people who want to be police officers, thousands who want to be sheriffs' deputies, thousands who want to work in the state police, and thousands who want to work in the highway patrol. There are thousands who want to work in the FBI, the CIA, the DEA, and the Secret Service; thousands who want to work as park rangers, intelligence officers, postal police officers, and IRS agents; thousands who want to work as customs inspectors, U.S. park police officers, and border patrol agents.

There are thousands of people who want to work as federal police officers, federal parole officers, federal protection officers, and deputy marshals. There are thousands who want to work as state corrections officers and federal correctional officers.

There are thousands who want to work as university police officers, state parole officers, state park police, and state attorney general investigators; there are thousands who want to work as district attorney investigators, private investigators, private security guards, and bodyguards.

There are thousands who want to be lawyers, judges, paralegals, court reporters and bailiffs and thousands of people who want to work in the business and administration areas of law enforcement. And don't forget all the people who want to work in the peripheral segments of the law enforcement industry encompassing journalism, communications, sales, and more.

I can almost hear you say, "That is a lot of competition. Can I make it? Can I succeed?"

To that I answer a definitive, "Yes! Lots of people succeed in all aspects of law enforcement. Why shouldn't one of them be you?"

Here's the challenge. How can you stand out in a positive way? What attributes do you have or what can you do so people choose you over others?

"I don't like calling attention to myself," many people tell me. "I just want to blend into the crowd."

Unfortunately, that isn't the best thing to do if you want to make it. Why? Because the people who get the jobs, the ones who succeed, the ones who make it, are the ones who have found a way to set themselves apart from others. And it you want success, you are going to have to find a way too.

How? Perhaps it's your personality or the energy you exude. Maybe it's your sense of humor or the way you organize things. Perhaps it's your calm demeanor in the eye of a storm. Maybe it's your smile or the twinkle in your eye. Some people just have a presence about them.

It might be the special way you have of dealing with others. Perhaps you have a way of explaining something difficult in an easy-to-understand manner. Maybe it's the way you calm down a situation or make people feel better. Possibly it's the way you make others feel special themselves.

⭐ The Inside Scoop

Successful people usually have something special about them, something that sets them apart from others. Sometimes it is related to their career; sometimes it isn't. If you don't take advantage of your expertise, whatever it is, you might not gain the success you deserve.

Perhaps it's the way you write grants that bring in huge sums of money. It might be the way you can look at an accounting ledger and *see* the error while everyone else has been trying to find it.

Maybe it's the way you motivate people or inspire them. Maybe it's the way you can take a complicated project and can just make it easier to understand. Perhaps it is that you are not only a visionary but have the ability to bring your visions to fruition.

Maybe it's the way you can calm a domestic call. Perhaps it's the way you can negotiate so that both sides feel they are getting what they want.

Everyone is special in some way. Everyone has a special something they do or say that makes them stand out in some manner. Most people have more than one trait. Spend some time determining what makes you special in a positive way so that you can use it to your advantage in your career.

How to Get Noticed

Catching the eye of people important to your career is another challenge. How are you going to bring your special talents and skills to the attention of the people who can make a difference to your career? This is the time to brainstorm.

First of all, instead of waiting for opportunities to perform to present themselves, I want you to actively seek them out. You are also going to want to actively market yourself. We're going to discuss different ways to market yourself later, but at this point you need to take some time to try to figure out how to make yourself and your accomplishments known to others.

Consider joining a not-for profit or civic organization whose mission you believe in. And don't just join—get involved. How? That depends what your passion is and where your talents lie. You might, for example, offer to do the marketing, publicity, or public relations for a civic group, not-for-profit organization, or one of their events. You might volunteer to do fund-raising for a not-for-profit or even suggest a fund-raising idea and then chair the project.

You might offer to handle security issues for a concert sponsored by a civic group. You might volunteer with a literacy program and teach adults to read or children to read better. You might volunteer to work at a food bank or a library. You might volunteer with abused or neglected children or perhaps abused or neglected animals.

Why volunteer when you're trying to get a job? Why volunteer when you're trying to climb the career ladder? What's the point? What does this have to do with a career in law enforcement? Aside from doing something for someone else, it can help you get noticed.

"I can see volunteering in something related to some area of law enforcement," you say, " but what will volunteering for an unrelated industry and not even getting paid for it do for my career?"

It will give you experience. It will give you exposure. And maybe…just maybe, someone else involved in that not-for profit or civic group for which you're volunteering may have some contacts in the area of law enforcement where you are seeking a job.

"What does that have to do with anything?" you ask.

You want to stand out in a positive manner. If a position is chosen, for example, from the top three candidates on an exam, you want to make sure that, in addition to your test score, you stand out and shine in other areas. You want to give yourself every advantage to get the job or the promotion you want.

Need some other ideas? Think creativity. What about giving a class in preparing healthy snacks? How about a workshop on helping kids do homework? What about a seminar in keeping kids safe? How about a workshop on personal safety? What about giving a class at a local community center on making your home safer? Don't forget to call the media and send out a press release on your activities.

What about coordinating a fund-raiser for the Patrolmen's Benevolent Association? How about offering to develop a Web site for your local police department? What about volunteering to put together a community cookbook for a not-for-profit organization?

Just keep coming up with ideas and writing them down as you go. You can fine-tune them later.

Why are you doing this? You want to get your name out there. You want to call attention to yourself in a positive manner. You want to set yourself apart from others. You want people in law enforcement and others in the position to hire you not only to know you exist but to think of you and remember you when opportunities for employment or promotions arise.

Have you won any awards? Have you been nominated for an award (even if you didn't win)? Honors and awards always set you apart from others and help you get noticed.

Have you presented a paper at a conference? Have you spoken at a conference or convention? These events can help set you apart from others as well.

What have you done to set yourself apart? What can you do to accomplish this goal? Think about these possibilities. Can you come up with any more? As you come up with answers, jot them down in a notebook. That way, you'll have something to refer to later. Once you determine the answers, it's easier to move on to the next step of writing your plan.

What Should Your Basic Action Plan Include?

Now that you've done some research and brainstormed some great ideas, you are on your way. It's time to start developing your action plan?

What should your basic action plan include?

Career Goals

One of the most important parts of your action plan will be defining your career goals. Are you just starting your career? Are you looking for a new job or career? Are you already in the industry and want to climb the career ladder? Are you interested in exploring a different career in law enforcement, other than the one you're in now?

Are you a municipal police officer interested in becoming an FBI agent? Do you want to climb the career ladder by becoming a detective? Do you want to become a border patrol agent? What about a supervisor?

Is it your dream to be a crime reporter for a major metropolitan newspaper? What about the crime reporter for a network television station?

What is your dream? The sky is the limit once you know what your goals are.

When defining your goals, try to make them as specific as possible. So, for example, instead of writing in your action plan that your goal is to be a police officer, refine your goal to be a respected police officer working in New York City (or wherever you want to work). Instead of writing that your goal is to be involved in some aspect of law enforcement, you might refine your goal to be a special agent for the FBI in charge of a large city field office.

Instead of writing that your goal is a career in journalism, refine your goal to a crime reporter for the *New York Times* (or the paper of your choice). Instead of writing that your goal is to be an author, revise it to a best-selling novelist of crime mysteries.

Instead of defining your goal to be involved in communications in some manner, you might want to define your goal to being the director of communications for a large metropolitan police department. Instead of defining your goal to work in a prison, you might define it as being a corrections officer in a federal prison.

When thinking about goals, you might include your short-range goals as well as your long-range ones. You might even want to include mid-range goals. That way, you'll be able to track your progress, which gives you inspiration to slowly but surely meet your goals.

For example, let's say you're interested in pursuing a career as a municipal police officer. Your short-range goals might be to go to college and get your bachelor's degree with a major in criminal justice. Your mid-range goals might be to take the written police exam, go through the police training academy, and get a job as a municipal police officer in a suburban police department. Your long-range goal might be to become the chief of police.

Keep in mind that goals are not written in stone and it is okay to be flexible and change them along the way. The idea is that no matter what you want, moving forward is the best way to get somewhere.

What You Need to Reach Your Goals

The next step in your action plan is to put in writing exactly what you need to reach your goals? Do you need some sort of training or more education? Do you need to learn new skills or brush up on old ones? Do you need to move to a different geographic location? Do you need to network more? Do you need to make more contacts? Do you need to get in better shape? Do you need to prepare to take the written exam?

Your Actions

This is the crux of your action plan. What actions do you need to attain your goals?

◎ Do you need to get a bachelor's degree?
  ▫ Your actions would be to identify colleges and universities that offer the degree you are looking for, apply, and graduate with the degree you need.
◎ Do you need to find ways to do better on the written exam needed to become a police officer? Do you need to find ways to do better on the test needed for a promotion?
  ▫ Your actions would be to locate a college or school offering classes on taking the necessary exams. Actions also might be to get study guides and books on preparing for each specific exam you need to take and practicing to increase your scores.

◎ Do you need to take some classes or attend some workshops?

  ▫ Your actions would be to identify, locate, and take classes and workshops.

◎ Do you need to get in better shape?

  ▫ Your actions would be to go on a diet, investigate potential trainers and gyms, and find ways to lose weight, get in shape, and increase your strength, endurance, and agility.

◎ Do you need to learn another language to become more employable?

  ▫ Your actions would be to find a course to help you quickly learn a new language.

◎ Do you need to move to another geographic location?

  ▫ Your actions would be to find a way to relocate.

◎ Do you need to attend industry events, conferences, and conventions?

  ▫ Your actions would be to locate and investigate events, conferences, and conventions and then attend them.

◎ Do you need to find more ways to network or just network more?

  ▫ Your actions would be to develop opportunities and activities to network and follow through with those activities and opportunities.

◎ Do you need more experience?

  ▫ Your actions might include becoming an intern, volunteering, or finding other ways to get experience. Talk to people who might be able to help you find opportunities to volunteer. Your actions might also include working at one job until you get the experience you need to go after another job you want.

◎ Do you need to determine exactly what area of law enforcement in which you want to work?

  ▫ Your actions would be to locate people working in various segments of the industry and talk to them about their job. Your actions might also be to do research on various career options.

Your Timetable

Your timetable is essential to your action plan. In this section, you'll list what you're going to do (your actions) and when you're going to do it. The idea is to make sure you have a deadline for getting things done so your actions don't fall through the cracks. Just saying "I have to do this or I have to do that" is not effective.

Remember that there is no right or wrong way to assemble your action plan. It's what you are comfortable with. You might want yours to look different in some manner, have different items, or even have things in a different order. That's okay. The whole purpose of action plans is to help you achieve your career goals. Choose the one that works for you.

Let's look at a couple of examples. First, let's look at a couple of different examples of what basic action plans might look like. Then look at the same plan partly filled in by someone with specific career goals.

Tip from the Coach

Try to be realistic when setting your timetable. Unrealistic time requirements often set the groundwork for making you feel like you failed.

Example 1

My Basic Action Plan

Career Goals

Long-range goals:
Mid-range goals:
Short-range goals:

My market:

What do I need to reach my goals?

How can I differentiate myself from others?

How can I catch the eye of people important to my career?

What actions can I take to reach my goals?

What actions do I absolutely need to take now?

What's my timetable?
   Short-range goals:
   Mid-range goals:
   Long-range goals:

Actions I've taken: Date completed:

Example 2

My Basic Action Plan

Career Goals

Long-range goals: To become a chief of police in a large metropolitan police department. To lead the department in finding ways to keep the community safe; to substantially lower the crime rate in my city; to get my doctorate in criminal justice; and eventually after I've retired, act as a consultant to other law enforcement agencies.

Mid-range goals: To become a police sergeant; to get my master's in criminal justice.

Short-range goals: To become a respected police officer; to become a detective.

My market (short term): Municipal police departments throughout the country.

My market (long term): Large metropolitan police departments.

Possibilities for employment after completing police academy training: Municipal police departments.

Possibilities for employment in the long term: Large metropolitan police departments. (I would love to work in New York City, Chicago, Los Angeles, or Philadelphia.)

What do I need to reach my goals?
Graduate from college; take written tests, physical tests, and psychological tests.
Go through police academy.
Apply for and secure job in municipal police department.
Get experience.
Go to school part time and work toward my master's degree.
Search out opportunities.
Using study guides, practice taking exams for promotion to detective.
Take exam to become a detective.
Get the promotion—become a detective.
Be recruited to work in larger police department.
Get more experience.
Look for doctoral program in criminal justice.
Apply for program.
Get promoted to sergeant.
Get experience.
Receive promotion to sergeant.   *(continues)*

Example 2, continued

Continue getting experience.
Complete doctoral program.
Get more experience.
Become assistant chief of police.
Become assistant chief of police at larger police department.
Become chief of police.
Look for other opportunities.
Be recruited for chief of police of large metropolitan police department.
Get the job!!!

How can I differentiate myself from others? I volunteer in a program for at-risk youth; I received an award for one of the projects I developed to help keep youngsters out of gangs. I've networked and have a number of good contacts. I interview well and test well. I'm in great physical condition. I'm continuing my education.

How can I catch the eye of people important to my career? Continue my involvement in projects that help keep kids out of gangs. Become a respected, committed police officer.

What actions can I take to reach my goals? Explore seminars and workshops in teaching at-risk teens. Continue my education; talk to a number of people involved in this area to make sure this is the path I want to follow.

What actions do I absolutely need to take now? Get my undergraduate degree. Continue volunteering and working with at-risk youth; network.

What's my timetable?
   Short-range goals: Within the next four years
   Mid-range goals: Within the next eight years
   Long-range goals: Within the next 12 years (I want it sooner, but I want to be realistic).

Actions I've taken:
Finished two years of college toward my bachelor's degree.
Spoken to my advisor about my goals.
Talked to Dr. Bennet about program working with at-risk teens.
Spoken to a number of people in different capacities working in law enforcement. (This is the industry for me!)
Bought a study guide on passing the police exam. (It's early, but I want to get started.)
Continue with actions.

Here's a different type of action plan.

Example 3

My Personal Action Plan

CAREER GOALS (Long-range):

CAREER GOALS (Short-range):

Action to Be Taken	Comments	Timetable/ Deadline	Date Accomplished
Short-range			
Contact Any City Police Department	Informational seminar on January 16	ASAP	December 22
Attended informational seminar	This was great. This is what I want to do with my life.	January 16	January 16
Get study guide for police officer tests	Purchased and found people interested in forming a study group	ASAP	October 10
Get in shape	Work out consistently, eat sensibly	Now	
Mid-range			
Long-range			

After reviewing these samples, use the blank plan provided to help you create your own personal action plan. Remember, you can start your action plan at whatever point you currently are in your career.

Copy this worksheet and fill it in to create your own personal action plan. Feel free to change the chart or add in sections to better suit your needs

My Personal Action Plan

CAREER GOALS (Long-range):

CAREER GOALS (Short-range):

ACTION TO BE TAKEN	COMMENTS	TIMETABLE/ DEADLINE	DATE ACCOMPLISHED
SHORT RANGE			
LONG RANGE			

- Take seminars, workshops, and classes.
- Get a college degree.
- Make business cards.
- Perform research online.
- Learn about industry trends.
- Make cold calls to obtain job interviews.
- Read books about law enforcement.

Now look at some actions you might have if your career aspiration is to become a police officer, sheriff's deputy, state police officer, highway patrol officer, and so on. Specific actions will, of course, be dependent on the particular area of law enforcement you are targeting. Remember, this list is just to get you started thinking. It is by no means a complete list.

- Send letter of application.
- Fill in application.
- Get study guides to help do better on exams.
- Practice taking exams.
- Exercise and work out to assure optimum physical fitness.
- Go through police academy.
- Join trade associations.
- Join appropriate unions.

Now let's say you might be interested in a career as a personal security consultant. What other actions might you add?

- Take courses, seminars, and workshops in training and techniques.
- Check out licensing requirements.
- Take courses in public speaking and facilitating.
- Make up business cards.
- Research companies.
- Send out cover letters and resumes to companies, corporations, and individuals.

The Inside Scoop

Don't start panicking when you think you are never going to reach your career goals. Just because you estimate that you want to reach your long-range goals within the next five years or seven years, or whatever you choose, does not mean that you can't get there faster. Your timetable is really just an estimate of the time you want to reach a specific goal.

Specialized Action Plans

What things might be in your specialized action plan? Once again, that depends on the area in which you're interested in working and the level you currently are at in your career.

Let's first look at some general actions you might take. Remember, these are just to get you started. When you sit down and think about it, you'll find tons of actions you're going to need to take.

- Identify your skills.
- Identify your talents.
- Identify your passions.
- Look for internships.
- Develop different drafts of your resume.
- Develop cover letters tailored to each position.
- Network.
- Go to industry events.
- Make contacts.
- Volunteer to get experience.
- Obtain reference letters.
- Get permission to use people's names as references.
- Develop your career portfolio.
- Attend career fairs.
- Look for seminars, workshops, etc. in your area of interest.

- Place cold calls to large corporations.
- Find relevant trade magazines and read them on a regular basis.
- Get experience training.

When developing your own action plan, just keep adding new actions as you think of them.

Using Action Plans for Specific Jobs

Action plans can be useful in a number of ways. In addition to developing a plan for your career, you might also utilize action plans when looking for specific jobs. Let's look at an example.

Action Plan Looking for Specific Job

Job title: Probation Officer

Job description: Supervise convicted offenders on probation or parole through personal contact with the offenders and their families; meet with offenders in their home and/or place of work.

Company name: Some County Probation Department

Contact name: Lisa Sheriden

Secondary contact name: None

Company address: Some County Probation Department, Government Center, Some County, NY 11111

Company phone number: (123) 333-5555

Company fax number: (123) 222-1111

Company Web site address: None

Company e-mail: somecountyprobation@somecounty.org

Secondary e-mail: probation@somecountyprobation@somecounty.org

Where I heard about job: Saw ad in *The Record*

Actions taken: Asked for application. Filled in application. Tailored resume and cover letter to job; spoke to references to tell them I was applying for job and make sure I could still use them as references; faxed application, resume, and cover letter. Mailed application, resume, and cover letter.

Actions needed to follow up: Review career portfolio; make extra copies of my resume; call if I don't hear back within three weeks.

Interview time, date, and location: Received call on 6/11 asking me to come in for interview; interview set for 2:00 P.M. on 6/17 with Lisa Sheriden.

More actions to follow up on: Get directions to office; pick out clothes for interview; try everything on to make sure outfit looks good; rehearse giving answers to questions most likely to be asked during interview.

Comments: Went to interview; very nice people working there; I would like the job; Ms. Sheriden seemed impressed with some of my volunteer activities; she also seemed interested in my career portfolio; she said she was conducting interviews for the next week and would get back to me one way or another in a couple of weeks.

Extra actions: Write note thanking Ms. Sheriden for interview.

Results: 6/30—Ms. Sheriden called and asked me to come back for another interview to meet with some others people.
6/31—Ms. Sheriden called and asked if I would be interested in the job!!! She asked me to come in next week to discuss salary and benefits!

Copy the blank plan provided to use when you find specific jobs in which you're interested to keep track of your actions.

Fill in this worksheet for any of the jobs you apply to. Feel free to change the chart or add sections to better suit your needs.

How to Use Your Action Plan

Creating your dream career takes time, patience, and a lot of work. In order for your action plan to be useful, you're going to have to use it. It's important to set aside some time every day to work on your career. During this time, you're going to be *taking actions*. The number of actions you take, of course, will depend on your situation. If you are currently employed and looking for a new job, you may not be able to tackle as many actions as someone who is unemployed and has more time available every day. Keep in mind that some actions may take longer than others.

For example, putting together your career portfolio will take longer than making a phone call. So if you're working on your portfolio, you might not accomplish more than one action a day.

Working out to make sure you are in shape takes longer than a phone call. Taking practice tests might take longer than working out.

Try to make a commitment to yourself to take at least one positive action each day toward getting your dream career or becoming more successful in the one you currently have. Do more if you can. Whatever your situation, just make sure you take *some* action every single day.

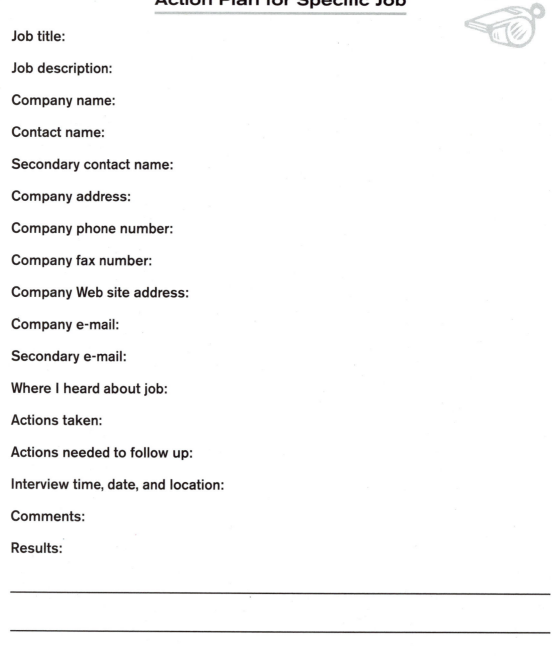

Action Plan for Specific Job

Job title:

Job description:

Company name:

Contact name:

Secondary contact name:

Company address:

Company phone number:

Company fax number:

Company Web site address:

Company e-mail:

Secondary e-mail:

Where I heard about job:

Actions taken:

Actions needed to follow up:

Interview time, date, and location:

Comments:

Results:

_____

_____

_____

In addition to an action plan, you'll find it helpful to keep an action journal recording all the career-related activities and actions you take on a daily basis. Use the journal to write down all the things that you do on a daily basis do to help you attain your career goals. You then have a record of all the actions you have taken in one place. Like your action plan, your action journal can help you track your progress.

I can hear you telling me, "I don't remember hearing about anyone else looking for a job in law enforcement going through all this. Why am I doing it?"

Here's the answer. First of all, just because you haven't heard that someone was doing all this doesn't mean they aren't doing it. Second of all, as we have discussed previously, chances are, you don't just want a job. You are trying to craft a career. If it takes a little longer or you have to do a little more, in the long run, it will be worth it.

How do you do this? Here's a sample to get you started. Names and phone numbers are fabricated for this sample.

The Inside Scoop

Once you start writing in your daily action journal, you'll be even more motivated to fulfill your career goals.

Daily Action Journal

Sunday, June 8

Read Sunday papers.
Checked papers for interesting stories and articles on law enforcement, crime prevention, and so on.
Read through classifieds. Found four openings I was interested in.
Surfed Internet looking for job openings in other areas.

Monday, June 9

Refined resume for specific jobs.
Wrote cover letter for each job.
Downloaded applications.
Mailed resumes, cover letters, and applications.

Tuesday, June 10

Read daily newspapers and checked out classifieds.
Wrote Charles David (cdavid@somecitypolice.org), Some City Chief of Police, an e-mail telling him I was interested in volunteering for project he discussed on TV news yesterday regarding helping seniors secure their homes.
Surfed Internet looking for stories about crime prevention and law enforcement.

(continues)

(continued)

Wednesday, June 11

Read daily paper and scanned classified section.
Read employment section of a couple of Sunday papers online.

Thursday, June 12

Worked on my career portfolio.
Continued actions.

With your daily action journal, you can look back and see exactly what you've done, who you've called, who you've written to, and what the result was. Additionally, you have the names, phone numbers, times, dates, and other information at your fingertips. As an added bonus, as you review your daily action journal, instead of feeling like you're not doing enough, you are often motivated to do more.

Your Personal Career Success Book

In this section, we've discussed being your own career manager, and we've talked about developing action plans and putting together a daily action journal. The next step is to discuss your personal career success book.

What is your personal career success book? It's a folder, scrapbook, notebook, binder, or group of notebooks where you keep all your career information. Eventually, you might have so much that you'll need to put everything in a file drawer or cabinet, and that's okay too. That means your career is progressing.

You will find your personal career success book useful no matter what segment of education you are pursuing.

What can go in your personal success career book? You can keep your action plans, your daily action journals, and all of the information you have and you need to get your career to the level you want to reach.

What else can go into your personal success career book? What about career-related correspondence? It's always a good idea to keep copies of all the letters you send out for your career, as well as the career-related ones you receive. Don't forget copies of e-mail messages.

Why do you want to keep correspondence? First of all, it gives you a record of people you wrote to as well as people who wrote to you. You might also find ways to make use of letters people send you. For example, instead of getting a rejection letter, reading it, crumpling it up, and throwing it in the trash, take the name of the person who signed it, wait a period, and see if you can pitch another idea, another job possibility, or anything that might further your career or get you closer to where you want to be. Call that person and ask if he or she can point you in another direction. Ask what you could have done better or differently. Take the advice constructively (whatever it is) and then use it for next time.

My Daily Action Journal

Date:

Date:

Date:

Date:

Date:

Will the person at the other end always help? Probably not, but they might and all you need is one good idea or suggestion to get you where you want to go. It's definitely worth the call or the letter.

What else can go in your book? Keep copies of advertisements for jobs that you might want or be interested in now and even in the future. Keep copies of information on potential companies you might want to work for or may offer employment opportunities. Keep copies of advertisements of jobs you might aspire to in your long-range plans or even interesting job opportunities you might not have heard of.

"I don't need to write it down," you say. "I'll remember it when I need it."

Maybe you will and maybe you won't. Haven't you ever been in a situation where you do something and then say to yourself, "Oh, I forgot about that. If I had only remembered what it was, I wouldn't have done it like that?" Or, "It slipped my mind." Writing things down means you're not leaving things to chance.

Keep lists in this book of potential support staff, people who might be helpful in your career. Keep names and addresses of recruiters, headhunters, and so on. You might not need an attorney now, but if you needed one quickly, who would you call? If you needed an accountant, who would you use? How about a printer or banker? As you hear of professionals who others think are good, write down their names. That way you'll have information when you need it.

If everything is in one place, you won't have to search for things when you need them.

What else? You might keep lists of media possibilities, names, addresses, phone and fax numbers, and e-mail addresses. Let's say you're watching television and see an interesting interview about something in the area of the law enforcement in which you're interested. It might be an interview with a police chief, an FBI agent, an investigator, a journalist, or an author. At the time, you think you're going to remember exactly what you saw, when you saw it, and who the reporter or producer was. Unfortunately, you will probably forget some of the details. You now have a place to jot down the information in a section of your book. When you need it, you know where to look!

Don't forget to clip out interesting interviews, articles, and feature stories. Instead of having them floating all over your house or office, file them in this book. Want to network a bit? Write the reporter a note saying you enjoyed his or her piece and mention why you found it so interesting. Everyone likes to be recognized, even people in the media. You can never tell when you might make a contact or even a friend.

It goes without saying that you should also clip and make copies of all articles, stories, and features that appear in the print media about you. Having all this information together will make it easier later to put together your career portfolio.

What else is going into your personal career success book? Copies of letters of recommendation and notes from supervisors, colleagues, and so on. Even letters from students thanking you for doing such a good job.

As your career progresses, you will have various resumes, background sheets, and CVs. Keep copies of them all in your book as well (even after you've replaced them with new ones). What about your networking and contact worksheets? They now have a place too.

We've discussed the importance of determining your *markets* and potential employers.

This is where you can keep these lists as well. Then, when you find new possibilities, just jot them down in your book. With your personal career success book, everything will be at your fingertips.

If you are like most people, you may attend seminars or workshops and get handouts or take notes. You now know where to keep them so you can refer back to them when needed. The same goes for conference and convention material. Keep it in your personal career success book.

You know how sometimes you just happen to see a place where you would love to work? You just know you would fit right in. Until you have a chance to brainstorm and get your foot in the door there, jot down your ideas. You'll be able to come back to them later and perhaps find a way to bring that job to fruition.

You'll find that success is easier to come by if you're more organized and have everything you need in one place.

If you're now asking, "Isn't there a lot of work involved in obtaining a career you want?" the answer is a definite yes.

"Can't I just leave everything to chance like most people and hope I get what I want?" you ask.

You can, but if your ultimate goal is to succeed in some aspect of law enforcement, the idea is to do everything possible to give yourself the best opportunity for success.

Planning for a successful career does take some work. As your own career manager, you are going to be responsible for your career every step of the way. In the end, however, it will be worth it. You will be rewarded with the wonderful career that you want and deserve.

4

GET READY, GET SET, GO: PREPARATION

Opportunity Is Knocking: Are You Ready?

Guess what? Opportunity might be knocking! Are you ready to open the door and let it in?

Whether I'm giving seminars on getting the career of your choice, a workshop on obtaining success in some other facet of life, or coaching someone on the phone, I always ask the same question.

While there are those who quickly say, "Yes," others say "What do you mean?" "If opportunity knocks, I'll *get* prepared."

Unfortunately, that's not the way it always works. Sometimes you don't have a chance to prepare. Sometimes you need to be prepared at that very moment or you could lose out on an awesome opportunity.

Let's look at a couple of scenarios. First, imagine you are walking along the beach thinking about your career. "I wish I had a job in law enforcement," you say out loud, even though no one is there to hear you. "I wish I could find a really great job opening as a police officer in a large police department and then move up to become a detective," you continue, planning how success might come your way. As you're walking, the surf washes up and you see something shiny. You reach down to see what it is and pick

up what appears to be a small brass lamp. All this time, you're still planning your career as you're walking. "I wish I had an interview for that job right now," you say as you absentmindedly rub the side of the lamp.

You see a puff of smoke and a genie appears. "Thank you for releasing me," he says. In return for that, I will grant you your three wishes."

Before you have a chance to ask, "What wishes?" you find yourself in an office sitting in front of a desk where the police chief is asking you questions and interviewing you for the job of your dreams. Evidently, the genie had been listening to you talking to yourself and picked up on your three wishes.

Here's the opportunity you've been wishing for! You're sitting at the interview you wished for and being interviewed by the chief of police of a large police department. Are you ready? Or is this big break going to pass you by because you're not prepared?

Let's look at another scenario. In this scenario imagine you have a fairy godmother, who comes to you one day and says, "I can get you that interview you've been wanting with someone in charge of hiring for the FBI." The only catch is you have to be ready to walk in his office door in half an hour. Would you be ready? Would you miss your big break because you weren't prepared? If your answer is, "Hmm, I might be ready…well, not really," then read on.

Want to think about another one? Let's imagine you are on your way to Las Vegas. The plane you were supposed to take was overbooked and the airline offered to give you a first class ticket on the next flight. You sit down in your seat on the plane and a man sits down next to you. You've seen him before…but where?

"I don't know why you look so familiar?" you ask him.

All of a sudden it hits you. The gentleman sitting next to you, behind the dark glasses, is the star of the movie you just saw last night.

"I just saw your new movie last night," you say to him. "It was great."

"Thank you," he says. "Are you on your way to Vegas for some fun?"

"I'm going to a conference," you tell him. "I thought I would mix some business with pleasure."

"What line of work are you in?" he asks.

"I'm a newly retired police officer," you tell him. "Not as exciting as being a movie star, but it was a good job. I've always wanted to do private security, so when I saw this conference on security for high-level executives a few years ago, it looked interesting and I've been going every year since then. They offered some classes and seminars that were great. I'm going to take a new one this week too."

"Really," the star says. "I didn't know business people needed security. I thought it was just people in the entertainment field. My co-star had someone who handled her security issues who is leaving. I think the traveling was too hard on his family life."

"I would love a job like that," you tell him. "Traveling wouldn't be a problem for me. I nev-

er even thought about doing private security for celebrities, but it probably has some of the same challenges as dealing with high-level executives."

"Do you have a card?" he asks. "I can't promise anything, but I would be glad to pass it on. You never can tell."

Do you have a card with you? Can you take advantage of the opportunity sitting right next to you? Or would you let the opportunity pass you by?

Here's the deal on opportunity. It may knock. As a matter of fact, it probably will knock, but if you don't open the door, opportunity won't stand there forever. If you don't answer the door, opportunity, even if it's *your* opportunity, will go visit someone else's door.

While you might not believe in genies, fairy godmothers, or even the concept that you might just be in the right place at the right time, you should believe this. In life and your career, you will run into situations where you need to be ready "now" or miss your chance. When opportunity knocks, you need to be ready to open the door and let it in.

How can you do that? Make a commitment to get ready now. It's time to prepare. Ready, set, let's go!

Look Out for Opportunities

Being aware of available opportunities is essential to taking advantage of them. While it's always nice when unexpected opportunities present themselves, you sometimes have to go out looking for them as well.

How many times have you turned on the television or radio and learned about an opportunity you wished you had known about so *you* could have taken advantage of it? How many times have you opened the newspaper and read that about an opportunity someone else experienced?

⭐ The Inside Scoop

For some reason, which we never understood, my grandmother always kept a suitcase packed. "Why?" we always asked her.

"You can never tell when you have an opportunity to do something or go someplace," she replied. "If you're ready, you can go. If you're not prepared, you might miss an opportunity."

Evidently she was right. While she didn't work in law enforcement, her story does prove a point. Here's her story.

My grandfather was a physician. After he died, my grandmother worked at a number of different jobs, both to keep herself busy and to earn a living. At one point, she worked as a sales associate in a women's clothing store in a well-known resort hotel. The hotel always had the top stars of the day in theater, music, film, and television performing night club shows on holiday weekends. One weekend, Judy Garland was doing a show at the hotel. According to the story we were told as children, Judy Garland evidently wanted a few things from the clothing store and called the store to see if someone could bring up a few pieces for her to choose from.

The store was busy and the manager assigned my grandmother the job. She quickly chose some items and brought them up to the star's room. Judy was pleased with my grandmother's choices and, after talking to her for a short time, was evidently impressed with her demeanor and attitude.

While signing for the purchases, she said to my grandmother, "I need a nanny for my children. I think you would be the right one for the job. I'm leaving tomorrow morning. If you're interested, I need to know now." Without missing a beat, my grandmother took the job and by the next afternoon was on the road with Judy Garland serving as nanny to her children.

While clearly she didn't give two weeks' notice to her sales job, being at the right place at the right time certainly landed her an interesting job she seemed to love. I don't really remember how long she kept the position. What I do know, however, is that when an interesting opportunity presented itself, my grandmother was ready. Had she not been ready or hesitated, no doubt, someone else would have gotten the job.

What does this have to do with you? It doesn't matter what industry you are working in. The moral of the story is when opportunity knocks, you have to be ready to open the door.

Would you rather open up the newspaper and read a feature story profiling a police detective who solved a major case or be the detective being profiled? Would you rather see a press release congratulating the new police chief or be the new police chief?

Would you rather have a chance meeting with the director in charge of training for the FBI or hear from your friend that she ran into the individual?

Whatever your goal is in law enforcement, whatever area of the industry you aspire to work in, you want to be the one taking advantage of every available opportunity. Here's the deal: If you don't know about opportunities, you might miss them. It's therefore important to take some time to look for opportunities that might be of value to you.

Where can you find opportunities? You can find them all over the place. Read through the papers, listen to the radio, look through the trade journals, and watch television. Check out newsletters, colleges, universities, trade associations, organizations, and Web sites.

Even if you're not a student, schools, universities, and colleges often offer seminars or have programs that might be of interest and are open to the public for a small fee. Contact associations and ask about opportunities. Call local, county, state, and federal law enforcement agencies. Network, network, network, and network some more, continually looking for further opportunities.

What kind of opportunities do you have? What types of opportunities are facing you? Is a well-known police commissioner giving a presentation on decreasing crime? Is your local college giving a seminar on careers in law enforcement? Have you heard that the newspaper is looking for ideas for new weekly columns? Perhaps you want to suggest a column on crime prevention. Maybe you want to suggest a column about staying safe.

Is there an upcoming fund-raiser at one of the local schools? Is a local civic organization looking for a speaker? Will a trade association conference be hosting a career fair? Is an acclaimed judge speaking at a conference?

Have you heard of an opening as a detective in the department in which you're working? Did you hear a news story on the radio discussing the need for FBI agents? Did you read in the newspaper that they are looking for border control agents?

Have you heard that the local sheriff is retiring? Are you considering running for the position? Does your local chamber of commerce hold networking events? Is there an interesting conference on law enforcement being held at the same time in the same city you are vacationing in? These are all potential opportunities. Be on the lookout for them. They can be your keys to success.

Keep track of the opportunities you find and hear about in a notebook or, if you prefer, use the Opportunities Worksheet provided. Here is a sample to get you started.

Opportunities Worksheet

The local mall is hosting a seminar for its employees given by someone in the Secret Service on spotting counterfeit money. Good networking possibility. June 14, 8:00 p.m. Call 222-2222 to get more info and see if I can attend.

Conference of Police Chiefs taking place when I'm on vacation. See if I can find a way to attend. Maybe see if I can do a story for local newspaper for better networking opportunities.

Newspaper had article on need for more law enforcement officers.

Chamber of Commerce is holding large networking event and recognizing the local law enforcement community. September 16. Make reservation.

Daily News looking for people to interview to talk about why they chose law enforcement as a career.

Opportunities Worksheet

_____

_____

_____

_____

_____

_____

_____

_____

Self-Assessment and Taking Inventory

Let's now make sure you're ready for every opportunity. One of the best ways to prepare for something is by first determining what you want and then seeing what you need to get it. Remembering that you are your own career manager, this might be the time to do a self-assessment.

What's that? Basically, your self-assessment involves taking an inventory of what you have and what you have to offer and then seeing how you can relate it to what you want to do. Self-assessment involves thinking about you and your career goals.

Self-assessment helps you define your strengths and your weaknesses. It helps you define your skills, interests, goals, and passions, giving you the ability to see them at a glance. Your self-assessment can help you develop and write your resume and make it easier to prepare for interviews.

Do you know what you want? Do you know what your strengths and weaknesses are? Can you identify the areas in which you are interested? Can you identify what's important to you in your career?

"But I already _know_ what I want to do," you say. "This is a waste of my time. Do I _have_ to do this?"

No one is going to make you do this. However, many people find that answering these questions now can help their career dreams come to fruition quicker. It may give you insight into something you hadn't yet thought of. It might help you fine-tune an idea for a career. It often helps give you the edge others might not have.

Doing a self-assessment is a good idea no matter what segment of law enforcement you are interested in pursuing. Before someone takes a chance on you, they are going to want to know about you. If you have this done, you'll be prepared.

Strengths and Weaknesses

We all have certain strengths and weaknesses. Strengths are things you do well. They are advantages that others may not have. You can exploit them to help your career. Weaknesses are things you can improve. They are things you don't do as well as you could.

What are your strengths and weaknesses? Can you identify them? Why are these questions important? Because once you know the answers, you know what you have to work on.

For example, if one of your weaknesses is you're shy and you don't like speaking in front of groups of people, you might take some public speaking classes or you might force yourself to network and go into situations that could help make you more comfortable around people.

Are you a good salesperson who could be great? Think about taking some classes or workshops in selling. Are you a good presenter who could be spectacular? Think about taking a workshop or seminar in presenting? Do your computer skills need tweaking? Consider taking a quick class or workshop. Do you want to improve your writing skills? Take a class!

Tip from the Top

If there is something that you need to do or determine that can help you in your career, do it now! Don't procrastinate. In other words, don't put off until tomorrow what could have been done today (or at least this week). If you need more education, certification, additional skills, or anything else, don't put it off until "you have time." Get it now! If you need to lose weight or get in shape, do it now. Don't wait until you absolutely need to do it and you're under pressure. If you need to work on your resume or your portfolio, do it now and get it done. Procrastinating can seriously affect your career because it means you didn't get something done which needed to be accomplished. Just the sheer thought about *having* to get something done takes time and energy. Instead of thinking about it, do it!

Do your interpersonal skills need some help? A class or seminar might be what you need. Do you need to learn how to organize your time better? Look for a time management seminar. Are you always stressed? Take a course in stress management. Do your negotiation skills need fine-tuning? You know what you need to do. Take a class.

Is it hard for you to stay in shape? Get a personal trainer. Go to a gym and make a commitment to improve your fitness level.

Take some time now to define your strengths and weaknesses. Then jot them down in a notebook or use the Strengths and Weaknesses Worksheet provided on page 75. Be honest and realistic. Here are a couple of sample worksheets to help you get started. The first is for someone who wants a career as a police officer. The next is for someone interested in a career as a private investigator.

Strengths and Weaknesses Worksheet:
Career as a Police Officer

My strengths:
I have a lot of energy.
I can get along with almost everyone.
I can follow instructions.
I'm a team player, yet can work on
   my own.
I am good at explaining things in a
   simple-to-understand manner.
I'm creative and a good problem solver.
I'm thorough.
I have a good memory.
I am great at motivating and inspiring
   others to do their best.

My weaknesses:
I'm shy.
I'm not good with numbers.
I don't test well.
I'm not organized.

What's important in my career?
I want to be municipal police officer in a mid-sized police department. Big enough to be challenging, yet small enough so I get to know people in the community. I want to help keep my community safe. I want people to be able to feel safe in their homes and on the street. I want to be a role model to young people. I eventually want to be a detective.

Strengths and Weaknesses Worksheet:
Career as a Private Investigator

My strengths:
I get along with others.
I have strong interpersonal skills.
I have great communications skills.
I'm a team player.
I have a degree in criminal justice.
I have great problem-solving skills.
I'm innovative.

My weaknesses:
I am not organized.
I have a difficult time being on time for things.
I don't know how to use PowerPoint or Excel.

What's important in my career?
I really want to be a private investigator. I want to help people get information they might not otherwise be able to obtain easily. I want to help locate missing people. I want to be an integral part of legal cases where I can help prove someone's innocence. I want to do something interesting each and every day.

Strengths and Weaknesses Worksheet

My strengths:

_____

_____

_____

My weaknesses:

_____

_____

_____

What's important in my career?

_____

_____

_____

_____

Tip from the Top

Accept the fact that at almost every interview you go on you will be asked about your strengths and weaknesses. Preparing a script ahead of time so you know what you are going to say and are comfortable saying it gives you the edge.

Tip from the Coach

If a human resource director, headhunter, recruiter, interviewer, police chief, or interview panel asks what your weaknesses are, try to indicate a weakness that might also be thought of as a strength. For example, you might say something like, "I'm a perfectionist. I like things to be done right." Try not to give anyone in those positions information on any of your *real* weaknesses. Remember that as friendly as these people might seem during interviews, their job is screening out candidates. You don't want to give an interviewer or anyone else a reason not to hire you.

⭐ Tip from the Coach

A good way to deal with an interviewer asking you how you will deal with a specific weakness that *they* identify is by telling them that you are actively trying to change it into a strength. For example, if one of your weaknesses is you don't like speaking in public, you might say you are working on turning that into a strength by taking a public speaking class. If you are disorganized, you might tell the interviewer that you are taking a class in organization. Telling an interviewer you are working on your shortcomings helps him or her form a much better picture of you.

Now that you know some of your strengths and weaknesses, it's time to focus on your personal inventory. Your combination of skills, talents, and personality traits is what helps determine your marketability.

What Are Your Skills?

Skills are acquired things that you have learned to do and you can do well. They are tools which you can use to help sell yourself. Keep in mind that there are a variety of relevant skills. There are job-related skills that you use at your present job. Transferable skills are skills that you used on one job and that you can transfer to another. Life skills are skills you use in everyday living such as problem-solving, time management, decision-making, and interpersonal skills. Hobby or leisure time skills are skills related to activities you do during your spare time for enjoyment. These might or might not be pertinent to your career. There are also technical skills connected to the use of machinery. Many of these types of skills overlap.

Most people don't realize just how many skills they have. They aren't aware of the specialized knowledge they possess. Are you one of them?

While it's sometimes difficult to put your skills down on paper, it's essential so you can see what they are and where you can use them in your career. Your skills, along with your talents and personality traits, make you unique. They can set you apart from others and help you not only land the career of your dreams but succeed in it as well.

Once you've given some thought to your skills, it's time to start putting them down on paper. You can either use the worksheet provided or a page in a notebook.

Begin with the skills you know you have. What are you good at? What can you do? What have you done? Include everything you can think of, from basic skills on up, and then think of the things people have told you you're good at.

Don't get caught up thinking that "everyone can do that" and so a particular skill of yours is not special. *All* your skills are special. Include them all in your list.

Review these skill examples to help get you started. Remember, this is just a beginning.

- ◎ Computer proficiency
- ◎ Public speaking
- ◎ Time management
- ◎ Analytical skills
- ◎ Sharp shooting skills
- ◎ Organizational skills
- ◎ Presentation skills
- ◎ Counseling skills
- ◎ Writing skills
- ◎ Listening skills
- ◎ Verbal communications
- ◎ Management
- ◎ Selling
- ◎ Problem solving
- ◎ Language skills
- ◎ Leadership
- ◎ Math skills
- ◎ Decision-making skills
- ◎ Negotiating skills

- ◎ Art skills
- ◎ Money management
- ◎ Word processing skills
- ◎ Computer repair
- ◎ Teaching skills
- ◎ Customer service
- ◎ Cooking

- ◎ Web design
- ◎ Singing
- ◎ Songwriting
- ◎ Acting
- ◎ Playing an instrument
- ◎ Interior decorating
- ◎ Playing a sport

Skills Worksheet

Tip from the Coach

Don't limit the skills you list to just those that relate to the area of law enforcement in which you are interested. Include all your skills. Even when a skill seems irrelevant, you can never tell when it might come in handy.

Your Talents

You are born with your talents. They aren't acquired like skills, but they may be refined and perfected. Many people are reluctant to admit what their talents are, but if you don't identify and use them, you'll be wasting them.

What are your talents? You probably already know what some of them are. What are you not only good at but better at than most other people? What can you do with ease? What has been your passion for as long as you can remember? These will be your talents.

Are you a talented problem solver? Does your talent lie in being able to come up with creative ways to solve even the most complicated problems?

Are you a talented teacher (either formal or informal), inspiring people to want to learn? Does your talent lie in being able to make even complicated things easy to learn?

Are you a talented negotiator? Can you bring two sides to an agreement when no one else can? Are you a prolific writer? A great fund-raiser? Can you tell stories in such a manner people that

Tip from the Top

Keep in mind that some skills also need *talent*. For example, writing is a skill. It can be learned. To be a great writer, however, you generally need talent. Cooking is a skill. To be a great chef, you need talent. Teaching is a skill. The best teachers, however, are also talented. Negotiating is a skill. Most good negotiators are also talented.

listening want to hear more? Do you tell jokes in such a style that those listening just can't stop themselves from laughing? Can you make people feel comfortable with a simple look?

Does your talent fall in the science area? How about math? What about art? Do you have that "eye" to be able to see just the right employee for a specific job? Can you look at someone and just *know* that, with a little training and work, they can be great?

Think about it for a bit and then jot your talents in your notebook or on the Talents Worksheet. Here are a couple of examples to get you started.

Sample 1

Talents Worksheet

I have good interpersonal skills. I get along with most people.

People feel comfortable telling me things.

I am multilingual and can speak English, Spanish and French. I can also pick up most languages quickly and easily.

People feel they can relate to me.

I have the ability to make people around me feel good about themselves.

Sample 2

Talents Worksheet

I am a talented negotiator and can bring two sides together easily.

I am very creative.

I have a great sense of humor. I can make almost everyone I'm around feel better by making them laugh.

I get along well with people in all walks of life.

I have the ability to inspire people.

I have the ability to motivate people.

I am a great public speaker.

I am very persuasive.

I am talented writer. I can bring stories to life with my words.

I'm a talented athlete.

Talents Worksheet

_____

_____

_____

_____

_____

_____

_____

Your Personality Traits

We all have different personality traits. The combination of all these traits is what sets us apart from others. There are certain personality traits that can help you move ahead no matter what aspect of law enforcement you want to pursue. Let's look at some of them.

- ability to get along well with others
- adaptable
- ambitious
- analytical
- assertive
- caring
- charismatic
- clever
- compassionate
- competitive
- conscientious
- cooperative
- creative
- dependable
- efficient
- energetic
- enterprising
- enthusiastic
- flexible
- friendly
- good listener
- hard worker
- helpful
- honest
- imaginative
- innovative
- inquisitive
- insightful
- life-long learner
- observant
- optimistic
- organized

Personality Traits Worksheet

_____

_____

_____

_____

_____

_____

_____

◎ outgoing
◎ patient
◎ passionate
◎ personable
◎ persuasive
◎ positive
◎ practical
◎ problem solver
◎ reliable
◎ resourceful
◎ respectful
◎ sense of humor
◎ self-confident
◎ self-starter
◎ sociable
◎ successful
◎ supportive
◎ team player
◎ trustworthy
◎ understanding

What are your special personality traits? What helps make you unique? Think about it, and then jot them down in your notebook or on the Personality Traits Worksheet.

Special Accomplishments

Special accomplishments make you unique and often will give you an edge over others. What are your special accomplishments?

Have you won any awards? Were you awarded a scholarship? Were you asked to deliver a paper at a national conference? Have you won a writing competition? Did you do especially well in school? Have you been awarded a special commendation? Were you first in your class at the police academy?

Were you the chairperson of a special event? Have you won a community service award? Were you nominated for an award even if you didn't win?

Special Accomplishments Worksheet

_____

_____

_____

_____

_____

_____

_____

Has an article about you appeared in a regional or national magazine or newspaper? Have you been a special guest on a radio or television show? Are you sought out as an expert on some subject in law enforcement? Are you sought out as an expert on subjects outside of law enforcement? Being an expert on anything will set you apart from others.

Did you get a medal in the military? What about a commendation?

All these things are examples of some of the special accomplishments you may have experienced. Think about it for a while and you'll be able to come up with your own list. Once you identify your accomplishments, jot them down in your notebook or on the Special Accomplishments Worksheet on page 81.

Education and Training

Education and training are important to the success of your career no matter what you want to do. For most jobs in law enforcement, a college education is preferred, if not mandatory. In many cases, the amount of education you have also impacts your salary.

Depending on your career aspirations, you may also need specialized training. You may, for example, be required to go through the police academy or other training programs. If your career aspirations are working with federal agencies such as the FBI, you will need to go through specialized training provided by that agency. Similarly, if your aspiration is to work with the CIA, you're going to need to go through a different training program. Each agency generally has

its own training program to help assure that you will be totally prepared to be the best at your job.

In addition to your formal education, there may be other opportunities that will prove useful in your career. These may encompass classes, courses, seminars, workshops, programs, on-the-job training, and learning from your peers. Every opportunity you have to learn anything can be a valuable resource in your career and your life.

What type of education and training do you already possess? What type of education and training do you need to get to the career of your dreams? What type of education and training will help you get where you want to go?

Would some extra classes help you reach your career goal? Is there a special seminar that will help give you the edge? Classes don't necessarily have to be directly related to your career choice to be useful. How about a course in public speaking? What about a class in time management? How about a stress management seminar? What about a seminar in facilitating? How about an immersion class in a second language?

Do you need some classes to get you certified in your field or to help move your career forward? Do you need additional education to keep any licenses or certifications you hold?

Do you need to get your master's degree? What about your PhD? How about taking some workshops or seminars? What about attending some conferences? The options are yours.

Education and Training Worksheet

What education and training do I have?

_____

_____

What education or training do I need to reach my goals?

_____

_____

What classes, seminars, workshops, and courses have I taken which are useful to my career aspirations?

_____

_____

_____

What classes, seminars, workshops, and courses can I take to help advance my career?

_____

_____

_____

Now is the time to determine what education or training you have and what you need so that you can go after it.

Fill in the Education and Training Worksheet with your information so you know what you need to further your career and meet your goals.

Location, Location, Location: Where Do You Want to Be?

Location can be an important factor in your career. What are the best locations to live if you want a great career in law enforcement? Is one location better than another? Here's the good news!

Location Worksheet

Type of area in which I currently reside:

_____

Location of job or career choice I want:

_____

Other possible locations:

_____

Careers in law enforcement are available throughout the country. With that being said, there is a caveat. Every job is not available in every location.

There are a ton of options, however. Depending on what you want to do, you might work in a rural setting, the suburbs, or a large city. You might work on the East Coast, the West Coast, or the middle of the country. Depending on your career situation, you might even work in another country. Sometimes you get to choose. Other times you have to go where the jobs are. Of course, if you want to work in a specialized agency, you may need to relocate.

Will the biggest cities be the best? Not always. If you're just starting out, you might find it easier to locate opportunities in smaller areas.

That way you can get some experience, make some contacts, and hone your skills. Working in law enforcement in small, rural areas may also provide different experiences and challenges than those in larger metropolitan cities.

Where is the right location for you? While you need to be in the location where there are openings, remember that you want to be in an area where you will be comfortable. If you love the hustle and bustle of a city, you might not be comfortable setting up your life in a small, rural town. On the other hand, if you grew up in a rural area and love that type of life, you might not _want_ to live in a city. Some people are more flexible than others. Only you can decide where you want to be.

You might want to use the Location Worksheet to help you decide where you want to look for a job.

Reviewing Your Past

Let's now look at your past. What have you done that can help you succeed in your career in whatever specialization you have chosen in law enforcement?

Words from the Wise

You should be aware that if your career aspirations are working in a federal law enforcement agency, in many situations, you must be willing to go wherever you are assigned.

Make a list of all the jobs you have had and the general functions you were responsible for when you held them. Then make a list of the volunteer activities in which you have participated. Look at this information and see what functions or skills you can transfer to your career in law enforcement.

Remember that many skills are transferable. It doesn't necessarily matter if all your skills are directly related to law enforcement, although that wouldn't hurt.

"Give me some examples," you say.

Were you in the military? Military experience is great for those seeking a career in law enforcement. Have you been a security guard? Did you handle the security for a concert in college? The skills utilized in these activities may help you in your career.

Have you worked as the director of a summer camp? Were you a key holder in a retail store? Have you held jobs in corporate America? The skills used in any of these situations might help if you are seeking a career in the administration segment of law enforcement.

Did you have a part-time job working as a clerk in a police department? Have you worked as a dispatcher? Do you have experience as an EMT?

Have you held a job as a reporter for a local newspaper? That shows that you know how to develop and write an article or news story and can do it in a timely fashion. These skills can easily be transferred if you are interested in a career as a beat or crime reporter or journalist. They might also be transferred if you are interested in writing textbooks in a subject area in which you have expertise.

Have you worked in public relations? What about communications? These skills can be transferred to skills needed to be a communica-

tions specialist in a police department as either a civilian or officer.

Have you worked as a bookkeeper? What about a job in the bookkeeping department of a prison? With some education and certification, you might be able to fulfill your goals of working as a CPA. Have experience in accounting? The FBI often looks for individuals with that specialty. Have experience as an attorney? The FBI might be looking for someone with your skills as well.

Have you volunteered and helped a not-for-profit organization execute a special event? Were you the fund-raising chairperson for a local not-for profit organization? Did you bring in thousands of dollars for the organization when you ran the membership drive? You might use those talents doing fund-raising for a PBA. You might also transfer your skills to a position doing the fund-raising for an association related to some aspect of law enforcement.

Remember, the idea is to use your existing education, training, talents, skills, and accomplishments to get your foot in the door of a job you want. Once in, you can find ways to move up the ladder so you can achieve the career of your dreams. When going over your list of past positions, include both part-time jobs as well as full-time ones. Look at the entire picture, including not only your jobs but your accomplishments and see what they might tell about you.

"Like what?" you ask.

Did you graduate from high school in three years instead of four? That illustrates that you're driven and can accomplish your goals. Were you the chairperson for a not-for-profit charity event? That illustrates that you can take initiative, work well with people, delegate, and organize well. Do you sing in your church choir? Have you volunteered to handle the choir's music? This shows you can sing and that you have

Using Your Past to Create Your Future

Past Job/ Volunteer Activity/ Accomplishment	Parts of Job/ Volunteer Activity/ Accomplishment which I Enjoyed	Skills I Learned and Can Transfer to Career in Law Enforcement

the dedication to attend rehearsals. Handling the music illustrates your organizational skills.

Have you volunteered for a program for youth? When you were in school, were you a peer drug and alcohol counselor? All these things can help you move closer to the career you want.

Now that you have some ideas, think about what you've done and see how you can relate it to your dream career. Everything you have done in your life, including your past jobs, volunteer and civic activities, and other endeavors, can help create your future dream career in law enforcement.

Using Your Past to Create Your Future

When reviewing past jobs and volunteer activities, see how they can be used to help you get closer to the career you are seeking. Answer the following questions:

◎ What parts of each job accomplishment or volunteer activity did you love?
◎ What parts made you happy?
◎ What parts gave you joy?
◎ What parts of your previous jobs excited you?
◎ What skills did you learn while on those jobs?

⭐ Tip from the Top

If you're just out of school, your accomplishments will probably be more focused on what you did while in school. As you get more established in your career, your accomplishments will be more focused on what you've done *during* your career.

◎ What skills can be transferred to your career in the segment of law enforcement you are interested in pursuing?
◎ What accomplishments can help your career in law enforcement?

Jot down your answers in your notebook or use the Using Your Past to Create Your Future worksheet provided.

The more ways you can find to use past accomplishments and experience to move closer to success in your career in law enforcement, the better you will be. Look outside the box to find ways to transfer your skills and use jobs and activities as stepping-stones to get where you're going.

Passions and Goals

Once you know what you have, it's easier to determine what you need to get what you want. You've made a lot of progress by working on your self-assessment, but you have a few more things to do. At this point, you need to focus on exactly what you want to do.

In what area of law enforcement do you want to be involved? What is your dream career? There are so many opportunities. It's all up to you.

You began working on determining exactly what you wanted to do earlier in the book. Continue to refine your list of things that you enjoy and want to do. Previously, you defined your career goals. Now that you've assessed the situation, are they still the same?

What are your passions? What are your dreams? Think about these things when making your career choices. You owe it to yourself to have a career that you love, that you're passionate about, and that you deserve. With a little bit of preparation, you're going to be on your way!

5

JOB SEARCH STRATEGIES

If you've decided that your dream career is in some aspect of law enforcement, you're in luck. There are thousands and thousands of jobs in the various segments of the industry as well as the peripherals. One of them can be yours!

The question is, where are they? How do you find the job of your dreams?

We've covered some of the various opportunities in previous chapters. You probably know of some others. It's important to continue to remember that careers in law enforcement are not just limited to the traditional jobs that come to mind when most people think about law enforcement. They are not just limited to those who want to work as police or peace officers; they are not just limited to those who want to work in security; they aren't just limited to those who want to work in compliance; they aren't just limited to those who want to work in investigative work; they aren't limited to those who want to work in justice or corrections; and they aren't just limited to those who want to keep their community, country, or even the world safe. In addition to these, there are thousands of jobs providing support to the groups. There are thousands that are on the periphery. And there are even thousands of jobs available in closely associated areas of law enforcement, if you only look outside the box.

Some jobs are easier to obtain. Some may be more difficult. This section will cover some traditional and not-so-traditional job search techniques.

It's important to recognize that *getting* the job is just the beginning. What you want is a career.

Using a Job to Create a Career

Unfortunately, you can't just go to the store and *get* a great career. Generally, it's something you have to work at and create. How do you create your dream career? Developing the ultimate career takes a lot of things, including sweat, stamina, and creativity. It takes luck and being in the right place at the right time. It takes talent and experience. It takes education and training. It takes perseverance and passion. And it takes a faith in yourself that if you work hard for what you want, and don't give up, you will get it.

You have to take each job you get along the way and make it *work* for you. Think of every job as a rung on the career ladder, every assignment within that job as a stepping-stone. To complete the puzzle takes lots of pieces and lots of work, but it will be worth it in the end.

Every job you get along the way helps sharpen your skills and adds another line to your resume. Every situation is an opportunity to network, learn, and to get noticed in a positive manner.

If you know what your ultimate goal is, it is much easier to see how each job you do can get you a little closer. Every situation, no matter how small or insignificant you think it may be, gives you another experience, hones your skills, helps you gain confidence, and gives you the opportunity to be seen and discovered. Every job can lead you to the career you've been dreaming about no matter what area of law enforcement in which you aspire to succeed.

One of the things you should know is that while almost anyone can get a *job*, not everyone ends up with a career. As discussed earlier in the book, the difference between a job and a career is that a job is a means to an end. It's something

you do to get things done and to earn a living. Your career, on the other hand, is a series of related jobs you build using your skills, talents, and passions. It's a progressive path of achievement.

When you were a child, perhaps your parents dangled the proverbial carrot on a stick in front of you, tempting you to eat your dinner so that you could have chocolate ice cream and cake for dessert. Whether dinner was food you liked, didn't particularly care for, or a combination, you probably ate it most of the time to get to what you wanted—dessert. In this case, your dessert will be ultimate success in your career in some segment of law enforcement.

Use every experience, every job, and every opportunity for the ultimate goal of filling your life with excitement and passion while getting paid. Will there be things you don't enjoy doing and jobs you wish you didn't have along the way? Perhaps, but there will also be things you love doing and jobs you look back on and remember with joy.

Your Career: Where Are You Now?

Where are you in your career now? Are you still in school? Are you just starting out? Are you in another field and want to move into a career in law enforcement? Are you currently working in one segment of law enforcement yet want to work in another? Are you looking for a lateral change? Do you know what you want to do with the rest of your life? If any one of these scenarios is yours, read on.

Moving Into Law Enforcement: Career Changing

Are you currently working in another industry but really want to be in some segment of law enforcement? If so, you're not alone. Many people wanted a career in law enforcement from the time they were very young but, for a variety of reasons, ended up working in other industries. Is this you? If so, read on.

Perhaps at the time you needed a job. Possibly it looked too difficult to obtain a career in law enforcement. Maybe you couldn't afford the time or money to finish your education. Maybe you just didn't know how to go about it. Maybe you weren't ready. Maybe you weren't in good physical shape. Maybe people around you told you that you were pipe dreaming.

Maybe someone told you that a career in law enforcement *was not* what you wanted to do. Maybe you were frightened. Or maybe someone offered you a job in a different industry and you took it for the security. There might be hundreds of reasons why you wanted a career in law enforcement but didn't pursue it at the time. The question is, do you want a career in law enforcement now?

"Well," you say. "I do, but . . . ."

Before you go through your list of *buts,* ask yourself these questions. Do you want to give up your dream? Do you want to live your life saying, "I wish I had," and never trying?

Wouldn't you rather find a way to do what you *wanted*, than never really be happy with what you are doing? Wouldn't it be great to look at others who are doing what they want and know that *you* are one of them? Here's the good news. You can! You just have to make the decision to do it!

Tip from the Coach

Are you living someone else's dream? Are you doing what someone else wanted you to do? You can't change your past, but you can change your future. If your dream is to work in a segment of law enforcement, go for it now. Things might not change overnight, but the first step you take toward your new career will get you closer to your dream. Every day you put it off is one more day you're wasting doing something you don't love. You deserve more. You deserve the best.

How can you move into a career in law enforcement from a different industry? How can you change your career path? Of course, it will depend on the segment of the industry in which you aspire to work, but it's not as hard as you think. What you need to do is take stock of what you have and what you don't have. Then see how and where you can transfer your skills and accomplishments to find ways you can use them in the career of your choice.

Of course, depending on your career choice, you probably will need additional training and most likely will have to learn some new skills. If you want to be a police officer, state trooper, highway patrol officer, deputy sheriff and so on, you will probably need to go through some sort of police training such as the police academy. That doesn't mean the skills you have are useless. Careers in this field utilize a variety of skills, some of which you may already have, others which you may need to pick up.

If you want to work with a federal agency such as the FBI, you should also know that in most cases in order to even be considered for employment, you need at least three years of professional experience. What that means is

---

Tip from the Top

Don't get so caught up in getting to your goal that you don't enjoy your journey.

that in addition to transferring skills, you will be transferring prior work experience.

Some individuals who want to take this route, for example, come out of a police background. Others may be lawyers or accountants, businesspeople, or even teachers. The important thing to realize is that whatever you have done and wherever you have worked previously, your skills and experiences can be helpful in your new career. You should also know that even if you have come out of a police background, you will still need to go through specialized training.

Do you have an MBA? Want to work in law enforcement? You might use your administrative skills in a variety of ways. Perhaps you want to work in administration. Perhaps you want to work for the CIA. Maybe you want to become an FBI special agent. Perhaps you want to work in some area of corrections. By transferring your education and skills and maybe taking some additional classes, you will be on your way.

Do you have people skills? Are you motivating and inspiring? Do you have leadership skills? Are you fair? Maybe you want to work in a correctional facility. Perhaps you want to work in probation? What about working as a parole officer? Maybe you want to be a judge?

What if you don't want to be a police officer? What if you don't want to work hands-on in police work yet still want to work in some aspect of law enforcement? Can you do it? Absolutely! There are a ton of other opportunities.

Do you have strong writing skills? Think about writing a column on crime prevention. Think about writing textbooks. Think about writing training materials or test-prep books for those who want to work in law enforcement. What about a job as a crime reporter for a newspaper? What about a career as a television crime reporter?

Do you have strong communications skills? Consider seeking out a position with a large police department in the communications department. What about the community relations area? Some of these positions are held by law enforcement officers, while others are held by civilians. What about starting a Web site geared toward some aspect of law enforcement? What about working as an editor for a law enforcement Web site? What about working for a law enforcement trade association?

Are your skills in the number-crunching area? What about seeking out a position in a prison accounting or bookkeeping department? The FBI also has openings for people with skills in that area. What about becoming a special agent with the IRS?

Do you have office skills? Are you a good manager? Do you have good organizational skills? Consider a job as an administrative assistant in a police department. What about in the administrative office of a correctional facility?

Do you have computer skills? Are you skilled in information technology (IT)? Are you a webmaster? Are you an expert in IT security? Specialized computer skills are a tremendous asset in law enforcement and easily transferred.

Are your skills in sales? Lucky you! The possibilities are endless. Every industry needs salespeople. Whether you're selling equipment, books, educational materials, ads on a law enforcement Web site, or anything else, there are always opportunities in sales.

Do you have an inquiring mind? Do you have investigative skills? Maybe you want to use your skills to become a criminal investigator. Perhaps you want to become an investigative crime reporter. What about becoming a fugitive investigator? Perhaps you want to become a private investigator? There is a wide array of opportunities. You just have to look for them.

"Wait a minute," you say. "What if I don't want to work in the area where my skills are? What if I want to do something totally different? What then?"

Here's the deal. If you have skills and talents that can help you get your foot in the door, use them. Once in, you have a better opportunity to move into the area you want.

Can you do it? Can you find the career of your dreams? Yes! Thousands of people are successful in the industry. You can be too!

Should you quit your present job to go after your dream? And if so, when should you make the move? Good questions. Generally, you are much more employable if you are employed. You don't have that desperate "I need a job" look. You don't have the worries about financially supporting yourself and your family. You don't have to take the wrong job because you've been out of work so long that *anything* looks good.

It's best to work on starting your dream career while you have a job to support yourself. Ideally, you'll be able to leave one job directly for another much more to your liking.

Of course, in some situations, that idea doesn't work. In some situations you might want

The Inside Scoop

In your journey to obtaining your perfect career in law enforcement, you might take some jobs that, while considered stepping-stones, are not where you ultimately want to end up career-wise. No matter what type of career you aspire to, it is essential that you remember your ultimate goal. Don't get so wrapped up in the job you have that you forget where you're going.

to (or need to) devote most of your time to your career. Only you can make the decision on how to go about your starting your career. Take some time to decide what would be best for you.

It's essential to focus on exactly what you want to do, set your goals, prepare your action plan, and start taking action now. The idea is to begin moving toward your goals every day. This can be a job in itself, but it is a job that can lead to the career of your dreams and so well worth the effort.

Over the years I've often seen people take jobs because the "money" was there even though they weren't exactly what they wanted. Then as time goes on, they are offered more money or promotions and find it difficult to "give it up" even to pursue their goals. Don't get so busy that you forget where you're going and what you want. If you have a dream, don't forget your goals.

The question many ask is, "When do I quit the job that I have to go after the job that I want?" No one can answer this for you, but try to be realistic. You don't want to be in the position where you *can't* do what you want because you don't have any funds. Do you have a nest egg put away? In order to have the best shot at what you want to do, you need to be as financially stable as possible.

Words from the Wise

If you are working at another job until you get the one you want, it's not a good idea to keep harping on the fact that you're only there until you get your big break or the job of your dreams. If your supervisor thinks you are planning on leaving, not only will you probably not get the choice assignments, but coworkers who are *stuck* in the job you are using as a stepping-stone often feel jealous.

We've already discussed that you are usually more marketable if you are currently employed. This doesn't mean you shouldn't work toward your goals. Continue searching out ways to get where you're going.

"Working takes all my energy," you say. "I don't have time to do everything. If I'm working, I just don't have enough time to put into creating my dream career."

You're going to have to make time. It's amazing how you can expand your time when you need to. Remember your action plan? It's imperative that you carve time out of your day to perform some of your actions.

If you think you don't have the time, look at your day a little closer. What can you eliminate doing? Will getting up half an hour early give you more time to work on your career? How about cutting out an hour of TV during the day or staying off the computer for an hour? Even if you can only afford to take time in 15-minute increments, you usually can find an hour to put into your career.

Moving from One Segment of Law Enforcement to Another

Are you currently working in one segment of law enforcement and want to work in another? Are you a police officer who wants to become a detective? Are you a detective who aspires to become an FBI agent? Are you a private investigator who wants to become a police officer? Are you a newspaper crime reporter who wants a career writing crime novels?

Are you a highway patrol officer who wants to work with homeland security? Are you a border patrol agent who wants to become a supervisor?

If your situation is similar to any of these scenarios, find out what you need to do to get the career of your dreams and then do it! Don't procrastinate. Check out the requirements of the job you are seeking. Look into what education you need to reach your goals. Look into the training needed. Check out what type of exams you need to take. Find a mentor. Ask questions.

What should you *not* do? To begin with, don't give up before you get started. Don't get so caught up in how difficult something will be that you don't look for a way to do it. Most of all, don't discount your dreams.

Let's say you are a police officer who wants to become a detective. What would you do? You might speak to your supervisor and find out when the next detective exam will be given. You might then get some test-prep books and start taking practice tests. You might even find a class or seminar to help you do better on the exam.

Is your goal instead to move into a job with a federal law enforcement agency? Check out their Web sites. See what you need to get the job. Contact one of their field offices. Don't give up until you know what you have to do and get started on the path.

No matter what area of law enforcement you want to move from and what area of law enforcement you are considering moving to, if you research what you need to do and take it step by step, you will be on your way to getting the job of your dreams.

Finding the Job You Want

Perseverance is essential to your success no matter what you want to do, what area of the industry you want to enter, and what career level you want to achieve. Do you want to know why most people don't find their perfect job? It's because they gave up looking *before* they found it.

Difficult as it might be to realize at this point, remember that your job, your great career, is out there waiting for you. You just have to locate it. How do you find that elusive position you want? You look for it!

Basically, jobs are located in two areas: the open job market and the hidden job market. What's the difference? The open job market is composed of jobs which are advertised and announced to the public. The hidden job market is composed of jobs which are not advertised or announced to the public.

Where can you find the largest number of jobs? Are they in the hidden job market or the open job market? That depends on what you specifically want to do in the industry. Positions in local, state, and federal law enforcement agencies and facilities are generally advertised in the open market. As a matter of fact, in most cases, openings are mandated by law to be advertised.

You should be aware, however, that there are also a great many jobs in other areas of the law enforcement industry that may not be advertised. Why?

There are a few reasons. Some employers don't want to put an ad in the classified section of the newspaper, because it might mean that there could be hundreds of responses, if not more.

"But isn't that what employers want?" you ask. "Someone to *fill* their job openings?"

Of course they want their job openings filled, but they don't want to have to go through hundreds of resumes and cover letters to get to that point. It is much easier to try to find qualified applicants in other ways, and that is where the hidden job market comes in.

The smart thing to do to boost your job hunt is utilize every avenue to find your job. With that being said, let's discuss the open job market a bit, and then we'll talk about the hidden job market in more detail.

The Open Job Market

When you think of looking for a job, where do you start? If you're like most people, you head straight for the classifieds. While, as we just noted, in certain situations this strategy may not always be the best bet, it's at least worth checking out, especially if you are looking for a position in a local, state, or federal law enforcement agency. Let's go over some ways to increase your chances of success in locating job openings this way.

The Sunday newspapers usually have the largest collection of help-wanted ads. Start by focusing on those. You can never tell when an employer will advertise job openings, though, so you might also want to browse through the classified section on a daily basis if possible.

Will you find a job you want advertised in your local hometown newspaper? That depends on what type of job you're seeking and where you live. If you live in a small town and you're looking for a position as a special FBI agent or an agent working with the DEA, probably not. If you're looking for a position as a municipal police officer, deputy sheriff, state police officer, or highway patrol officer, your chances are better.

What do you do if you don't live in the area where you want to look for a job? How can you get the newspapers?

There are a number of solutions. Large bookstores and libraries often carry Sunday newspapers from many cities in the country. If you're interested in getting newspapers from specific areas, you can also usually order short-term subscriptions. One of the easiest ways to view the classified sections of newspapers from around the country is by going to the newspapers' Web sites. The home page will direct you to the classified or employment section. Start your search from there.

What do you look for once you get to the classified or employment section? That depends on the specific job you're after, but generally look for key words. You might look for key words such as *police officer, law enforcement, state police officer, highway patrol officer, deputy marshal, corrections officer, deputy sheriff, security officer, probation officer, parole officer, law clerk, warden, paralegal, attorney,* or *court clerk.*

Don't forget to look for specific company or organization names as well.

Keep in mind that in many situations, large police departments, correctional facilities, or agencies may also display classified ads. These are large ads that may advertise more than one job and usually have a company name and/or logo.

The Trades, Newsletters, Bulletins, and Web Resources

Where else are jobs advertised? The trades are often a good source. Trades are periodicals geared toward a specific industry. Every industry has these industry publications, and law enforcement is no exception. Generally, each segment of the industry has its own trades.

Where do you find them? Contact trade associations geared toward the specific area of the industry in which you are interested. (Trade associations are listed in the appendix in the back of this book.)

How can you use the trades to your advantage? Read them faithfully. If you don't want to invest in a subscription, go to your local or college library to see if they subscribe. Many of the trades also have online versions of their publications. Browse through the "Help Wanted" ads in the classified section of each issue to see if your dream job is there.

Newsletters related to the various areas of law enforcement might offer other possibilities

for job openings. What about Web sites such as Monster.com, Hotjobs.com, and other employment sites? Don't forget Web sites oriented toward the area of law enforcement in which you are interested. Many local and state law enforcement agencies have Web sites. So do federal law enforcement agencies. Many of these sites have specific sections listing career opportunities. It's worth checking out.

Are you already working in the industry and seeking to move up the career ladder? Are you a police officer who wants to become a detective? Are you a detective who wants to move up another rung on the ladder? Are you a police chief hoping to land a job in a larger department? Are you a highway patrol officer who wants to advance your career? Are you a border patrol agent who aspires to climb the career ladder? Are you a state police officer who aspires to become a sergeant? These agencies generally post their employment listings in human resources departments, employee newsletters, and bulletins.

What do you do if you don't have a job in one of those agencies and are interested in finding out about internal postings? This is where networking comes into play. A contact at the organization can help keep you informed. While employment listings for these agencies are generally available

---

★ Words from the Wise

If you are going to use an employment agency to help you find a job, remember to check *before* you sign any contracts to see who pays the fee, you or the company. There is nothing wrong with paying a fee. You simply want to be aware ahead of time of what the fee will be.

to the public, it's always good to know what is happening first so you can prepare.

If you're still in college or you graduated from a school that has programs in the area in which you are interested, check with the college placement office. Organizations seeking to fill specific positions often go to these schools in hopes of finding qualified candidates.

Employment Agencies, Recruiters, and Headhunters

While the majority of the traditional jobs you probably think about in law enforcement do not generally utilize employment agencies, recruiters, or headhunters, there are some jobs both in the industry and on the peripherals that might. With that in mind, let's take a few minutes to discuss employment agencies, recruiters and headhunters. What are they? What's the difference? Should you use them?

Employment agencies may fall into a number of different categories. They may be temp agencies, personnel agencies, or a combination of the two. Temp agencies work with companies to provide employees for short-term assignments or fill-in work. These agencies generally specialize in a number of career areas. Some agencies even provide workers for longer-term projects.

How do they work? Basically, a company tells an agency what types of positions they are looking to fill and the temp agency recruits workers who they feel are qualified for those positions. The business then pays the agency and the agency pays the employee.

When you work in this capacity, you are not working for the company. You are an employee of the temp agency. This might be the case, for example, if you are working for a private security temp agency. Generally, in this type of situation, you do not pay a fee to be placed.

Personnel agencies, on the other hand, work in a different manner. These agencies try to match people who are looking for a job with companies that have openings. When you go to a personnel agency, they will interview you, talk about your qualifications, and, if the interviewer feels you are suitable, send you to speak to companies, agencies, or organizations that have openings for which you are qualified. You may then meet with an HR director or someone else in the human resources department of the company with the opening. You may or may not get the job. There are no guarantees using a personnel agency.

If you do get the job, you will generally have to pay a portion of your first year's salary to the personnel company that helped you get the job. In some cases, the employer will split the fee with you. Check ahead of time so you will have no surprises.

You should not be required to pay anything up front. You may be asked to sign a contract. Before you sign anything, read it thoroughly and understand everything. If you don't understand what something means, ask.

Don't forget about the federally funded and state-operated Public Employment Service known as the Job Service, which may know of openings in a variety of areas of law enforcement. The services of this agency are free.

Recruiters, headhunters, and executive search firms are all similar. These firms generally

---

★ ## Words from the Wise

Employment agencies in most states are required to be registered with the department of labor and licensed. Check out employment agencies *before* you get involved.

have contracts with employers who are looking for employees with specific skills, talents, and experience. It is their job to find people to fill those positions.

The difference between recruiters, headhunters, executive search firms, and the employment or personnel agencies we discussed previously is that you (as the job seeker) are not responsible for paying a fee. The fee will instead be paid for by the employer.

How do these companies find you? There are a number of ways. Sometimes they read a story in the paper about you or see a press release about an award you received. Sometimes someone they know recommends you.

In some cases, they just cold call people who have jobs like they are trying to fill and ask if they know anyone who might be looking for a similar job. You might recommend someone or you might even say you are interested yourself.

What if no one calls you? Are you out of luck? Not at all. It's perfectly acceptable to call recruiters and headhunters yourself.

What you need to do is find the firms that specialize in the area of the industry in which you are interested. How do you find them? There are more than 5,000 executive recruiting agencies in the United States. You can search out firms on the Internet or look in the Yellow Pages of phonebooks from large metropolitan areas.

You might also check out trade magazines and periodicals. Many have advertisements for recruiters in their specific career area.

Why do companies look to recruiters to find their employees? Generally, it's easier. They have someone screening potential employees, looking for just the right one. As recruiters don't generally get paid unless they find the right employee, they have the perfect incentive.

The Inside Scoop

The National Directory of Law Enforcement Administrators is a book published annually by the National Public Safety Information Bureau, containing the names, addresses, and phone numbers of smaller police departments throughout the country. It also includes the names of the current police chiefs or administrators. This book is useful if you are interested in contacting departments in a specific area of the country to inquire about openings.

Should you get involved with a recruiter? As recruiters bring job possibilities to you, there really isn't a downside. As a matter of fact, even if you have a job that you love, it's a good idea to keep a relationship with headhunters and recruiters. You can never tell when your next great job is around the corner.

Here are a few things that can help when you are working with a recruiter.

◎ Tailor your resume or CV to the specific sector of the industry in which the recruiter works. You want your qualifications to jump off of the page.
◎ Make sure you tell your recruiter about any companies to which you do not want your resume sent. For example, you don't want your resume sent to your current employer. You might not want your resume sent to an organization where you just interviewed, either.
◎ Call the recruiter on a regular basis.

The Hidden Job Market

While as we just discussed, a good majority of jobs in law enforcement *are* advertised, let's talk a bit about the hidden job market. Although this section won't apply to positions in local, state, and federal law enforcement, which are advertised, if your career aspirations are on the peripherals, this section will be helpful.

Many people think that their job search begins and ends with the classified ads. If they get the Sunday paper and their dream job isn't in there, they give up and wait until the next Sunday. I am betting that once you have made the decision to have a career in law enforcement, you're not going to let something small like not finding a job opening in the classifieds stop you. So what are you going to do?

While there may be job openings in which you are interested advertised in the classifieds, as we just discussed, it's essential to realize that some jobs are not advertised at all. Why? In addition to not wanting to be bombarded and inundated by tons of resumes and phone calls, some employers may not want others in a competing company to know that they are looking for a new employee until they hire one. As a matter of fact, they may not want the person who currently holds the job to know that he or she is about to be let go. Whatever the reason, once you're aware that all jobs aren't advertised, you can go about finding them in a different manner.

Why do you want to find jobs in the hidden job market? In a nutshell, it gives you a better shot at getting the job. Why? There are a number of reasons. To begin with, there is a lot less competition. As these positions aren't being actively advertised, there aren't hundreds of people sending in resumes trying to get the jobs.

Not everyone knows how to find the hidden job market, nor do they want to take the extra time to find it, so you also have an edge over other potential job applicants. Many applicants in the hidden job market also often come recommended by someone who knew about the opening. This means that you are starting off with one foot in the door.

The hidden job market can be valuable whether you are just beginning your career or you are climbing the career ladder. How does the hidden job market work? Basically, when a company or organization needs to fill a position, instead of placing an ad, they quietly look for the perfect candidate. How do they find candidates without advertising? Let's look at some ways this is accomplished and how you can take advantage of each situation.

◎ Employees may be promoted from within the company or organization.
  ▫ That is why it is so important once you get your foot in the door and get a job to keep yourself visible in a positive manner. You want supervisors and other powers that be to think about you when an opening occurs.
◎ An employee working in the company may recommend a candidate for the position.
  ▫ This is another time that networking helps. Don't keep your dreams to yourself. Tell others what type of job you're looking for and what your qualifications are. You can never tell when a position becomes available. Employers often ask their staff if they know anyone who would be good for this job. If you shared your qualifications and dreams, someone just might remember and recommend you.
◎ Someone who knows about an opening may tell their friends, relatives, or coworkers, who then apply for the job.
  ▫ In some cases, it's not another employee who knows about an opening, but it might be someone

who has contact with the company. For example, an attorney might be at a conference and hear that the director of a legal aid agency is leaving for another position. He might then tell his brother's neighbor to call up and apply for the job. He might also mention it to a colleague, who mentions it to someone else.

◎ Sometimes it may be someone outside the organization who hears about the job. The FedEx delivery person, for example, may be delivering packages to a large law office when he hears that they are considering hiring an investigator. If you had networked with the FedEx delivery person and he knew you were looking for a position as an investigator, he might contact you and then all you'd need to do is make a cold call and see if you could nab the job. Conversely, he might tell someone in the law office about you and you might just get a call.

The UPS delivery person may be delivering packages to a police department when she hears that they are looking for someone to fill in as a civilian dispatcher. If you had networked with the UPS delivery person and mentioned you were looking for a job, she might stop by and tell you about the opportunity. Then, all you would have to do is contact the police department.

A police officer may be assigned to work at a local arena handling crowd control during a major concert event. During that time, he may hear that the recording artist performing at the concert is looking for a personal bodyguard. The police officer might mention what he heard to a friend of his whom he knows has been

looking for that type of job. There is an array of possibilities. You just have to look for them.

◎ People may have filled in applications or sent resumes and cover letters to the company, asking that they be kept on file. When an opening exists, the human resources department might review the resumes and call one of the applicants.

⊡ Even if there are no jobs advertised, it is often worth your while to send a letter and your resume to the human resources department, asking about openings. Be sure to ask that your resume be kept on file.

◎ Suitable candidates may place cold calls or write letters at just the right time.

⊡ Difficult as it can be to place cold calls, it might pay off. Consider committing yourself to making a couple of cold calls every day. Do some research. Then, depending on the area in which you are interested in working, call the director of human resources or hiring director in an attempt to set up an interview. Who can you call? Depending on what type of job you are looking for, you might call legal aid offices. You might call trade associations involved in various aspects of law enforcement. How about companies selling equipment needed by law enforcement agencies or their personnel? What about contacting television station news shows to see if they might need a courtroom sketch artist? What about contacting a station like Court TV to see if you can sell a new show idea? What about contacting Web sites

⭐ The Inside Scoop

When making a cold call, try to get the name of the person you're trying to reach ahead of time so you can ask for someone by name. How? Just call up and ask the receptionist.

geared toward some aspect of law enforcement? The beauty of a "cold call" is that it can be made to anyone.

◎ People may have networked and caught the eye of those who need to fill the jobs.

    ▫ Finding positions in the hidden job market is a skill in itself. One of the best ways to do this is by networking. Through networking you can make contacts and your contacts are the people who will know about the jobs in the hidden market.

Networking in Law Enforcement

Often, it's not just what you know but who you know. Contacts are key in every industry, and law enforcement is no exception. Networking is, therefore, going to be an important part of succeeding. It is so important that, in some situations, it can often make you or break you.

"How so?" you ask.

If you don't have a chance to showcase your skills and talents to the right people, it's difficult to get the jobs you want, the promotions you want, and the career of your dreams.

"But I thought all I had to do was do well on an exam," you say.

While it is true depending on the type of job you are going after, you may need to do well on qualifying exams, remember that the people in charge of hiring generally have a choice among a number of qualified candidates, even if they have to choose them from the top three or five or even 10 high scorers of an exam. If you have networked, made contacts, and have resources, you will have an edge over others.

Networking is important in every area of law enforcement, no matter what segment of the industry you aspire to work in. The fact of the matter is that without the power of networking it is often difficult to get your foot in the door. That doesn't mean you *can't* get your foot in the door; it just may be harder to do so.

Earlier chapters have touched on networking, and, because of its importance to your career success, we will continue discussing it throughout the book. What is essential to understand is that networking isn't just something you do at the beginning of your career. It's something you're going to have to continue doing for as long as you work.

How do you network? Basically, you put yourself into situations where you can meet people and introduce yourself. Later in the book, we discuss more about networking basics and offer some networking exercises that you'll find useful. However, what you should be doing at this point is learning to get comfortable walking up to people, extending your hand, and introducing yourself.

"Hi, I'm Gregg Johnson. Isn't this an interesting event? What a great opportunity this was

⭐ Tip from the Top

If you look at some of the most successful people working in various segments of law enforcement, you will generally find that they are the ones who continually networked throughout their career. If it worked for them, it can work for you.

to learn more about gangs' influence in rural areas," you might say at a seminar.

The person you meet will then tell you his or her name and perhaps something about him or herself. You can then keep talking or say, "It was nice meeting you. Do you have a card?"

Make sure you have your business cards handy, and when you are given a card, offer yours as well.

Every situation can ultimately be an opportunity to network, but some may be more effective than others. Look for seminars, workshops, and classes that professionals in the area of law enforcement in which you are interested might attend.

Why would an industry professional be at a workshop or seminar? There are many rea-

sons. They might want to network just like you, they might want to learn something new, or they might be facilitating the seminar or workshop.

If you are already working in some segment of the law enforcement industry, you probably will have the opportunity to network with other people in the industry in the course of your day. Instead of just letting opportunities pass you by, when a situation arises, introduce yourself. Make a contact. You can never tell when a contact might come in handy down the line.

How else can you get to the right people? Sometimes all it takes is making a phone call. Consider calling a trade association, for example, asking to speak to the communications director or public relations director and telling him or her about your career aspirations. Ask if he or she would be willing to give you the names of a couple of industry people that you might call. What about contacting the communications director of a large police department to see who might be able to give you insight into career opportunities? What about contacting a college offering a degree in criminal justice and asking to speak to an advisor? What about contacting the police department, telling them about your career aspirations and asking if you might do a ride-along to see what police work is really like. Get creative and you just might be surprised.

"Why would anyone want to help me?" you ask.

Most people like to help others. It makes them feel good. Don't expect everyone to be courteous or to go out of their way for you, but if you find one or two helpful people, you may wind up with some useful contacts.

"But what if I ask someone something and they say no?" you ask. "What if they won't help?"

Well, that might happen. The conversation may not go in the direction you want it to. Some people will say "No." So what? If you don't ask, you'll never know.

"But what do I say if someone says no?"

Simply thank them nicely for their time and hang up. Don't belabor the point. Just say, "Thanks anyway. I appreciate your time."

It might be difficult the first couple of times you make calls like that, but as you begin to reach out to others, it will get easier. Pretty soon, you won't even think about it.

Where else can you network? A lot of that depends on what segment of the industry you are trying to target. Look for opportunities.

"How else can I network with industry professionals?" you ask.

You're going to have to be creative. For example, let's say you read a press release in the paper about an upcoming event to benefit a PBA. Or perhaps you see that the local sheriff is being honored. There might be any number of similar situations. How do you use these types of events to your advantage? What do you do?

First of all, make sure you go. Then get creative. You want to stand out from the crowd, if you can. If you can volunteer to help with the event in any manner, do so. Call up and ask. Volunteer to help do the publicity. Volunteer to be a host or hostess. Offer to help serve. See if you can cover the event for the newspaper. Think outside of the box.

Events don't always have to be geared specifically to the law enforcement industry to be good networking opportunities. What they need to be, however, are events where people in the segment of the law enforcement industry in which you are interested might congregate. For example, you might want to join the Kiwanis or Rotary clubs or another similar civic organization. You might want to join the chamber of commerce and go to their events. Why? Industry professionals attend these events. When you meet people in these situations, you are meeting them on a more even playing field.

Remember that these are business functions. Behave professionally and make sure to watch for any opportunities to network (the main reason that you're there). Here are some tips on what to do and what not to do:

- Do not bring anyone with you. Go alone. It will give you more opportunities to meet people.
- Do not smoke even if other people are. You can never tell what makes someone remember you. You don't want it to be that you smell of tobacco.
- Don't wear strong perfume, cologne, or aftershave. Aside from the possibility of some people being allergic to it, you don't want this to be the reason people remember you.
- While this goes without saying, do not use any illegal drugs.

Here are some things you *should do.*
- Do bring business cards to give out to everyone.
- Do bring a pen and small pad to take down names and phone numbers of people who don't have cards.

Tip from the Coach

Remember that networking is a two-way street. If you want people to help you, it's important to reciprocate. When you see something you can do for someone else's career, don't wait for them to ask for help. Step in, do it, and do it graciously.

◎ Do meet as many people as possible. If given the opportunity, briefly tell them what your goal is and ask if they have any suggestions about who you can contact.

Follow up on the contacts and information you gather at these meetings. Don't neglect this step or you will have wasted the opportunity. Call, write, or e-mail contacts you have made in a timely fashion. You want them to remember meeting you.

The Right Place at the Right Time

Have you ever looked down while you were walking and seen money sitting on the ground? It could have been there for a while, but no one else happened to look down. You just happened to be in the right place at the right time.

It can happen anytime. Sometimes you hear about an interesting job opening from an unlikely source. You might, for example, be standing in a long line at the bakery. The woman in back of you asks if you would mind very much if she went ahead of you because she is rushing out of town to visit her daughter. It seems she needs to pick up the bakery's famous chocolate cake because it is her daughter's favorite and she misses it since moving away to take a job in the city.

You agree to let her get ahead of you. While standing in line chatting, the portfolio you are carrying slips out of your hand and a few of your sketches fall out. The woman helps you pick them up and looks at them. "Wow," she said. "These are amazing. Are you an artist?"

You mention that while you just finished college and your dream is to work as a courtroom sketch artist, you probably are going to have to do something else.

"It must be difficult to find a job like that," the woman says to you. "But you really are good," she says, looking at your sketches.

"It's your turn," you say to the woman. "Have a good trip. Here's my card. Maybe you'll run into someone who needs someone like me."

"I hope I do," the woman says. "Thanks for letting me go ahead of you."

You forget about the incident until a few weeks later when you get a phone call.

"Hi, this is Mary Jean Morrow. You don't know me, but you met my mom in the bakery a couple of weeks ago. She said you let her get ahead of you. Do you remember?"

"Yes, she was going to visit you and she was in a rush," you say.

"Well, I know this is coming out of left field, but I'm a news producer for WABA TV and my mom was telling me about meeting you while we were eating the chocolate cake. She told me you are an amazing sketch artist. You'll never believe this, but the station really needs to find a courtroom sketch artist pronto. I'm not sure what your qualifications are, but I hear your sketches are great. Would you be interested in something like that?"

"I would love a job like that," you say.

"I can't promise anything, but if you are as good as my mom says, we would love to see your portfolio. I don't suppose you would be available to come into the city in the next couple of days to meet with my boss. Our sketch artists left and we have a position open—immediately. You probably have heard the Jerome trial is starting next week. It's going to be a long trial, I think."

"I can fax my resume as soon as we get off the phone," you say, "and my portfolio is ready. I can drive into the city tomorrow morning if that would be good for you. I'm so excited. I can't tell you how glad I am we both have a sweet tooth; your mom was in a hurry and I gave her my card."

"I'm glad you gave my mom your card too," she says. "Let me give you our fax number and the address and I'll see you tomorrow."

Think things like this can't happen? They can and do. It's just a matter of being in the right place at the right time.

There is no question that being in the right place at the right time can help. The question is, however, what is the right place and the right time and how do you recognize it?

The simple answer is, it's almost impossible to know what the right place and right time is. You can, however, stack the deck in your favor. How? While you never know what the right place or the right time to be someplace is, you can put yourself in situations where you can network. Networking with people outside of the industry can be just as effective and just as important as networking with industry professionals.

The larger your network, the more opportunities you will have to find the job you want. The more people who know what you have to offer and what you want to do, the better.

Who do you deal with every day? Who do these people know and deal with? Do any of these people in your network and your extended network know about your dream career?

If you aren't currently employed and don't have to worry about a boss or supervisor hearing about your aspirations, spread the news about your job search. Don't keep it a secret. The more people who know what you're looking for in a career, the more people who potentially can let you know when and where there is a job possibility.

If I haven't stressed it enough, if at all possible, do not keep your career aspirations to yourself. Share them with the world.

Cold Calls

What exactly is a cold call? In relation to your career, a cold call is an unsolicited contact in person, by phone, letter, or e-mail with someone you don't know in hopes of obtaining some information, an interview, or a job. It is a proactive strategy.

Let's focus on the cold calls you make by phone. Many find this form of contact too intimidating to try. Why? Because not only are you calling and trying to sell yourself to someone who may be busy and doesn't want to be bothered, but you are also afraid of rejection. None of us like rejection. We fear that we will get on the phone, try to talk to someone, and they will not take our call, hang up on us, or say no to our requests.

The majority of telemarketing calls made to homes every day are cold calls. In those cases, the people on the other end of the phone aren't trying to get a job or an interview. Instead, they are attempting to sell something such as a product or a service. When you get those calls, the first thing on your mind is usually how to get off the phone. The last thing you want to do is buy anything from someone on the other end. But the fact of the matter is that people do buy things from telemarketers if they want what they're selling.

With that in mind, your job in making cold calls is to make your call compelling enough that the person on the other end responds positively. Why would you even bother making a cold call to someone? It's simply another job search strategy, and it's one that not everyone attempts, which gives you an edge over others.

How do you make a cold call? It's really quite simple. If you want to make a cold call to a potential employer, you just identify who you want to call, put together a script to make it easier for you, give yourself a boost of confidence, and then make your call.

Keep track of the calls you make. You may think you'll remember who said what and who you didn't reach, but after a couple of calls, it gets confusing. Check out the Cold Call Tracking Worksheet sample below for the type of information you should record. Then use the Cold Call Tracking Worksheet provided.

> **Voice of Experience**
>
> You will find it easier to make cold calls if you not only create a script but practice it as well. In order to be successful in cold calling, you need to sound professional, friendly, and confident.

Who do you call? That depends on who you're trying to reach and what you're trying to accomplish. You might call private security firms. You might call the management of entertainers, celebrities, and sports stars to see if they are interested in private security or the services of a private body guard.

You might call high-level corporate executives who may need the services of private security for

Cold Call Tracking Worksheet

Company	Phone Number	Name of Contact	Date Called	Follow-up Activities	Results
Tri County Investigators	111-222-2222	Jim Parish	5/6	Send resume.	Asked for resume, will get back to me after reviewing my qualifications.
Cone & Border Legal	111-111-1111	Janice Cone	5/9	Send resume.	Will keep resume on file, no current opening. Call back in a few months.
Genesee Legal Services	111-222-3333	Mike Edwards	5/9	E-mailed resume.	Will review resume and get back to me.
Tyler Taylor Inc.	111-999-9999	Tyler Taylor	5/11	Call back in two weeks.	

Cold Call Tracking Worksheet

Company	Phone Number	Name of Contact	Date Called	Follow-up Activities	Results

themselves or their company. You might cold call large corporations searching out a position handling their computer security issues.

You might call law firms to see if they need a private investigator. You might call law firms to see if they need another attorney. You might call legal aid offices to see if they need the services of an attorney or perhaps a paralegal. It all depends on your qualifications and your career aspirations.

You might call police chiefs or hiring managers. You might call a federal law enforcement agency. You might call a correctional facility.

What about contacting newspapers or television stations to see if you can create a position as a crime reporter? How about calling a television station to see if they might need a courtroom artist to illustrate courtroom activity on air?

Every call you make is a potential opportunity that can pan out for you.

Need an example to get you started? Read on.

You: Hi, Mr. Block. This is Janice Masters. I'm not sure you're the right person to speak to, but I was hoping I could tell you what I was looking for and perhaps you could point me in the right direction. Are you in the middle of something now or would it be better if I called back later?

Mr. Block: What can I do for you?

You: I have my bachelor's degree in criminal justice and I'm working toward completing my master's. I have a number of certifications in IT security and I was wondering if you knew who I would talk to about possible career opportunities I might pursue in your company?

Mr. Block: What do you specifically want to do?

You: I'm interested in designing and overseeing corporate IT security programs.

Mr. Block: We don't have any positions like that here. Sorry.

You: I understand and I thank you for your time. I'm just trying to get some leads on where to call. Do you have any suggestions?

Mr. Block: You probably could call our main office. They might be able to tell you more about positions in that area. We have nothing to do with that in our office.

You: Thanks so much. Who would I call there?

Mr. Block: Why don't you try speaking to Josh Barnes. His number is 222-4444.

You: Thanks for your help.

Josh Barnes: Josh Barnes, can I help you?

You: Hi, Mr. Barnes, this is Janice Masters. Mr. Block suggested I call you. I was trying to find out more about opportunities in your company for IT security? Are you the right person to speak to?

Josh Barnes: What kind of background do you have?

You: I have a bachelor's in criminal justice, and I'm working toward completing my master's. I have a number of certifications in IT security and I did an internship with American Bank in the IT security department.

Josh Barnes: That's pretty impressive. We don't really have any positions open right now in that area, but any company would be lucky to have someone with those qualifications.

You: Do you have any suggestions of people I might call?

Josh Barnes: Not really. You know, why don't you come in and we can chat. Do you have any time next week? Wednesday would be good for me. How about you?

You: Wednesday would be great. Thank you.

Josh Barnes: Why don't you come in around 1:00 p.m. You have our address, don't you?

You: Yes, 123 Broadway, right?

Josh Barnes: I'm on the 16th floor. See you next week.

You: Thanks. I look forward to meeting you.

As you can see, it's not all that difficult, once you get someone on the phone.

"But what if they say no?" you ask.

So they say no. Don't take it personally. Just go on to your next call and use your previous call as practice.

Where do you find people to call? Browse Web sites for names. Read trade journals. Read the newspaper. Look for magazine articles and feature stories. Watch television and listen to the radio. Go through the Yellow Pages. You can get names from almost anyplace. Call up. Take a chance. It may pay off.

Depending on where you're calling and the size of the organization, in many cases when you start your conversation during a cold call, the person you're speaking to will direct you to the human resources (HR) department. If this

> **Tip from the Coach**
> Expect rejection when making cold calls. Some people may not want to talk to you. Rejection is a lot easier to deal with when you decide ahead of time that it isn't personal.

is the case, ask whom you should speak to in HR. Try to get a name. Then thank the person who gave you the information and call the HR department asking for the name of the person you were given. Being referred by someone else in the company will often get you through.

Believe it or not, the more calls you make, the more you increase your chances of success in getting the information you want, potential interviews, or the job you want.

If you're really uncomfortable making the calls, or you can't get through to the people you're trying to reach by phone, consider writing letters. It takes more time than a phone call, but it is another proactive method for you to potentially get through to someone.

Creating Your Own Career

Do you want one more really good reason to find the hidden job market? If you're creative and savvy enough, you might even be able to *create* a position for yourself, even if you are only on the first or second rung of the career ladder. What does that mean?

It means that if you can come up with an idea for a job, even if that job doesn't currently exist, and are creative and persuasive in selling that idea, you often can create your own job.

Let's go back to Janice Masters for a moment. In this scenario, let's say she instead meets an online retailer. Janice explains to their CEO that many customers are uncomfortable

The Inside Scoop

There is a wide array of potential employers for those interested in pursuing a career in law enforcement. Below is a listing to get you started.

Airports	Periodicals
Banks	Police departments, local
Casinos	Police departments, state
Celebrities	Private investigation companies
Central Intelligence Agency	Probation departments
Colleges and universities	Public defenders office
Correctional facilities (local, state, federal)	Radio stations
Criminal courts	Railroads
Department of Homeland Security	Retail stores
Drug Enforcement Agency	Security organizations
Entertainment venues	Sports personalities
Family courts	Sports venues
Federal Bureau of Investigation	State departments of agriculture
Federal Trade Commission	State departments of insurance
Forensic laboratories	Television producers
Hotels	Television stations
Internal Revenue Service	Transit authorities
Juvenile courts	U.S. Bureau of Alcohol, Tobacco, Firearms, and
Juvenile justice programs	Explosives
Law enforcement agencies, federal	U.S. Customs and Border Protection
Law firms	U.S. Department of Agriculture Forest Service
Legal aid offices	U.S. Department of Justice
Military police	U.S. Immigration and Naturalization Service
National Park Service	U.S. Marshals Service
National Security Agency	U.S. Postal Inspection Service
Newspapers	U.S. Secret Service
Parole departments	Web sites
Pentagon Force Protection Agency	

giving out their personal information online because of the fear of security breaches. She suggests to the CEO that, with her credentials and background, she could develop a program where not only would information be safe and secure, but she would be the company spokesperson explaining that security to potential customers. She explains that if people felt more secure when buying online, it could positively affect that company's bottom line. And guess what? The CEO heard that and decided to create a position.

"That kind of thing doesn't really happen," I hear you saying.

The truth of the matter is that people create their own positions more often than you know.

If you are creative, have some initiative, and are assertive enough to push your idea, you can do the same. What you have to do is come up with something you can do for an organization, law enforcement agency, corporation, or other entity that isn't being done now or you might do better. Then pitch it to the correct people.

Do you have any ideas? Put fear aside and think outside the box. Get creative. Come up with an idea, develop it fully, put it on paper so you can see any problems, and then fine-tune them. Then call up a company or organization that you want to work with, lay out the idea, and sell them on it. You've just created your own job!

Whether you use traditional job search strategies or get a little creative, the idea is to stack the deck in your favor. By taking a little time and doing a bit of research, you might just uncover the job you have been dreaming about.

6

TOOLS FOR SUCCESS

The right tools can make it easier to do almost any job. Imagine, for example, trying to paint your house without the right brushes, high-quality paint, and a good ladder. It could happen, but it would probably be more difficult to do a really good job. Imagine trying to bake a cake without measuring spoons, measuring cups, pans, and a good oven. You might be able to do it, but your chances of success are diminished.

Obtaining jobs and creating a great career is a project in itself. Tools can make it easier. Every trade has its own set of tools that help the tradesman (or woman) achieve success. Not having these tools would make their job more difficult, if not impossible, to accomplish.

Whatever area of law enforcement you are pursuing, there are certain tools that can help you achieve success faster as well. These may include things like your resume, CV, business and networking cards, brochures, career portfolio and professional reference sheets, and good exam scores, among others. This chapter will help get you started putting together these tools.

Your Resume as a Selling Tool

There is virtually no successful company that does not advertise or market their products or services in some manner, whether it be through utilizing publicity, ads in newspapers or magazines, television or radio commercials, billboards, banners on the Web, or any other marketing vehicles.

Why do they do this? The foremost reason is to make sure others are aware of their products or services so they can then find ways to entice potential customers to buy or use a particular product or service.

What does this have to do with you? When trying to succeed in any career, it is a good idea to look at yourself as a *product*. What that means in a broad sense is that you will be marketing yourself so people know you exist, so they begin to differentiate you from others, and so that they see you in a better light.

How can you entice potential employers to hire you? How can you help people in the industry to know you exist? How can you get that all-important interview?

The answer is simple. Start by making your resume a selling tool! Make it your own personal printed marketing piece. Everyone sends out resumes. The trick is making yours so powerful that it will grab the attention of potential employers.

Resumes are important no matter what area of law enforcement you are pursuing.

> ⭐ **Tip from the Coach**
> Your resume will be useful at every level of your career. It is not a do-it-once, get-a-job-and-never-need-it-again document.

Does your resume do a great job of selling your credentials? Does it showcase your skills, personality traits, and special talents? Is your resume the one that is going to impress the employers or human resources directors who can call you in for that all-important interview and ultimately land you the job you are after? Is it going to land you the job you've been dreaming about?

If a potential employer doesn't know you, his or her first impression of you might very well be your resume. This makes your resume a crucial part of getting an interview that might ultimately lead to the job you are trying to land.

I can almost hear you asking, "Does it really matter what my resume looks like? I thought all I had to do was do well on the police exam (or the detective exam or the civil service exam and so on) and I'll be called in for an interview."

You might and you might not. Perhaps the powers that be liked the resume of one of the other top scorers. Why would you take a chance with something as important as your career?

A strong resume illustrates that you have the experience and qualifications to fill a potential employer's needs. How can you do this? To begin with, learn to tailor your resume to the job you're pursuing. One of the biggest mistakes people make in job hunting is creating just one resume and then using it every single time they apply for a position no matter the job.

If this is what you've been doing, it's time to break the habit. Begin by crafting your main resume. Then edit it to fit the needs of each specific job opening or opportunity you are applying for.

"But," you say, "I want to work in law enforcement. Can't I use the same resume for every job I apply for?"

Here's the answer in a nutshell. You can use the same resume only *if* you are going for the exact same type of job. For example, you might use the same resume if you are applying for two jobs as a police officer in similar types of departments.

However, if you are applying for one job as a police officer in a small municipal department and another as a university or college police officer, you might want to tailor your resume to each job a bit, highlighting any skills and experiences that might be relevant to each position. Even if you were applying for law enforcement jobs to two different federal law enforcement agencies, you most likely would want to tailor your resume for each job.

Similarly, if you are applying for one job as the director of communications for a community college and another job as director of communications in a large police department, you would probably want to tailor each resume for each specific position.

> ⭐ **Words from the Wise**
> If you're using different versions of resumes, make sure you know which one you send to which company. Keep a copy of the resume you use for a specific job with a copy of the cover letter you send. Do it *every* time. Otherwise, when sending out numerous resumes and letters, it's very easy to get confused.

Before computers became commonplace, preparing a different resume for every job was far more difficult. In many cases, people would prepare one resume and then have it professionally printed by a resume service or printer. That was it. If you wanted to change your resume, you had to go back to the printer and have it done again, incurring a major expense.

Today, however, most of us have access to computers, making it far easier to change resumes at will. Do you want to change your career objective? What about the order of the components on your resume? Do you want to add something? Do you want to delete something? You are in control. You can create the perfect resume every time with the click of a mouse.

Always keep a copy of your resume on your computer and make sure you note the date it was done and its main focus. For example, you might save your resumes as "Municipal Police Officer resume May 12;" "Any Town Police Officer resume May 15;" "FBI special agent resume June 19;" "DEA Agent resume June 21;" and so on. If you don't have your own computer, keep your resume on a CD or a flash drive so you always have access to it without having to type it all over again.

How can you make your resume a better marketing tool? Present it in a clear, concise manner, highlighting your best assets. Organize things in an order that makes it easy for someone just glancing at your resume to see the points that sell you the best and then want to take a second look.

The decision about the sequence of items in your resume should be based on what is most impressive in relation to the position you are pursuing. Do you have a lot of work experience? Put that information first. Are your accomplishments extraordinary? If so, highlight those first. Do you have little experience, but you just graduated cum laude with a degree in criminal justice? Then perhaps your education should be where your resume should start. Were you at the top of your class in the police academy? Then maybe your training should be highlighted.

Sometimes it helps when creating your own resume to imagine that you just received it in the mail yourself. What would make you glance at it and say *wow*? Would you continue reading or would you glance at it and hope that there was a more interesting resume coming in?

One of the most important things to remember is that there really is no *right* or *wrong* type of resume. The right one for you will end up being the one that ultimately gets you the position you want. There are so many ways to prepare your resume that it is often difficult to choose one. My advice is to craft a couple different ones, put them away overnight, and then look at them the next day. Which one looks better to you? That probably will be the style you want to use.

Here are some tips that might help:

◎ Tailor each resume for every position.

◎ Make sure you check for incorrect word usage. No matter what position you're pursuing, most employers prefer to have someone who has a command of the English language. Check to make sure you haven't inadvertently used the word "their" for "there," "to" for "too" or "two," "effect" for "affect," "you're" for "your," "it's" for "its," and so on.

◎ Don't rely solely on your computer's spell and grammar checker. Carefully go over your work yourself as well.

◎ Every time you edit your resume or make a change, check carefully for errors.

◎ It is very easy to miss a double word, a misspelled word, or a wrong tense. Have a friend or family member look over your resume. It is often difficult to see mistakes in your own work.

◎ Tempting as it is to use different-colored inks when preparing your resume, don't. Use only black ink.

◎ Use a high-quality paper, at least 40 pound weight for printing your resumes. Paper with texture often *feels* different, so it stands out. While you can use white, beige, or cream colored papers, soft

Words from the Wise

No matter what color paper you use for your resume and cover letters, make sure it photocopies well. Some colored papers photocopy dark or look messy. Even if you aren't photocopying your resume, a potential employer might.

light colors such as light blue, salmon pink, gray, or light green will help your resume stand out from the hundreds of white and beige ones.

◎ Make sure your resume layout looks attractive. You can have the greatest content in the world, but if your resume just doesn't look right, people may not actually read it.

◎ You know the saying, "You can't judge a book by its cover." Well, while you really can't, if you don't know anything about the book or its contents, you just might not pick it up *unless* the cover looks interesting.

◎ When sending your resume and cover letter, instead of using a standard number 10 business envelope and folding your resume, use a large manila envelope. That way you won't have to fold your resume, and your information gets there looking clean, crisp, and flat.

◎ Don't use odd fonts or typefaces. Why? In many large companies, resumes are scanned by machine. Certain fonts don't scan well. What should you use? Helvetica, Times, Arial, and Courier work well.

◎ Similarly, many fonts don't translate well when e-mailing or transmitting electronically. What looks great on the resume on your computer screen may end up looking like gibberish at the recipients end…and you probably will never know. Once again, use Helvetica, Times, Arial, or Courier.

◎ When preparing your resume, make your name larger and bolder than the rest of the content. For example, if your resume is done in 12 point type, use 14-, 16-, or 18-point type for your name. Your name will stand out from those on other resumes.

◎ Remember to utilize white space effectively. Margins should be at least one inch on each side as well as on the top and bottom of each page. White space also helps draw the reader's attention to information.

◎ Even if you view your resume on your computer screen, be sure to print out a copy to be sure the document looks good no matter how a potential employer sees it.

Redefining Your Resume

You probably already have a resume in some form. How has it been working? Is it getting you the interviews you want? If it is, great! If not, you might want to consider redefining it.

You want your resume to stand out. You want it to illustrate that you are successful in your past accomplishments. You want potential employers to look at your resume and say to themselves, "That's who I want working here!"

How do you do that? Make your resume compelling. Demonstrate through your resume that *you* believe in yourself, because if *you* don't believe in *you,* no one else will. Show that you have the ability to solve problems and bring fresh ideas to the table.

First decide how you want to present yourself. What type of resume is best for you? There are three basic types of resumes. The chronological resume lists your jobs and accomplishments beginning with the most current and going backwards. Functional resumes, which may also be referred to as skills-based resumes, emphasize your accomplishments and abilities. One of the good things about this type of resume is that it allows you to lay it out in a manner that spotlights your key areas, whether they be your qualifications, skills, or employment history. A combination resume is a combination of the chronological and functional resumes.

What's the best type of resume for you? That depends on a number of factors, including where and what level you are in your career. If you are just entering the job market and you haven't held down a lot of jobs but you have relevant experience through internships and/or volunteer activities, you might use the functional type. If, on the other hand, you have held a number of jobs in the field and climbed the ladder with each new job, you might want to use the chronological variety. As I noted earlier, there is no one right way. You have to look at the whole picture and make a decision.

Use common sense. Make sure your best assets are prominent on your resume. Do you have a lot of experience? Are your accomplishments above the bar? Did you graduate cum laude? Do

---

⭐ **Voice of Experience**
Your resume is your place to toot your own horn. If you don't, no one will know what you have accomplished.

you have a master's degree? Do you have a doctorate? Determine what would grab your eye and find a way to focus first on that.

What Should Your Resume Contain?

What should you include in your resume? Some components are required and some are optional. Let's look at some of them.

What do you definitely need? You absolutely need your name, address, phone number, and e-mail address if you have one. You also should have your education and any training as well as your professional experience. You want to include your work accomplishments and responsibilities so potential employers know what you have done and what you can bring to the table. What else? You should include certifications, licenses, professional affiliations and memberships, honors, awards, and any additional professional accomplishments.

What else *might* you want to put in your resume? Your career objective, a summary of skills, and a career summary. Anything else? How about any volunteer experience you might have?

What should you *not* put in your resume? Your age, marital status, religion, health problems, current or past salaries, and whether or not you have children. What else should you not include? Any weakness you have or think you have.

⭐ **Tip from the Top**

Many people sabotage themselves by giving more information than is required on their resumes. When preparing your resume, always stop and think, "Will this information help or hinder my career?"

Career Summary

Let's take a moment to discuss your career summary. While a career summary isn't a required component, it often is helpful when an employer gets huge numbers of resumes and gives each a short glance. A career summary is a short professional biography, no longer than 12 lines, that tells your professional story. You can do it in a number of ways. Here's an example:

> Dedicated police officer with more than six years of experience. Proven ability to effectively and efficiently handle a wide array of law enforcement duties. Exceptionally skilled in investigative procedures as well as legal liabilities related to arrest and law enforcement; accomplished in use of firearms and specialized police equipment. Certified EMT-paramedic; multilingual (English, Spanish, French, and Chinese, various dialects). Excellent management, organizational, communications, and human relations skills. Proven ability in undercover police work resulting in the conviction of more than 65 drug dealers in a two-year period. Diverse contacts in law enforcement field and community. Founding member of DDD (Dummies Don't Drink and Drive), a community-supported group whose goals are to stop teenage drinking and driving.

A potential employer looking at this might think, "This Eric Flay looks like a good candidate for our force. The ability to speak more than one language is always a plus. He is a certified EMT. He has been successful at undercover work and knows a great deal about legal liabilities. His cover letter states he is looking for a lateral transfer to be closer to his family, so he probably has ties to the community. He started a community-based organization to help stop teen drinking and driving. He was not number one on the exam, but even scoring third on the list, he looks better than the candidate who was the top scorer. Why don't I give him a chance to tell me more and bring him in for an interview?"

"What if I'm just out of college and have no experience?" you ask. "What would my career summary look like?"

In situations like this, you have to look to experience and jobs you held prior to graduating. How about this:

Recent graduate of State University with major in criminal justice (4.0 GPA). Member of college campus activities board assisting in the development of campus safety program. Held position for three years while in college as plainclothes security guard for Radsons Department Store working to prevent theft by customers and employees; helped apprehend shoplifting suspects prior to the arrival of the police. Successfully completed police academy.

If you prefer, you can use a bullet list to do your career summary.

- Recent graduate of State University with a major in criminal justice (GPA 4.0).
- Member of college campus activities board assisting in development of campus safety program.
- Instrumental in writing grant to get funding for program.
- Held position for three years as plainclothed security guard for Radsons Department Store, Any City, to prevent theft by customers and employees.
- Completed reports and testified in court when necessary to assure convictions.
- Completed Any City Police Academy.

Career Objective

Do you need a career objective in your resume? It isn't always necessary, but in certain cases it helps. For example, if you are just starting out in your career, having a career objective or a specific goal illustrates that you have some direction, that you know where you want to go in your career.

When replying to an advertisement for a job opening, make sure your career objective on your resume is as close to the job you are applying for as possible. For example, if you are applying for a job as a police chief of schools, you might make your career objective, "Combining my passions for working in law enforcement and keeping young people safe; utilizing my skills and talents to develop and oversee programs to provide a safe environment in which young people can learn and flourish."

If, on the other hand, you are sending your resume to a law enforcement agency, organization, or company, "cold" or not, for a specific job opening, don't limit yourself unnecessarily by stating a specific career objective. If you use a career objective in this type of situation, make sure it is general.

Education

Where should you place education on your resume? That depends. If you recently graduated from college, put it toward the top. If you have a 4.0 GPA, you might want to put it at the top. If you graduated a number of years ago, put your education toward the end of your resume. Do you need to put the year you graduated? Recent graduates might want to. Other than that, just indicate the college or university you graduated from, your major, and degree.

"What if I went to college but didn't graduate? What should I put on my resume?" you might ask.

If you went to college but didn't graduate, simply write that you attended or are taking coursework toward a degree. Will anyone question you on it? That's hard to say. Someone might. If questioned, simply say something like, "I attended college and then unfortunately found it necessary to go to work full time. I plan on getting my degree as soon as possible. I only have nine credits left to go, so it will be an easy goal to complete."

Similarly, if a job requires a master's or doctorate and you haven't completed the educational requirements, simply put down that you are taking the coursework toward your degree (if you are).

In addition to your college education, the police academy, and any other specialized training you may have gone through, make sure you add any industry-related seminars or workshops you have taken. Don't forget to include any relevant noncredit courses, seminars, and workshops you have attended as well as including any educational courses that are not industry oriented but might help you in your career, such as dispute resolution, public speaking, writing, grant writing, communications, or team work.

Professional and Work Experience

List your work experience in this section of your resume. What jobs have you had? Where did you work? What did you do? What were your accomplishments?

How far back do you go? That once again depends upon where you are in your career. Don't go back to your job as a babysitter when you were 15, but you need to show your work history.

In addition to your full-time jobs in or out of law enforcement, include any part-time work that relates to the area of law enforcement you are pursuing as well as any job that illustrates skills, accomplishments, or achievements.

Skills and Personality Traits

There's an old advertising adage that says something to the effect of, "Don't sell the steak; sell the sizzle." When selling yourself through your resume, do the same. Do not only state your skills and personality traits; make them sizzle! Do this by using descriptive language and key phrases.

Need some help? Here are a few words and phrases to get you started.

- creative
- dedicated
- hard working
- highly motivated
- energetic
- self-starter
- fully knowledgeable
- strong work ethic
- team player
- problem solver

Accomplishments and Achievements

What have you accomplished in your career, in or out of law enforcement? Were you instrumental in orchestrating a successful drug bust? Have you developed a program to decrease gang activity in the community? Were you a founding member of a community organization whose mission is to stop teen drinking and driving? Did you receive a commendation for saving someone's life? Have you been nominated as police officer of the year?

Have you written a weekly column on making your community safer? Have you won an industry award? Have you done the publicity for the PBA? Have you written a large grant? Have you written an acclaimed article on some aspect of law enforcement?

Have you implemented an innovative program? Have you supervised other officers? Were you the director of a legal aid office?

Have you been asked to speak at an industry conference? Were you the top scorer on the civil service test? Are you the president of a civic group or not-for profit?

Your achievements inform potential employers not only about what you have done but also about what you might do for them.

Sit down and think about it for a while. What are you most proud of in your career? What have you done that has made a difference or had a positive impact on the organization, agency, or company for which you worked? If you are new to the workforce, what did you do in school? What about in a volunteer capacity?

Just as you made your skills and personality traits sizzle and sparkle with words, you want to do the same thing with your accomplishments and achievements. Put yourself in the position of a human resources director, police chief, or owner of a company for a moment. You get two resumes. Under the accomplishments section, one says, "Worked as police officer, promoted to detective." The other says, "Worked as police officer in mid-sized police department; promoted to detective, then sergeant; planned, controlled, and directed investigations resulting in 128 arrests for trafficking cocaine and other illegal drugs; uncovered evidence and developed case against arsonist ring resulting in apprehension and conviction of 10 key individuals." Which resume would catch your eye?

You can help your accomplishments and achievements sizzle by adding action verbs to your accomplishments. Use words like *achieved, administered, applied, accomplished, assisted, strengthened,* and others.

Honors and Awards

When drafting your resume, include any honors you have received whether or not they have anything to do with law enforcement. These honors help set you apart from other candidates.

Did one of your newspaper articles win a journalism award? Did you run for the library board of directors and win the seat? Did you start a local Big Brothers/Big Sisters chapter? Did you win the Community Service Award from your local civic group? Were you elected president of the Rotary club? While these accomplishments might have nothing to do with law enforcement, they do show that you are a hard worker and good at what you do.

Community Service and Volunteer Activities

If you perform community service or volunteer activities on a regular basis, make sure you include it on your resume. These types of activities illustrate to potential employers that you "do a little extra." They demonstrate that you are involved in the community. Additionally, you can never predict when the person reviewing your resume might be a member of the organization with which you volunteer. An unexpected connection like that can help you stand out in a positive way. Additionally, illustrating that you are involved in civic groups and the not-for profit world may be a plus to potential employers.

Hobbies and Interests

What are your hobbies and interests? Do you collect old baseball cards? Do you have a collection of vintage baseball bats? Do you collect NASCAR memorabilia? Are you a hiker? Do you volunteer with a literacy program? Are you a Court Appointed Special Advocates (CASA) volunteer? Are you involved in pet rescue? While many career counselors feel that hobbies or personal interests have no place on a professional resume, I disagree. Why?

Here's a secret. You can never tell what will cause the person or persons reviewing the resumes to make a connection. Perhaps he or she has the same hobby as you. Perhaps he or she is a volunteer with a literacy program in which you participate. Anything that causes you to stand out in a positive manner or that causes a connection with your potential interviewer will help your resume garner attention helping you to land an interview.

References

The goal for your resume is to have it help you *obtain* an interview. If you list your references on your resume, be aware that someone may check them to help them decide if they should interview you. Of course, you will most likely have to give the names of references on your application. However, you don't really want people giving their opinions about you *until* you have the chance to sell yourself. With this in mind, it usually isn't a good idea to list your references on your resume.

If you are uncomfortable with this, include a line on your resume stating that "References are available upon request."

Tip from the Coach

Don't stress if you can't get your resume on one or two pages. While most career specialists insist a resume should only be one or two pages at most, I strongly disagree. You don't want to overwhelm a potential employer with a 10-page book, but if your resume needs to be three or four pages to get your pertinent information in, that's okay. Keep in mind, though, that lengthy resumes or CVs (curriculum vitae) are generally used by high-level professionals who have many years' experience and work history to fill the additional pages. If your resume is longer than normal, you should use a brief career summary at the beginning so a hiring manager can quickly see what your major accomplishments are. If they then want to take their time to look through the rest of the resume, your information will be there.

Your Resume Writing Style

How important is writing style in your resume? In two words…very important. Aside from conveying your message, your writing style helps to illustrate that you have written communication skills.

When preparing your resume, write clearly and concisely and do not use the pronoun "I" to describe your accomplishments. Instead of writing "I developed a program to decrease street crime," you might try, "Developed innovative program that decreased street crime by 30% within a one-year period." Note the inclusion of a time period. It's good to be specific about your achievements.

Instead of "I worked as director of a legal aid agency," you might try, "Managed large legal aid agency which provided legal services and representation in family matters, criminal matters, bankruptcy, landlord/tenant issues, and guardianships to low-income individuals. Directed staff of 49 including 35 attorneys."

Words from a Pro

If you are instructed to send references with your resume, attach them on a separate sheet with your cover letter.

Instead of "I want to work as a border patrol guard," try "Use my education, experience, talent, and skills to secure a position as a border patrol guard to help keep our country."

Creating Industry-Specific Resumes

How can you create resumes specific to the area of law enforcement you are pursuing? Once you've created your basic resume, tailor each resume for the specific position or area you are pursuing and find ways to relate your existing skills to that resume.

Use all your experiences, talents, and skills to help you obtain the career you want. Transfer skills and experience when you can.

One thing you should *never* do is lie on your resume. Don't lie about your education. Don't lie about experience. Don't lie about places you've worked. Don't lie about what you've done. Don't lie about your skills. If you haven't picked up on it yet, *do not lie*.

Being deceitful is wrong in any industry. In law enforcement, it can end your career. Once someone knows you have lied, that is what they will remember about you and they may pass on that information to others.

"Oh, no one is going to find out," you might say.

Don't bet on it. Someone might find out by chance, deduce the truth based on knowledge within the industry, or hear the facts from a coworker or industry colleague. Someone just by chance may be surfing the net and see your name. When the truth comes out, it can end up blowing up in your face.

"By that time, I'll be doing such a good job, no one will fire me," you say.

That's the best-case scenario and there's a chance that could happen, but think about this. Once someone lies to you, do you ever trust them again? Probably not and no one will trust you or anything you say. That will hurt your chances of climbing the career ladder. The worst-case scenario is that you will be fired, left without references, lose some of your contacts, and make it much more difficult, if not impossible, to find your next job.

If you don't have the experience you wish you had, try to impress the HR director, hiring manager, or recruiter with other parts of your resume and your cover letter. If you have the experience and you are trying to advance your career, this is the time to redefine your resume. Add action verbs. Add your accomplishments. Make your new resume shine. Create a marketing piece that will make someone say, "We need to interview this person. Look at everything he (or she) has done."

When creating your resume for a career in law enforcement, you want it to reflect your knowledge of the industry. Be sure your resume shows evidence of skills, experience, productivity, and your personal commitment to law enforcement.

Your CV: Curriculum Vitae

What exactly is a CV? CV is short for curriculum vitae. What's the difference between a CV and a resume? That depends who you ask. Some people use the words interchangeably. Some say a resume is a one- or two-page summary of your employment history, experience, and education and a CV is a longer, more comprehensive and

---

★ Words to the Wise

As people often use the words CV and resume interchangeably, don't assume that just because someone asks you for your CV they actually want that particular document. They might really want your resume.

⭐ **Tip from the Coach**

One of the mistakes that many people make when preparing their resume is that they keep adding accomplishments without deleting any of the earlier or less important ones. While it's very tempting to do this, it's not always the best idea.

detailed synopsis of your qualifications, education, and experience. So what's the answer?

Generally, it's somewhere in between. Your resume *is* a summary of your employment history and education that highlights your skills, talents, and education. Your CV is a longer, detailed synopsis of these things, plus teaching and research experience you might have, articles or papers you have published, research projects you have done, presentations you have made, and so on. The CV gives you the opportunity to list every paper, project, presentation, and so on.

How do you know which type of document to use? Generally, it depends on the type of job for which you are applying. You will often use your CV instead of a resume if you are applying for a job in research or administration or are running for an office such as sheriff, judge, or district attorney.

What About References?

We just discussed that it's not a good idea to list your references on your resume. That doesn't mean, however, that you don't need them. Ref-

⭐ **The Inside Scoop**

Instead of just making your resume an outline of your accomplishments, make it a powerful marketing tool.

erences are another of your selling tools. Basically, references are the individuals who will vouch for your skills, ethics, and work history when a potential employer calls. A good reference can set you apart from the crowd and give you the edge over other applicants. A bad one can seriously hinder your career goals.

It's always a good idea to bring the names, addresses, and phone numbers of the people you are using for references with you when you apply for a job or when you are going on an interview. If you're asked to list them on an employment application, you'll be prepared.

Who should you use for references? To begin with, you'll need professional references. These are people you've worked with or know you on a professional level. They might be current or former supervisors or bosses, maybe the chief of police, perhaps your lieutenant, maybe the director of a not-for profit organization you've worked with, internship program coordinators, former professors, instructors at the police academy, and so on.

Do your references have to be from within the law enforcement industry? If you have references in the industry, it can't hurt. What you are looking for, however, are people who you can count on to help sell you to potential employers. Those will be your best references.

Always ask people if they are willing to be a reference before you use them. Only use people you are absolutely sure will say good things about you. Additionally, when searching out your references, try to find people who are articulate and professional.

Who would be a bad reference? A boss who fired you, a supervisor you didn't get along with, or anyone who you had any kind of problem with. Do not use these people for references even if they tell you that they'll give you good ones. They might keep their word, but they might not and you won't know until it's too late.

| ⭐ | **Tip from the Coach** |

In some cases, employers might ask for personal references as well as professional references. Personal references are people such as family, friends, or neighbors who know you well. Be sure to have a list of three to five personal references as well as their contact information readily available in case you need it.

"What if I didn't get along with my supervisor?" you ask. "Isn't a potential employer going to call her anyway?"

You are right. Your potential employer probably *will* call your former supervisor. The trick is getting a list of three to five *good* references. That way, no matter what anyone else says, you will still look good.

You might be asked to list references on an employment application, but it's a good idea to prepare a printed sheet of your professional references that you can leave with the interviewer. Basically this sheet will contain your list of three to five references including their names, positions,

and contact information. As with your resume, make sure it is printed on a high-quality paper.

Here's an example to get you started.

Professional Reference Sheet for John Rivers

Mr. Dick Williams
Detective
Tri-Town Police Department
120 Main Street
Tri-Town, NY 11111
(111) 222-2222
dwilliams@tritownpd.org

Professor Amber Collins
State University
100 Route 9D
Some City, NY 11111
(111) 444-4444
acollins@steu.edu

Joseph Rosen
Intern Coordinator
New City PD
499 Broadway
New City, NJ 22222
(333) 666-6666
jrosen@newcitynj.com

Lieutenant George Andrews
Some State Police
538 Sunset Road
Some State, NY 11111
(333) 333-3333
gandrews@somestateny.com

Terri Hass
Assistant District Attorney, Some County
538 Government Plaza
Any City, NY 11111
(111) 888-8888
thass@anycityny.com

⭐ The Inside Scoop

If you give your references an idea of exactly what type of job you're pursuing, what skills are important in that position, or even what you want them to say, you stand a better chance of their leading the conversation in the direction you want it to go. You might tell a reference, for example, that you're applying for a position as a police dispatcher and that the job description calls for someone very organized with the ability to multitask and stay calm and focused. In most cases, when your reference gets a call, he or she will remember what you said and stress your important selling points.

Personal References

In addition to professional references, you might also be asked to provide personal references. These are friends, family members, or others who know you. You probably won't need to print out a reference sheet for your personal references, but make sure you have all their contact information in case you need it quickly.

As with professional references, make sure the people you are using know you are listing them as references. Give them a call when you're going on an interview to let them know someone might be contacting them. Ask them to let you know if they get a call.

Letters of Recommendation

As you go through your career, it's a good idea to get letters of recommendation from people who have been impressed with your work. Along with references, these help give potential employers a better sense of your worth. How do you get a letter of recommendation? You usually simply have to ask. For example, let's say you are close to completing an internship.

Say to your supervisor, "I've enjoyed my time here. Would it be possible to get a letter of recommendation from you for my files?"

Most people will be glad to provide this. In some cases, people might even ask you to write it yourself for them to sign. Don't forego these opportunities even if you feel embarrassed about blowing your own horn. The easiest way to do it is by trying to imagine you aren't writing about yourself. In that way you can be honest and write a great letter. Give it to the person and say, "Here's the letter we discussed. Let me know if you want anything changed or you aren't comfortable with any piece of it." Nine times out of ten, the person will just sign the letter as is.

Who should you ask for letters of recommendation? In many cases, the people you ask will be the same ones you ask to be your reference. If you are still in school or close to graduating, you might ask professors with whom you have developed a good relationship. Don't forget internship coordinators or supervisors, your instructors at the training academy, former and current employers, executive directors of not-for-profit, civic, or charity organizations you have volunteered with, and so on.

In some situations the people you ask may just write generic letters of recommendation, stating that you were a pleasure to work with or were good at your job. If the person writing the letter knows the type of position you're pursuing, he or she might gear the letter to specific skills, traits, and talents needed.

Your letters of recommendation will become another powerful marketing tool in your quest for career success in law enforcement. What do you do with them? Begin by photocopying each letter you get on high-quality white paper, making sure you get clean copies. Once that's done, you can make them part of your career portfolio, send them with your resume when applying for positions, or bring them with you to interviews.

Creating Captivating Cover Letters

Unless instructed otherwise by a potential employer or an advertisement, always send your resume with a cover letter. Why? Mainly because if your resume grabs the eye of someone in the position to interview you, he or she often looks at the cover letter to evaluate your written communications skills as well as to get a sense of your personal side. If your letter is a good one, it might just get you the phone call you've been waiting for. On the other hand, a poorly written letter might just keep you from getting that call.

What can make your letter stand out? Try to make sure your letter is directed to the name of the person to whom you are sending it instead of "hiring manager," "director of human resources," "Police Chief," "To Whom It May Concern," or "Sir or Madam."

"But the name of the person isn't in the ad," you say. "How do I know what it is?"

You might not always be able to get the correct name, but at least do some research. You might, for example, call the school or company advertising the opening and ask the name of the person to whom responses should be directed.

If you are sending your resume to an organization or company cold, it's even more important to send it to a specific person. It gives you a better shot at someone not only reviewing it, but taking action on it.

It's okay to call an organization or company and say to the receptionist or secretary, "Hi, I was wondering if you could give me some information? I'm going to be sending my resume to your company and I'm not sure who to send it to. Could you please give me the name of the human resources director [or police chief or whoever you are trying to target]?"

If he or she won't give it to you for some reason, say thank you and hang up. While most companies, organizations, and law enforcement agencies generally will freely give out this type of information, there may be some that for various reasons will not give out names easily.

How do you get around this? Wait until lunch time or around 5:15 p.m. when the person you spoke to might be at lunch or done with their workday, call back, and say something to the effect of, "Hi, I was wondering if you could please give me the spelling of your HR director's name [or whoever's name you are seeking]."

If the person on the other end of the phone line asks you to be more specific about the name, simply say, "Let's see I think it was Brownson or something like that. It sounded like Brown something."

Don't worry about sounding stupid on the phone. The person at the other end doesn't know you. This system usually works. Believe it not, most companies have someone working there whose name sounds like Brown or Smith.

The person on the phone may say to you, "No, we don't have a Brownson. What department are you looking for? It was HR, wasn't it?"

When you say yes, he or she will probably say, "Oh, that's not Brownson; it's John Campbell. Is that who you're looking for?"

Then all you have to say is, "You know what, you're right, sorry, I was looking at the wrong notes. So that's C-A-M-P-B-E-L-L?"

Voila. You have the name. Is it a lot of effort? Well, it's a little effort, but if it gets you the name of someone you need and ultimately helps get you an interview, isn't it worth it?

By the way, this technique not only works for getting names you need but other information as well. You might have to be persistent and it might take you a few tries, but it generally always gets you the information you need.

You also can sometimes get names from the Internet. Perhaps the company Web site lists the names of their key people. Key names for large companies may also often be located on Hoovers.com, an online database of information about businesses, but this is a paid service. If you are calling a police department, sheriff's office, or other law enforcement agency and the organization has a Web site, names of key personnel are often listed as well.

Do what you can to get the names you need. It can make a big difference when direct your letters to someone specific within the organization.

> ### ⭐ Words from the Wise
>
> Resist the urge to write a one-paragraph cover letter. Use your cover letter as another chance to *wow* the reader.

No matter which segment of law enforcement you are trying to locate a job, those who are in the position to hire you may be receiving a large number of resumes, letters, and phone calls. What can help your letters stand out? Make them grab the attention of the reader. How? Make sure your cover letters are creative.

Take some time and think about it. What would make *you* keep reading? Of course, there will be some situations when applying for jobs in law enforcement where you might be better off sending the traditional "In response to your ad" letter. But what about trying out a couple of other ideas when you can?

Take a look at the first sample cover letter. Would this letter grab your attention? Would it make you keep reading? Chances are it would. After grabbing the reader's attention, it quickly offers some of the applicant's skills, talents, and achievements. Would you bring in Robert Allen for an interview? I think most employers would.

ROBERT ALLEN
333 North Street
Another Town, NY 33333
Phone: (222) 333-5555
rallen@moreinternet.com

Ms. Ellen Mitchell
Any City Police Department
Any City, NY 11111

Dear Ms. Mitchell:
   CONGRATULATIONS!
   I'm pleased to inform you that you have just received the resume that can end your search for the Any City Police Department new director of media relations. In order to claim your "prize," please review my resume and call as soon as possible to arrange an interview. I can guarantee you'll be pleased you did!

In my current position as the assistant director of media relations for Mayor John Davis, I have developed a close working relationship with the local, regional, and national news media. During my three-year tenure in this position, I have implemented and conducted numerous press conferences and interviews, dealt effectively with media inquiries, provided spokespeople to assure the public receives accurate information when the mayor wasn't available, and handled spin control when necessary.

My responsibilities additionally include preparing statements for the mayor as well as his designated spokespeople and personally giving statements to the media when directed.

When the mayor's director of media relations went on maternity leave last summer, I was asked to step in and assume her responsibilities. During this period of time, I supervised the department of 16 employees.

Two years ago, with the help of the mayor, I instituted a program where young people interested in public service and helping the community could shadow the mayor for a day. Last year, we had more than 100 young people participate in four Shadow the Mayor Days.

While I love what I do now, my dream has always been a career where I could combine the skills garnered from my bachelor's in communications with my master's in criminal justice.

I would welcome the challenge and opportunity to work with the Any City Police Department and believe my experience, skills, talents, and passion will be an asset to your department.

I look forward to hearing from you.

Sincerely yours,
Robert Allen

While a creative cover letter may grab the attention of the reader, sometimes when applying for a position in law enforcement, creativity just isn't appropriate. Here's an example of a simple letter for someone applying for a job as a police chief.

WILLIAM BRENNER
332 G Avenue
Different Town, NY 33333
Phone: (666) 999-9999
williambrennerl@moreinternet.com

James Pless, Hiring Manager
Anytown Police Department
102 3rd Avenue
Anytown, NY 22222

Dear Mr. Pless:

I am submitting my resume for the position of Chief of Police in response to your advertisement in the July 15th edition of the *Anytown Times*. Fourteen years ago, I graduated from the police academy at the top of my class. The day I became a police officer was one of the best days of my life. It was then I could pursue the dream I had since I was a child.

Since that time, my life has been filled with wonderful challenges each and every day. Over the past fourteen years, I have earned ten promotions and three honorable decorations. While that should be the highlight of my career, it is not.

Instead, the highlights have been the things I did every day—some small, some larger—reuniting a child who was lost with her family; saving a child who was in the middle of a domestic situation with his abusive father; investigating the murder of a young mother and finding her killer; responding to a call from a senior citizen who was frightened when she heard a noise; working in conjunction with federal law enforcement agencies on a large drug bust; mentoring rookies; supervising other officers; being promoted to detective, sergeant, lieutenant, and assistant chief.

Every day has offered a new challenge. Every assignment has given me the experience that has prepared me for the job for which I now apply: the position of Anytown Chief of Police.

My philosophy for running a department is simple: Make sure the department is run with complete integrity, honesty, and fairness. Put together the best team of law enforcement officers, inspiring, motivating, and supporting them, and involve the residents of the area in keeping their community safe.

As you will note from my resume, I have a diverse background in law enforcement, including both formal education and on-the-job training. In addition to holding a master's degree in criminal justice, I have taken a wide array of seminars in areas from evidence collection and domestic violence investigation to hazardous material response and criminal law.

I would very much appreciate the opportunity to meet with you to further discuss this opportunity. I look forward to hearing from you.

Sincerely,
William Brenner

More Selling Tools—Business and Networking Cards

The best way to succeed at almost anything is to do everything possible to stack the deck in your favor. Most people use resumes to sell themselves. As we just discussed, done right, your resume can be a great selling tool. It can get you in the door for an interview. But putting all your eggs in one basket is never a good idea. What else can you do to help sell yourself? What other tools can you use?

Business cards are small but powerful tools that can positively impact your career if used

---

⭐ Tip from the Coach

Business cards are networking cards. You give them to people you meet so they not only remember you and what you do but how to contact you if necessary. These are important no matter what aspect of the law enforcement industry you aspire to succeed in.

correctly. We've discussed the importance of business cards throughout the book. Let's look at them more closely.

Whatever level you're at in your career, whatever area of the industry you're interested in pursuing, business cards can help you get further. If you don't have a job yet, business cards are essential. At this point, they may also be known as networking cards because that is what they are going to help you do. If you already have a job, business cards can help you climb the ladder to success. Get your business cards made up, and get them made up now! They will be very useful in your career.

Why are cards so important? For a lot of reasons but mainly because they help people not only remember you but find you. Networking is so essential to your success in the industry that once you go through all the trouble of doing it, if someone doesn't remember who your are or how they can contact you, it's almost useless.

How many times have you met someone during the day or at a party and then gone your separate ways? A couple days later, something will come up where you wish you could remember the person's name or you remember their name but have no idea how to get a hold of them.

The Inside Scoop

Don't try to save money making business cards on your computer. They never look professional and you don't really end up saving any money.

How bad would you feel if you found out that you met someone, told him or her that you were looking for a job, they ran into someone else who was looking for someone with your skills and talents, and they didn't know how to get a hold of you? Business cards could have helped solve that problem.

When was the last time you ran into someone successful who didn't have business cards? They boost your prestige and make you feel more successful. If you feel more successful, you'll be more successful.

So, what's your next step? Start by determining what you want your business cards to look like. There are a variety of styles to choose from. You might want to go to a print shop or an office supply store such as Staples or OfficeMax to look at samples or you can create your own style.

Samples of Business and Networking Cards

Howard Morton

Career Goal: Position in Federal Law Enforcement
Bachelor's Degree in Criminal Justice and
Business Administration
Master's Degree in Criminal Justice

PO Box 2900   Phone: (111) 888-9999
Anytown, NY 11111   Cell: (888) 999-0000
E-mail: hmorton@someinternet.com

Samples of Business and Networking Cards, continued

Charles Anthony
Information Systems Security Specialist

P.O. Box 909   Phone: 111-444-9999
Anytown, NY 11111   Cell: 888-111-1111
E-mail: canthony@someinternet.com

---

420 North Avenue
Anytown, NY 11111
lrodgers@internet.com

Laurie Rodgers

Career Goal—Law Enforcement Officer
Bachelor's Degree—Criminal Justice
Graduate—Police Academy

Phone: 111-444-0000
Cell: 888-888-9999

---

492 Circle Street
Anytown, NY 11111
E-mail: jevans@allinternet.com

Joseph Evans

Corporate Security
www.josephevanssecurity.com

Phone: 222-111-1111
Cell: 111-999-0000

Samples of Business and Networking Cards, continued

Jenny Caplow

Private Investigator
We find what you need
www.jennycaplowinvestigations.com

P.O. Box 1400   Phone: 111-444-5555
Anytown, NY 11111
E-mail: jcaplow@anytownelementary.edu

⭐ Tip from the Top

If you are currently employed, your employer will often provide you with business cards.

Order at least 1,000 cards. What are you going to do with that many cards? You're going to give them to everyone. While everyone might not keep your resume, most people in all aspects of business keep cards.

Simple cards are the least expensive. The more design, graphics, or features you add, the more the cost goes up.

What should your cards say? At minimum, include your name, address (or P.O. box), and phone number (both home and cell if you have one). It's a good idea to add your job or your career goal or objective. You might even briefly describe your talents, skills, or traits. Your business card is your selling piece, so think about what you want to sell. Check out some of the samples to get ideas.

Remember that business cards are small. The number of words that can fit on the card so the card looks attractive and can be read easily are limited. If you want more room, you might use a double-sided card (front and back) or a double-sized card that is folded over, in effect giving you four times as much space. I've seen both used successfully. The double-sized card can be very effective for a mini-resume.

You have a lot of decisions on how you want your business cards to look. What kind of cards stock do you want? Do you want your cards

⭐ Words from the Wise

If you don't feel comfortable putting your home address on your business cards, get a P.O. box.

⭐ Tip from the Coach

Look at other people's business cards in all industries to try to find a style you like. Then fit your information into that style.

smooth or textured, flat or shiny? What about color? Do you want white, beige, or colored cards? Do you want flat print or raised print? What fonts or type faces do you want to use? Do you want graphics? How do you want the information laid out? Do you want it straight or on an angle? The decisions are yours. It just depends on what you like and what you think will sell you the best.

Brochures Can Tell Your Story

While you're always going to need a resume, consider developing your own brochure, too. A brochure can tell your story and help you sell yourself. Sometimes something out of the ordinary can help grab the attention of someone important.

What's a brochure? Basically it is a selling piece that gives information about a product, place, event, or person, among other things. In this situation the brochure is going to be about you. While your resume tells your full story, your brochure is going to illustrate your key points.

Why do you need one? A brochure can make you stand out from other job seekers.

What should a brochure contain? While it depends to a great extent on what segment of the industry you are pursuing, there are some basic things you should include.

Of course, you need your name and contact information. Then add your selling points. Maybe those are your skills. Perhaps they are your talents or accomplishments. What about something unique or special that you do? Definitely try to illustrate what *you* can do for an organization, company, law enforcement agency, and so on and what benefits they will obtain by hiring you. A brief bio is often helpful to illustrate your credentials and credibility. What about three or four quotes from some of your letters of recommendation. For example:

◎ "One of the best interns we ever had participate in our internship program." Chief Lewis Bertinelli, Green City Police Department
◎ "A real team player who motivates the team." Danielle Jones, Sheriff, Tri-County Sheriff's Office
◎ "A true law enforcement professional." Judge Alexa Nixson

Keep your wording simple. Make it clear, concise, and interesting.

What should your brochure look like? The possibilities are endless. Brochures can be simple

---

or elaborate. Your brochure can be designed in different sizes, papers, folds, inks, and colors. You can use photographs, drawings, illustrations, or other graphics.

If you have graphic-design ability and talent, lay out your brochure yourself. If you don't, ask a friend or family member who is talented in that area. There are also software programs that help you design brochures. With these programs, you simply type your information in and print it out. Some people with access to a laser color copier and/or printer create their own professional-looking pieces.

The beauty of doing it yourself is that after you've sent out a number of brochures, you can improve and redesign them if they aren't doing anything for you and send out another batch. Be very sure, however, that your brochure looks professional or it will defeat the purpose.

If you want to design your brochure but want it printed professionally, consider bringing your camera-ready brochure to a professional print shop. Camera-ready means your document is ready to be printed, and any consumer print shop should be able to help guide you through the steps needed to prepare your work for them. In addition to print shops, you might consider office supply stores like Staples and OfficeMax that do printing.

If you don't feel comfortable designing your own brochure, you can ask a printer in your area if there is an artist on staff. Professional design and printing of a brochure can get expensive. Is it worth it? Only you can decide, but if it helps get your career started or makes the one you have more successful, probably the answer is yes.

Can brochures be effective? I certainly think so. Not only do I know a great number of people who have used them successfully in a variety of industries including law enforcement; I personally used one when I was breaking into the music business and have continued using them ever since. Here's my story.

At the time I was sending out a lot of resumes and making a lot of calls in an attempt to obtain interviews. I had learned a lot about marketing and noticed that many companies used brochures. My father, who was a marketing professional, suggested that a brochure might just be what I needed. By that time, I had realized that if I wanted to *sell* myself, I might need to market myself a little more aggressively than I was doing, so I decided to try the brochure idea.

We designed a brochure that was printed on 11-by-17-inch paper folded in half, giving me four pages to tell my story. We artistically mounted a head shot on the front page and printed it in hot pink ink. The inside was crafted with carefully selected words indicating my accomplishments, skills, talents, and the areas in which I could help a company who hired me. The brochures were professionally printed,

> **Tip from the Coach**
>
> You are going to use your brochure in addition to your resume, not in place of it.

and I sent them to various record labels, music instrument manufacturers, music publishers, music industry publicity companies, artist managers, and so on. I started getting calls from some of the people who received the brochures, obtained a number of interviews, and even landed a couple of job offers. None of them, however, interested me.

Five years after I sent out my first brochure, I received a call from a major record company who told me that at the time they first received my brochure they didn't need anyone with my skills or talents, but they thought the brochure was so unique that they kept it on file. Voila. Five years passed, they needed an individual with my skills, someone remembered my brochure, pulled it out, and called me. By that time I was already on the road with another group and couldn't take the job, but it was nice to be called.

What is really interesting, however, is that companies and people I originally sent that first brochure years ago still remember it. They can describe it to a tee and many of them still have it in their files.

When creating your brochure, make sure it represents the image you want to portray. Make it as unique and eye catching as possible. You can never tell how long someone is going to keep it.

Your Career Portfolio: Have Experience Will Travel

People in creative careers have always used portfolios to illustrate what they have done and can accomplish. You can do the same in your career in law enforcement.

What exactly is a career portfolio? Basically, it's a portfolio, binder, or book that contains your career information and illustrates your best work. In addition to traditional printed components of your portfolios, many people in education are also using multimedia components, including video, PowerPoint, and Web pages. Your portfolio is a visual representation of what you have done and often illustrates what your potential might be.

Why do you need one? Because your career portfolio can help you get the positions you want, and that is what this is all about.

Consider this question: What would you believe more—something someone told you or something you saw with your own eyes? If you're like most people, you would believe something you saw. And that's what a good career portfolio can do for you. It can provide illustrations of what you've done and what you can do.

For example, you might tell a potential employer that in your last job you helped decrease crime by 25 percent. If you have a copy of the newspaper story discussing the decrease in crime under your watch, he or she can see the decrease in black and white.

What would be more impressive to you? Looking over someone's resume and reading that they received the "Distinguished Law Enforcement Officer of the Year" award or actually seeing a copy of the award certificate? Reading that someone had developed an interesting program in a community or seeing a copy of the article and picture about it in the newspaper?

Have you successfully negotiated a hostage release? Has the story been in the paper?

Has someone done a feature story or article on you? Have you been quoted in your professional capacity? Have you received awards?

⭐ **Tip from the Top**

When compiling your portfolio, be careful not to use any confidential work or documents from an organization, law enforcement agency, or company, even if you were the one who wrote the report, letter, or document. A potential employer might be concerned about how you will deal with their confidential issues if you aren't keeping other confidences.

Copies of all these documents can be part of your career portfolio. Often, if you have buzz around you, potential employers feel you will be a commodity.

Don't think that your portfolio will only be useful when you are first trying to land a job. If you continue adding new accomplishments, skills, and samples of projects you've worked on, your portfolio will be useful in advancement throughout your career. Of course, as time goes on, omit some of your earlier documents and replace them with more current ones.

Having an organized system to present your achievements and successes is also helpful when going through employment reviews or asking for a promotion or raise. It also is very effective in illustrating what you've done if you're trying to move up the ladder at a different company.

Over the years, I've consistently gotten calls from people who have been to our seminars or called for advice who continue to use their portfolios in their careers in every industry. Work on developing your career portfolio and this simple tool can help you achieve success as well.

Your portfolio is portable. You can bring it with you when you go on interviews so you can show it to potential employers. You can make copies of things in your portfolio to give to potential employers or have everything at hand

when you want to answer an ad or send out cold letters.

How do you build a detailed portfolio illustrating your skills, talents, experiences, and accomplishments? What goes into it? You want your portfolio to document your work-related talents and accomplishments. These are the assets you will be *selling* to your potential employers. Let's look at some of the things you might want to include.

◎ Your profile
◎ Resume
◎ Bio
◎ Reference sheets
◎ Skill and abilities
◎ Degrees, licenses, and certifications
◎ Training
◎ Experience sheet
◎ Summary of accomplishments
◎ Professional associations
◎ Professional development activities (conferences, seminars, and workshops attended as well as any other professional development activities)
◎ Awards and honors
◎ Volunteer activities and community service
◎ Supporting documents
◎ Samples of work
◎ Your philosophy of law enforcement
◎ Newspaper, magazine, and other articles and/or feature stories about you
◎ Articles you have written and published
◎ Reports you've done
◎ Letters of recommendation
◎ Letters or notes people have written to tell you that you've done a good job.
◎ Photos of you accepting an award or at an event you worked on
◎ Photos of events you were involved in

◎ News stories or feature articles generated by your execution or supervision of a project (for example, if you are in charge of a program that raises money for children's toys for Christmas)

Remember that this list is just to get you started. Some of the components may relate to you, but some may not. You can use anything in your portfolio that will help illustrate your skills, talents, and accomplishments.

In order to make it easier to locate information in your portfolio, you might want to develop a table of contents and then utilize dividers.

Here's a sample of a profile that someone interested in a career in federal law enforcement

Sample of Profile for Career Portfolio

PROFILE
Lori Baker

Education:
- ◎ State University—Master's Degree
- ◎ Major: Criminal Justice
- ◎ State University—Bachelor's Degree
- ◎ Major: Criminal Justice

Additional Training:
- ◎ Seminar: Interviewing and interrogating
- ◎ Seminar: Technology in law enforcement
- ◎ Seminar: Forensic Investigation
- ◎ Seminar: School violence
- ◎ Seminar: Command operations procedures
- ◎ Seminar: Police labor relations
- ◎ Seminar: Issues in police administration
- ◎ Seminar: Leadership for police supervisors
- ◎ Grant Writing
- ◎ Workshop: Web page design and creation

Goals:
- ◎ Working in federal law enforcement agency

Qualifications:
- ◎ Passionate law enforcement officer
- ◎ Hard working, dedicated, focused, motivated and energetic
- ◎ Creative thinker
- ◎ Problem solver
- ◎ Ability to stay calm under any circumstances
- ◎ Computer skills
- ◎ Ability to develop and build Web sites
- ◎ Verbal and written communication skills
- ◎ Multilingual (English, Spanish, French)

⭐ Tip from the Top

Make high-quality copies of key items in your portfolio to leave with interviewers or potential employers, agents, and so on. Visit an office supply store to find some professional-looking presentation folders to hold all the support documents you bring to an interview.

might use in her portfolio. Use it to give you an idea on getting started on yours.

Whatever segment of the law enforcement you are pursuing, use every tool you can to make sure you get an edge over others who want the same success as you do.

7

GETTING YOUR FOOT IN THE DOOR

One of the keys to a great career is getting your foot in the proverbial door. If you can just get that door open—even if it's just a crack—you can slip your foot in, and then you're on the road to success. Why? Because once you get your foot in, you have a chance to sell yourself, sell your talent, and sell your products or services.

It seems easy, but the problem is sometimes the hardest part is getting your foot in the door. Whether you simply walk in off the street to see someone or call to make an appointment, you often are faced with the same situation. You need to get past the receptionist, the secretary, or whoever the "gatekeeper" happens to be between you and the person with whom you want to speak.

In many areas of law enforcement, in order to get the job, you are required to not only take a civil service or other exams but be one of the top scorers. This may be the case, for example, if you want to work as a police officer, state police officer, sheriff's deputy, corrections officer, probation or parole officer, and so on. And while you may not always need to get past a gatekeeper in these situations, you should be aware that there is still a gatekeeper.

It's also important to realize that not all jobs in law enforcement require you to take civil service or other exams. What you need to know is that when looking for almost any job, there will be a gatekeeper.

Whether I'm giving a career seminar or doing a career consultation, people looking for advice on getting that *perfect* job consistently tell me that if they only could get their foot in the door, they would be on their way. In a way, they're right.

Here's what you need to know. Whenever there is a job opening, someone will get the job and unfortunately someone won't. Rejection is often part of the process in getting a job. However, feeling rejected when you didn't even get the chance to really be rejected because you can't get through to someone is quite another thing.

It's not personal, but the secretary, receptionist, assistant, and even the person you're trying to reach often thinks of you and most other unsolicited callers as unwanted intruders who waste their time. It doesn't really matter whether you're trying to sell something or get a job; unless they can see what you can do for them, it's going to be hard to get through.

In reality, you are trying to *sell* something. You're trying to sell *you, your skills,* and *your talents.* You're trying to get a job. What you need to do, however, is try not to let these gatekeepers know exactly what you want.

I am in no way telling you to lie or even stretch the truth. What I'm telling you to do is find a way to change their perception of you and what you want. Get creative.

Some areas of the law enforcement industry are easier to enter than others. Some segments of the industry are more competitive. And while there generally always is a gatekeeper, sometimes it's easier to get past him or her.

You might not think you have to worry about getting past a gatekeeper if you are pursuing a career in one of the segments of the industry in great demand or, as we just discussed, in one of the segments of the industry where you will need to take a civil service exam. Still, you can never tell.

Being prepared for any situation always gives you the edge. My advice is to read over this section, get familiar with some of the ideas, and use them when needed. Keep in mind that even if the position you are pursuing is one which requires you to take and score well on a civil service exam or police exam, the people in charge of hiring have a choice. You want to be the one who is chosen whether you are the top scorer on an exam or the fifth one down on the list.

There are any number of scenarios in which you might run into a gatekeeper. You might want to go after a department head position. You might want to work as a corporate security specialist at a large corporation or go after a position as a bodyguard on the road with a hot recording group or artist. You might want to go after a job as an attorney specializing in criminal cases with a big law firm; you might want to create your own position in some private or public law enforcement company or agency. There are so many possibilities where there *could* be a gatekeeper in your way during your career that

you really need to know how to get past them just in case.

In many situations, you might be answering an advertisement or visiting the human resources offices of an agency or company to fill in an application. If, for example, you are applying for an advertised job as a corrections officer or police officer, you might not have to *worry* about getting past the gatekeeper, but that doesn't mean he or she isn't there. You might not see them, but they always are lurking in the background.

No matter which segment of the industry you are pursuing, there will be times when you need to get past a gatekeeper so you can get your foot in the door. Before you rush in and find the door locked, let's look at some possible keys to help you get in.

Will you need every key? Probably not, but once you learn what some of the keys are, you'll have them if you need them.

Getting Through to People on the Phone

Let's start with the phone. If your goal is to talk to a specific person or make an appointment, it's important to know that many high-level businesspeople don't answer their own phones. Instead, they rely on secretaries, receptionists, or assistants to handle this task. And that's not even counting the dreaded *voice mail.*

You can always try the straightforward approach. Just call and ask to speak to the person you are looking for. If that works, you have your foot in the door. If not, it's time to get creative. Let's look at a couple of scenarios and how they might play out. In the first scenario, Greg Baxter is trying to land an interview in an attempt to create a position as an investigator for a criminal law firm.

Scenario 1

Receptionist: Good afternoon, Brown, Ronald and Michaels.

You: Hello, this is Greg Baxter. Can I please speak to Ron Brown?

Receptionist: Does he know what this is in reference to?

You: No, I'm looking for a job as an investigator and would like to see if I could set up an interview.

Receptionist: I'm sorry, Mr. Brown isn't looking to fill any positions at this time. Thank you for calling.

You: Thanks. Good-bye.

With that said, you're done. Is there something you could have said differently that might have led to a better ending? Let's look at another scenario.

Scenario 2

Sometimes mentioning a job to the gatekeeper is not a good idea Let's say you are trying to create your own position or you are going after a position that is so coveted that those already working in the company or organization may not be that open about helping those on the outside. What can you do?

Creativity is the name of the game.

Secretary: Good afternoon, Brown, Ronald and Michaels.

You: Is Mr. Brown in please?

Secretary: Who's calling?

You: Greg Baxter.

Secretary: May I ask what this is in reference to?

You: Yes, I was trying to set up an informational interview. Would Mr. Brown be the person who handles this or would it be someone else?

[Asking the question in this manner means that you stand a chance at the gatekeeper giving you a specific name that you can call if Mr. Brown is the wrong person.]

Secretary: Informational interview for what purpose?

You: I was interested in exploring the possibilities of working on staff as an investigator in a law firm in relation to working as a consultant. I'm not looking for a job; I'm trying to see which direction would be better for me. Your firm is one of the most respected criminal law firms in the state. I thought Mr. Brown might be someone who might have some knowledge in that area. Would he be the right person?

[Make sure you are pleasant. This helps the person answering the phone want to help you.]

Secretary: You probably would be better off speaking to Mary Ronald. She deals more with investigators. Would you like me to switch you?

[What you are really doing is helping her get you off the phone, even if it means she is dumping you on someone else.]

You: Yes, that would be great. What was your name?

[Try to make sure you get the name. In this manner, when you get transferred, the person answering at the other end will be more apt to help you.]

Secretary: Kelly Jamison.

You: Thanks for your help. I really appreciate it.

Secretary: I'll switch you now.

Beth Clarkson: Mary Ronald's office. This is Beth, may I help you?

You: Hi, Ms. Clarkson; Kelly Jamison suggested that Ms. Ronald might be the right person for me to speak to. I'm interested in exploring the possibilities of working on staff as an investigator in relation to working as a consultant. I'm just looking for information at this point. Your firm is one of the most respected criminal law firms in the state. I thought someone there might be able to give me some insight into opportunities on a general basis, not necessarily with your firm.

Ms. Clarkson: What type of project are you working on? Is this a school project or something?

You: No, I'm out of school. As a matter of fact, I have a bachelor's in criminal justice and am working on getting my master's degree.

[Notice that you are not really answering her question at all. At this point, Ms. Clarkson probably will either say, sorry Ms. Ronald is very busy or keep pumping you for information.]

Ms. Clarkson: Ms. Ronald is out of the office this week on trial. She should be back next Monday.

You: I know she is busy. Do you think she would have ten minutes for me if I stop in sometime next week, or would it be better to call her? I'm really interested in hearing her thoughts in this area.

Ms. Clarkson: She is pretty busy next week, but she might be able to spare a few minutes on Wednesday. Would that work for you?

[Do not say, let me check my calendar. If at all possible, take the time you are given for the meeting, no matter what else you have to juggle.]

Ms. Clarkson: I'm going to double-check with Ms. Ronald later. If you don't hear from me, why don't you come over around 9:30 a.m. on Wednesday. Do you have our address?

You: It is 1500 E Broadway, isn't it?

Ms. Clarkson: That's where we are located. You might want to also speak to Christine Holmes. She is the director of the Tri-City Legal Aid Association. She might be able to give you some information as well. Her number is 333-333-3333. You can tell her I suggested that you call.

You: That is so nice of you. I'm going to give her a call as soon as I hang up. You have been really helpful. I'll see you on Wednesday morning.

Here's what you need to know. If you are going in for an informational interview, make sure you make it an *informational interview*. You can, of course, nonchalantly drop information about your qualifications, but make sure you ask questions and get the information you originally said you wanted. Otherwise, your credibility may be marred.

You may or may not be successful in planting a seed so Ms. Ronald thinks about creating an in-house position for you or even just uses your services when needed. However, no matter what, you have made another contact who may be useful in helping you attain your career goals. Ms. Ronald, for example, may tell a colleague about you, and voila—you have another opportunity.

I can hear you saying, "That kind of thing doesn't really happen."

To that I reply it can and it does. I've seen it happen numerous times. In order for it to happen, however, you have to find ways to get past the gatekeeper.

Here's another scenario.

Scenario 3

Receptionist: "Good afternoon, ABC Corporation."

You: "Hi, I'm working on a project involving Internet and data security careers. Do you know who in your company I might speak to that might know something about that area?"

[Here is where it can get a little tricky. If you are very lucky, he or she will just put you through to someone in publicity, public relations, or human resources. If you're not so lucky, he or she will ask you questions.]

Receptionist: "What type of project?"

You need to be ready with a plausible answer. What you say will, of course, depend on your situation. If you are in college, you can always put together a project with one of your professors and say you are working on a project for school. If not, you can say you are doing research on career opportunities in Internet or data security (or whatever area of the industry you are pursuing). If you have writing skills, you might contact a local newspaper or magazine to see if they are interested in an article on careers in Internet security, keeping information safe, or whatever segment of the industry you are target-

ing. If you can't find someone to write for, you can always write a story on "spec." This means that if you write a story, you can send it in to an editor on speculation. They might take it and they might not. Don't think about money at this point. Your goal here is to get the "right people" to speak to you and get an appointment.

This method of getting to know people is supposed to give you credibility. The idea will only be effective if you *really* are planning on writing an article or a story and carrying through.

One of the interesting things about writing an article (whether on spec or on assignment) is that you can ask people questions and they will usually talk to you. They won't be looking at you as they might be if you were looking for a job.

What you've done in these situations is changed people's perception about why you are talking to them. One of the most important bonuses of interviewing people about a career in various industries is that you are making invaluable contacts.

While it might be tempting, remember to use this opportunity to ask questions and network; *do not* try to sell yourself. After you write the article, you might call up one of the people you have interviewed, perhaps the human resources director, and say something like, "You made a career in Internet security so interesting, I'd like

---

⭐ **Voice of Experience**

Make sure you get the correct spelling of the name of everyone who helps you. Send a short note thanking them for their help immediately. This is not only good manners, but it also helps people remember who you are in a positive way.

to explore a career in that field. I believe I have the training. Would it be possible to come in for an interview or to complete an application?

What can you do if none of these scenarios work? The receptionist may not be very eager to help. He or she may have instructions on "not letting anyone through." It may be his or her job to block unsolicited callers and visitors from the boss. What can you do?

Here are a few ideas that might help. See if you can come up with some others yourself.

◎ Try placing your call before regular business hours. Many executives and others you might want to talk to come in early before the secretary or receptionist is scheduled to work.

◎ Try placing your calls after traditional business hours when the secretary probably has left. The executives and others you want to reach generally don't push a time clock and often work late. More importantly, even if people utilize voice mail, they may pick up the phone themselves after hours in case their family is calling.

◎ Lunch hours are also a good time to attempt to get through to people. This is a little tricky. Executives may use voice mail during lunch hour or may go out to lunch themselves. On the other hand, you might get lucky.

◎ Sometimes others in the office fill in for a receptionist or secretary and aren't sure what the procedure is or who everyone is. While you might not get through on the first shot, you might use this type of opportunity to get information. For example, you might ask for the person you want to speak to and when the substitute tells you he or

> ### ⭐ Words from the Wise
> Friday afternoon is the worst time to call someone when you want something. The second-worst time is early Monday morning.

she isn't in and asks if you want to leave a message, say something like, "I'm moving around a lot today. I'll try to call later. Is Mr. Brown ever in the office after 6:00 p.m.?" If the answer is yes, ask if you can have his direct extension in case the switchboard is closed.

Remember the three "Ps" to help you get through. You want to be:

◎ Pleasant
◎ Persistent
◎ Positive

Always be pleasant. Aside from it being general good manners to be nice to others, being pleasant to gatekeepers is essential. Gatekeepers talk to their bosses and can let them know if you were annoying or obnoxious. When someone tells you their boss "never takes unsolicited calls or accepts unsolicited resumes," tell them you understand. Then ask what they suggest. Acknowledge objections, but try to come up with a solution.

Be persistent. Just because you don't get through on the first try doesn't mean you shouldn't try again. Don't be annoying, and don't be pushy, but don't give up. People like to help positive people. Don't moan and groan about how difficult your life is to the secretary. He or she will only want to get you off the phone.

Persistence and the Guilt Factor

Don't forget the guilt factor. If you consistently place calls to "Mr. Keane" and each time his secretary tells you he is busy, unavailable, or will call you back and he doesn't, what should you do? Should you give up? Well, that's up to you. Be aware that persistence often pays off. In many cases, after a number of calls, you and the secretary will have built up a "relationship" of sorts. As long as you have been pleasant, he or she may feel "guilty" that you are such a nice person and his or her boss isn't calling you back. In these cases, the secretary may give you a tip on how to get through, tell you to send something in writing, or ask the boss to speak to you.

Voice mail is another obstacle you might have to deal with. This automated system is often more difficult to bypass than a human gatekeeper. Many people don't even bother answering their phone, instead letting their voice mail pick up the calls and then checking their messages when convenient.

Decide ahead of time what you're going to do if you get someone's voice mail. Try calling once to see what the person's message is. It might, for example, let you know that the person you're calling is out of town until Monday. What this will tell you is that if you are calling someone on a cold call, you should probably not call until Wednesday, because they probably will be busy when they get back in town.

If the message says something to the effect of "I'm out of town, if you need to speak to me today, please call my cell phone" and then

provides a phone number, don't. You don't *need* to speak to him or her; you *want* to. There is a big difference between *needs* and *wants*. You are cold calling a person who doesn't know you to ask for something. It is not generally a good idea to bother them outside the office.

If you call a few times and keep getting voice mail, you're going to have to make your move. Leave a message something like this.

> **You:** "Hi, this is Sam Harris. My phone number is (111) 999-9999. I'd appreciate it if you could give me a call at your convenience. I look forward to hearing from you. Have a great day."

If you don't hear back within a few days, try again.

> **You:** "Hi, Mr. Ryan. This is Sam Harris. (111) 999-9999. I called a few days ago. I know you're busy and was just trying you again. I look forward to hearing from you. Thanks. Have a great day."

You might not hear from Mr. Ryan himself, but one of his assistants might call you. What do you do if you don't get a call back? Call again. How many times should you call? That's hard to say. Persistence may pay off. Remember that the person on the other end may start feeling guilty that he or she is not calling you back and place that call.

Be prepared. When you get a call back, have your ducks in a row and be ready to sell yourself. Practice ahead of time if need be and leave notes near your phone.

I suggest when making any of these calls that you block your phone number so that no one knows who is calling. To permanently block your phone number from showing on the receiver's caller ID, call your local phone company. Most

> ### ⭐ Words from the Wise
> Be aware that even if you block your number, certain companies pay to "see" your number. Generally these are companies utilizing toll-free numbers such as 1-800 phone numbers, but in certain cases, companies utilizing toll-free numbers may also unblock your number.

don't charge for this service. You can also block your phone number on a temporary basis by dialing *67 before making your call. Remember that as soon as you hang up, this service will be disabled, so you will need to do this for each call.

Will you need to use any of these tactics if you are pursuing a traditional civil service type job in law enforcement?

Getting Them to Call You

While persistence and patience in calling and trying to get past the receptionist is usually necessary, you may also need something else. You want something to set you apart so the busy executives not only want to see you but remember you. You want them to give you a chance to sell yourself.

What can you do? Creativity to the rescue! The amount of creativity will depend to a great extent on the specific company or organization to which you are trying to get through. Ideas you use to get someone's attention in a corporate situation will, of course, differ if you are pursuing a job with the FBI or CIA. Some will work in some situations but not in others. Use your judgment and the ideas with which you are comfortable.

Your goal is to get the attention of the important person who can give you a chance to sell yourself. Once you have his or her attention,

it's up to you to convince them that they should work with you.

Let's look at some ideas that I have either personally used or others have told me worked in their quest to get an individual's attention so they could get a foot in the door. Use these ideas as a beginning, but then try to develop some more of your own. You are limited only by your own creativity and ability to think outside of the box.

There are many unique ideas that can help you get the attention of important people who can give you a chance to sell yourself. I've given you a few that have been successful for others. I would love to see additional ideas that have worked for you and hear your stories. Go to http://www.shellyfield.com and drop me a note.

My Personal Number-One Technique for Getting Someone to Call You

I am going to share my number one technique for getting someone to call you. I have used this technique successfully over the years to get people to call me in an array of situations and in a variety of industries at various levels in my career. I first came up with it after I graduated from college when I was entering the workforce and wanted to get a job in the music industry.

At the time, there was no book to give me ideas. There was no career coach. There was no one who really wanted to help, and I desperately needed help to get the job I wanted.

I had tried all the traditional methods. I tried calling people, but most of the time I couldn't get past the gatekeeper. When I did, no one called me back. I had tried sending out resumes. As I had just graduated college, I had no "real" experience. I didn't know anyone and didn't even know anyone who knew anyone. I needed a break. Here's what I did.

When I was younger my parents used to take raw eggs, blow out the contents, and then decorate the shells. Every one always commented on how nice they were and how different they were. One day, for some reason, the eggs popped into my mind, and I came up with my method to get people to call me back. Here's how it works.

Get a box of eggs. Extra-large or jumbo work well. While either white or brown eggs can be used, because of the coloration differences in brown eggs, start with white ones. Wash the raw eggs carefully with warm water. Then dry the shells thoroughly.

Hold one egg in your hand and using a large needle or pin, punch a small hole in the top of the egg. The top is the narrower end. Then, carefully punch a slightly larger hole in the other end of the egg. You might need to take the needle or pin and move it around in the hole to make it larger. Keep any pieces of shell that break off.

Now, take a straw and place it on the top hole of the egg. Holding the egg over a bowl, blow into the straw, blowing the contents of the egg out. This may take a couple of tries. Because of concerns with salmonella, do not put your mouth directly on the egg.

Keep in mind that the bigger you have made the hole, the easier it will be to blow the contents out of the egg. However, you want the egg to look as "whole" as possible when you're done. The bigger the hole, the harder this is to accomplish.

After blowing the contents out of the egg, carefully rinse out the shell, letting warm water run through it. Get the egg as clean as possible. Shake the excess water out of the egg and leave it to dry thoroughly. Depending on the temperature and humidity when you are preparing the eggs, it might take a couple of days.

Do at least three eggs at one time in case one breaks or cracks at the next step. You might want to do more. After you get the hang of this, you're going to want to keep a few extra prepared eggs around for when you want to get someone's attention fast and don't have time to prepare new ones.

Next, go to your computer and type the words, "Getting the attention of a busy person is not easy. Now that I have yours, could you please take a moment to review my resume." You can customize the message to suit your purposes by including the name of the recipient if you have it or specifying your background sheet, CV, or whatever you want the recipient to look at and consider. Then type your name and phone number.

Use a small font to keep the message to a line or two. Neatly cut out the strip of paper with your message. Roll the strip around a toothpick. Carefully insert the toothpick with the strip of paper into the larger of the holes in the egg. Wiggle the toothpick around and slowly take the toothpick out of the egg. The strip of paper should now be in the shell.

Visit your local craft store and pick up a package of those small moveable eyes, miniature plastic or felt-shaped feet, and white glue or a glue gun. Glue the miniature feet to the bottom of the egg, covering the hole. Make sure you use the glue sparingly so none goes on your message. Now, glue on two of the moving eyes making the egg look like a face.

Go back to your computer and type the following words. "CRACK OPEN THIS EGG FOR AN IMPORTANT MESSAGE." Print out the line and cut it into a strip. You might want to use bright-colored paper. Glue the strip to the bottom of the feet of the egg.

Now you're ready. Take the egg and place it in a small box that you have padded with cotton, bubble wrap, or foam. These eggs are very fragile, and you don't want the egg to break in transit!

Wrap the egg filled box in attractive wrapping paper and then bubble wrap to assure it won't move around. Put your resume (or CV, background sheet, and so on) and a short cover letter into an envelope. Put it on the bottom of a sturdy mailing box. Place the egg box over it.

Make sure you use clean boxes and pack the egg as carefully as possible. Address the box. Make sure you include your name and return address. Then mail, UPS, FedEx, Airborne, or hand-deliver it to the office of the person you are trying to reach. Even if that person has a secretary opening his or her mail, the chances are good that the "gift" will be opened personally. In the event that a secretary opens the package, he or she will probably bring the egg into the boss to crack.

Now the recipient has the egg in front of them. He or she will probably break it open, see the message, and glance at your resume. Here's the good news. By the time the person breaks open the egg, he or she won't even notice the hole on the bottom and usually has no idea how you got the message in there. Generally, people who have seen this think it is so neat that they want to know how you did it, and so they call you to ask. (Believe it or not, everyone has someone else they wish they could get to call them back.)

Once you have them on the phone, your job is to obtain an interview. You want to get into their office and meet with them. When you get that call, tell the recipient that you would be glad to show him or her how you did it; but it's kind of complicated explaining it on the phone. Offer to show them how it is done and ask when they would like you to come in.

Voila, you have an appointment. Now all you have to do is sell yourself.

Is your resume sitting in a pile of countless others? Do you want your resume to stick out among the hundreds that come in? Do you want an interview but can't get one? Are you

having difficulty getting people to call you back?

While I love the egg idea and have used it to obtain appointments, call backs, and to get noticed throughout my career, there are other ideas that work too. You might want to try a couple of these.

Have you ever considered using these simple items to help you succeed? If you haven't, perhaps now is the time.

◎ Fortune Cookies
◎ Chocolate Chip Cookies
◎ Candy Bars
◎ Mugs
◎ Pizzas
◎ Shoes
◎ Roses

Fortune Cookies

Almost no one can resist cracking open a fortune cookie to see what the message says. This can be good news for your career.

Some fortune cookie companies make cookies similar to the ones you get in Chinese restaurants but with personalized messages inside. What could you say? That depends on what you are looking for. How about something like, "Human Resources Director who interviews Paul Evans will have good luck for the rest of the day. Paul's lucky number: 111-222-3333."

Whatever message you choose, remember that you generally need to make all the messages the same or it gets very expensive to have the cookies made. You also need to print cards on your computer or have cards printed professionally that read something to the effect of "Getting the attention of a busy person is not easy. Now that I have yours, could you please take a moment to review my resume?" Or, "Getting the attention of a busy person is not easy. Now that I have yours, I was hoping you would take a few moments to give me a call." Or set up an appointment or anything else you want. Make sure your name and phone number are on the card.

Put a couple of cookies with the card and your resume or other material in a clean, attractive mailing box and address it neatly. Make sure you address the box to someone specific. For example, don't address it to President, ABC Security Company. Instead, address it to Mr. Mike Carlson, President, ABC Security Company. Don't send it to Director, Brean Forensic Research. Instead, send it to Andrew Brooks, Director, Brean Forensic Research.

"I've heard of sending fortune cookies," you say. "What else can I do?"

Here's a twist. Send the same package of cookies, the card, and whatever else you sent (your resume, CV, or background sheet) every day for two weeks. Every day, after the first day, also include a note that says, "Cookies for [Name of person] for Day 2," "Cookies for [Name of Person] for Day 3," and so on. At the end of the two-week period, stop. By now your recipient will probably have called you. If not, he or she will at least be expecting the cookies. If you don't hear from your recipient, feel free to call the office, identify yourself as the fortune cookie king or queen, and ask for an appointment.

This idea can be expensive, but if it gets you in the door and you can sell yourself or your idea, it will more than pay for itself.

Words from the Wise

Make sure cookies are individually wrapped and factory sealed. Otherwise, some people may just toss them.

The Inside Scoop

To avoid potential problems with people who have allergies, do not send any food with nuts as an ingredient. Nothing can ruin your chances of getting a job better than causing an allergic reaction in the person you're trying to impress.

Another great idea that can really grab the attention of a busy executive or anybody else for that matter is sending them a gigantic fortune cookie with a personalized message. There are a number of companies that specialize in making cookies like this which are often covered in chocolate, sprinkles, and all kinds of goodies and almost command people to see who sent it. Send these cookies with the same types of messages and supporting material as the others. The only difference is that if you choose to send the gigantic cookies, you probably only need to send one. If you don't get a call within the first week, feel free to call the recipient yourself.

Chocolate-chip Cookies

Chocolate chip cookies are a favorite of most people. Why not use that to your advantage? Go to the cookie kiosk at your local mall and order a gigantic pizza-sized cookie personalized with a few words asking for what you would like done. For example:

◎ "Please Review My Resume . . . Donna Jones"

◎ "Please Call Me for an Interview . . . Toni Harrison"

Keep your message short. You want the recipient to read it, not get overwhelmed. Generally, the cookies come boxed. Tape a copy of your resume or whatever you are sending to the inside of the box.

Write a short cover letter to your recipient stating that you hope he or she enjoys the cookie while reviewing your resume or giving you a call. Put this in an envelope with another copy of your resume, or other material. On the outside of the box, neatly tape a card with the message we discussed previously, stating "Getting the attention of a busy person is never easy. Now that I have yours, would you please take a moment to review my resume?" Or ask them to give you a call or whatever you are hoping they will do. Make sure your name and phone number are on the card.

If the cookie company has a mail or delivery service, use it even if it is more expensive than mailing it yourself. It will be more effective. If there is no mail or delivery service, mail or deliver the cookie yourself. You should get a call from the recipient within a few days.

There have been a number of studies that tout chocolate as a food that makes people happy or at least puts them in a good mood. Keeping this in mind, you might want to use chocolate to grab someone's attention and move them to call you. Most people love chocolate and are happy to see it magically appear in their office. There are a number of different ways you can use chocolate to help your career.

◎ Buy a large, high-quality chocolate bar. Carefully fold your resume or

a letter stating what you would like accomplished and slip it into the wrapping of the chocolate bar.

◎ Buy a large, high-quality chocolate bar. Wrap the chocolate bar with your resume or the letter stating what you would like accomplished.

◎ There are companies that create personalized wrappings for chocolate bars. Use one to deliver your message.

◎ Create a wrapping on your computer. Make sure you leave the original wrapping intact and cover it with your custom wrapping.

Whatever method you choose, put the candy bar in an attractive box, and attach the card with the message, "Getting the attention of a busy person is never easy. Now that I have yours, could you please take a moment to review my resume [or whatever action you are asking your recipient to take]?" Add a cover letter and send it off.

When was the last time you threw out a mug? Probably not for a while. How about using this idea to catch the attention of a potential employer? Depending on your career aspiration, have mugs printed with replicas of your business or networking card, key points of your resume, CV, or background sheet, along with your name and phone number.

Add a small packet of gourmet coffee or hot chocolate and perhaps an individually wrapped biscotti or cookie and, of course, the card with the message stating, "Getting the attention of a busy person is never easy. Now that I have yours, could you please take a moment to check out my resume?" Put the mug, a short cover letter, and your resume, background sheet, or other material in a box and mail or deliver to your

---

★ **Voice of Experience**

Do not try to save money by making the cookies yourself. In today's world, many people won't eat food if they don't know where it came from or if it wasn't prepared by a commercial eatery.

recipient. Remember to always put your return address on the box.

Want to make sure your resume or background sheet gets attention? Have it delivered to your recipient with a fresh, hot pizza. This technique can be tricky but effective. It does have some challenges, however.

Here they are. In order to guarantee the pizza gets there with your information, you really need to be in the same geographic location as the company or organization you're trying to reach. You will need to personally make sure that your information is placed in a high-quality zip-lock bag or, better yet, laminated and then taped to the inside cover of the pizza box. You also not only have to know the name of the person for this to be delivered to but that he or she will be there the day you send it and won't have a lunch date. It's difficult to call an office where no one knows you and ask what time the recipient goes to lunch. So you are taking the risk that you will be sending a pizza to someone who isn't there. One way to get around this is by sending it in the late afternoon instead. That way your recipient can have a mid-afternoon "pizza break." And even if your recipient isn't there, his or her employees will probably enjoy the pizza and tell their supervisor about it the next day.

If you do this, make sure that you have the pizzeria delivering the pizza tape the card with the message about getting a busy person's attention on the front of the box, so even if the receptionist gets the pizza, he or she will know who it came from.

If you don't get a thank-you call that day, call the recipient the next morning. You probably will speak to the secretary or receptionist first. Just tell whomever you speak to that you were the one who sent the pizza the day before in hopes of getting the attention of the recipient so you might set up a job interview.

Over the years, many people have told me that they were successful in garnering interviews after sending their resume in a shoebox with one shoe in it and a note that says something to the effect of "I'm sending you this shoe to try to get my foot in the door. I would like to get both feet in and tell you more about myself and how I can help your company."

If you are considering this idea, make sure you send a new shoe. It doesn't have to be a $200 shoe, but it does need to be new. What kind of shoe do you send? That depends. While most people who have told me about this idea used an adult-sized shoe in a shoe box, there have been others who have used children's shoes, doll's shoes, and even miniature shoes from a craft shop.

One man I know even created a sculpture out of the shoe so that it would be a conversation piece. A woman I know crafted a planter in her shoe. If you are a man, by the way, send a man's shoe. If you are a woman, send a woman's shoe.

A very effective but pricey way to get your recipient's attention is to have a dozen roses delivered to his or her office. No matter how many things you have tried with no response, there are very few people who will not place a thank-you call when they receive a dozen roses.

Talk to the florist ahead of time to make sure that the roses you will be sending are fragrant. Send the roses to your recipient with a card that simply says something to the effect of "While you are enjoying the roses, please take a moment to review my resume sent under separate cover." Or, "While you and your staff are enjoying the roses, please take a moment to review my resume, sent under separate cover." Sign it "Sincerely hoping for an interview," and include your name and phone number.

It is imperative to send your information so it arrives on the same day or, at the latest, the next day so the roses you sent are still fresh in the recipient's mind.

It's Who You Know

While, of course, some areas of law enforcement are easier to enter, there generally still is always some amount of competition to get most jobs. There are also individuals who are talented or skilled but yet never get past the front door. Knowing someone who can get you in the door most certainly will help.

Of course, as we've discussed, for many positions, you will need to go through a civil service process that normally entails not only taking an exam but scoring well. However, even if that is the case, those in the position to hire usually have leeway to choose the *best* candidate from the top scorers. What that means is in certain situations, contacts may help.

Before you say, "Me? I don't know anyone," stop and think. Are you sure? Don't you know someone, anyone, even on a peripheral basis who might be able to give you a recommendation, make a call, or be willing lend his or her name?

What about your mother's aunt's husband's friend's neighbor's boss? Sure, it might be a stretch. But think hard. Who can you think of who might know someone who might be able to help? This is not the time to be shy.

"But I don't need any help," you say. "I can do this on my own."

You might be able to and you might not, but why wouldn't you give yourself every edge possible? You're going to have to prove yourself once you get in the door. No one can do that for you.

What if you don't have a relative who has a contact down the line? What about your son's teacher's wife? What about one of your sister's

> **Tip from the Top**
>
> If you are currently working in the industry and are planning on moving to another location, your current supervisor may be able to put in a good word for you. Don't be afraid to ask.

neighbors? Does he or she know someone at the company or agency where you want to apply? What about a friend who is already working in the agency or company where you want to work? What about the officer who gave the workshop on personal safety you attended?

What about your UPS delivery person? Your mailman or mail lady? Your clergyman or woman? What about one of your physicians? Your pharmacist? The possibilities are endless if you just look.

The trick here is to think outside the box. If you can find someone who knows someone who is willing to help you to get your foot in the door, then all you have to do is sell yourself.

If someone does agree to lend their name, make a call, or help you in any manner, it's important to write thank-you notes immediately. These notes should be written whether or not you actually get an interview or set up a meeting.

If you do go on an interview, it's also a good idea to either call or write another note letting your contact know what happened.

Meeting the Right People

You think and think and you can't come up with anyone you know with a connection to anyone at all in the area of law enforcement in which you are trying to succeed. What can you do? Sometimes you have to find your own contacts. You need to meet the right people. How can you do this? The best way to meet the right people in the area of law enforcement you want to pursue is to be around people working in or around law enforcement. There are several possible ways you might do this.

To begin with, consider joining industry organizations and associations. Many of these organizations offer career guidance and support. They also may offer seminars, workshops, and other types of educational symposiums. Best of all, many have periodic meetings and annual conventions and conferences. All of these are treasure troves of possibilities to meet people in the industry. Some of them may be industry experts or insiders. Others may be just like you: people trying to get in and succeed. The important thing to remember is to take advantage of every opportunity.

Workshops and seminars are great because not only can you make important contacts, but you can learn something valuable about the industry. Most have question-and-answer periods built into the program. Take advantage of these. Stand up and ask a good question. Make yourself visible. Some seminars and workshops have break-out sessions to encourage people to get to know one another. Use these to your advantage as well.

During breaks, don't run to the corner to check your voice mail. Walk around and talk to

Words from a Pro

Don't just blend in with everyone else at a seminar or workshop. Make yourself visible and memorable in a positive way. Ask questions and participate when possible. During breaks, don't rush to make calls on your cell phone. Instead, try to meet more people and make more contacts.

people. Don't be afraid to walk up to someone you don't know and start talking. Remember to bring your business or networking cards and network, network, network!

After the session has ended, walk up, shake the moderator's hand, and tell him or her how much you enjoyed the session, how much you learned, and how useful it will be in your career. This gives you the opportunity to ask for his or her business card so that you have the correct spelling of the person's name, as well as his or her address and phone number. This is very valuable information. When you get home, send a short note stating that you were at the session the person moderated, spoke to him or her afterwards, and just wanted to mention again how much you enjoyed it.

You might also ask, depending on their position, if it would be possible to set up an informational interview with them at their convenience or if they could suggest someone you might call to set up an appointment. If you don't hear back within a week, feel free to call up, identify yourself, and ask again. These interviews might just turn into an interview for a job or even a job itself.

Another good way to meet people in the industry is to attend industry or organization annual conventions. These events offer many opportunities you might not normally have to network and meet industry insiders.

Tip from the Top

When you go to industry events, it is important to have a positive attitude and not to have any negative conversation with anyone about anything at the seminar or in the industry. You can never tell who is related to who or what idea someone originated. You want to be remembered as the one who is bright and positive, not a negative sad sack.

Tip from the Top

If you are currently working in the industry, your employer may or may not pay for conventions, seminars, and workshops. If you approach your employer about one of these events and he or she can't pay (or doesn't want to pay), ask if you can have the time off if you pay for the event. If he or she agrees, when you return, be sure to share the knowledge you have learned.

There is usually a charge to attend these conventions. Fee structures may vary. Sometimes there is one price for general admission to all events and entry to the trade-show floor. Other times, there may be one price for entry just to the trade-show floor and another price if you also want to take part in seminars and other events.

The cost of attending these conventions may be expensive. In addition to the fee to get in, if you don't live near the convention location, you might have to pay for airfare or other transportation as well as accommodations, meals, and incidentals. Is it worth it? If you can afford it, absolutely! If you want to meet people in a specific area of law enforcement, these gatherings are the place to do it.

How do you find these events? Look in the appendix of this book for industry associations in your area of interest. Find the phone number and call up and ask when and where the annual convention will be held. Better yet, go to the organization's Web site. Most groups post information about their conventions online.

If you are making the investment to go to a convention or a conference, take full advantage of every opportunity. As we've discussed throughout this book, network, network, network, and network some more! Some events to take part in or attend at conventions and conferences might include:

- Opening events
- Keynote presentations
- Educational seminars and workshops
- Certification programs
- Break sessions
- Breakfast lunch and/or dinner events
- Cocktail parties
- Trade show exhibit areas
- Career fairs

There is an art to attending conventions and using the experience to your best benefit. Remember that the people you meet are potential employers and new business contacts.

This is your chance to make a good first impression. Dress appropriately and neatly.

Do not get inebriated at these events. If you want to have a drink or a glass of wine, that's probably okay, but don't drink excessively. You want potential employers or people you want to do business with to know you're a good risk, not someone who drinks at every opportunity.

It is essential to bring business cards with you and give them out to everyone you can. You can never tell when someone might hear about a position, remember meeting you, and give you a call.

Collect business cards as well. Then when you get home from the convention or trade

The Inside Scoop

Recruiters and headhunters often attend conferences and conventions in hopes of finding potential employees for their clients.

show, you will have contact names to call or write regarding business or job possibilities.

Walk the trade-show floor. Stop and talk to people at booths. They are usually more than willing to talk. This is a time to network and try to make contacts. Ask questions and listen to what people are saying.

If you have good writing skills, a good way of meeting people within the industry is to write articles or interview people for local, regional, or national periodicals or newspapers. We discussed the idea earlier when talking about using your writing skills to help you obtain interviews. It can be just as effective in these situations.

How does this work? A great deal of it depends on your situation, where you live, and the area of the industry you are targeting.

Basically, what you have to do is develop an angle or hook for a story on the segment of law enforcement in which you are interested in meeting people. For example, does the director of the probation department go on biking vacations in or out of the country? Perhaps his or her adventures might make a good story. Is one of police sergeants appearing on a game show? Does the director of the legal aid agency not only collect art but write about it in a major art magazine? Is one of the special FBI agents from a local office in your area giving a seminar on a subject of interest to the public? Has the captain of the state police barracks in

your area been asked to speak at a major law enforcement conference? Have a trio of triplets who graduated from the police academy become the third generation police officers and the only group of triplets to graduate at the same time? These are angles or hooks you might use to entice a local or regional periodical to let you do an article.

Your next step is to contact someone who might be interested in the story. If you're still in school, become involved with the school newspaper. If you're not, call up your local newspaper or a regional magazine and see if they might be interested in the article or feature story you want to write. You might even contact one of the trade magazines in your area of interest.

You probably will have to give them some samples of your writing and your background sheet or resume. You might also have to write on "spec" (speculation). What this means is that when you do the story, they may or may not use it. If they do, they will pay you. If not, they won't.

Your goal here (unless you want to be a crime reporter) is not to make money (although that is nice). Your goal is to be in situations where you have the opportunity to meet industry insiders. If you're successful, not only will you be meeting these people, you'll be meeting them on a different level than if you were looking for a job. You'll be networking on a different level as well.

Networking Basics

It's not always what you know but who you know. With that in mind, I'm going to once again bring up the importance of networking. You can never tell who knows someone in some area of the industry, so it is essential to share your career dreams and aspirations with those around you. Someone you mention it to might just say, "My cousin is an FBI special agent." Or "Really, I just heard that the Some State Correctional Facility is looking for correctional officers. They are giving the test in a couple of weeks." Or, "Did you see that the *Daily News* is looking for a new crime reporter?" Or "I just saw an advertisement in the classifieds for a job like that."

Think it can't happen? Think again. It's happened to me, it's happened to others, and it can happen to you!

A number of years ago, I was in Las Vegas giving a seminar on stress management. After the seminar was over, I was standing in the lobby and a man tapped me on the shoulder. He turned out to be a police officer I knew from across the country. I asked him what he was doing in Vegas and he told me that he had been attending a law enforcement seminar. We spoke for a while and then both went our separate ways.

I spoke to the officer a number of times after that when we were both on the East Coast. One day he called and told me he was leaving the department and the area. It seems that when he attended that seminar he mentioned to a number of people that he really wanted to work in the area of federal law enforcement.

Evidentially, one of the people he met at that seminar remembered what he had said and gave him a call when they heard of an interesting opening.

People always ask, "But do those things really happen?" and the answer is an unequivocal yes. These are not isolated incidents. Things like this happen all the time. Networking and sharing your dreams can and do work for others and can work for you. But in order for it to happen, you have to be proactive.

Knowing how important networking can be to your career, let's talk about some networking basics.

The first thing you need to do is determine exactly who you know and who is part of your network. Then you need to get out and find more people to add to the list.

When working on your networking list, add the type of contact you consider each person. Primary contacts are those people you know: your family members, teachers, friends, and neighbors. Secondary contacts are individuals referred to you by others. These include a friend of a friend, your aunt's neighbor, your attorney's sister, and so on.

You might also want to note whether you consider each person a close, medium, or distant relationship. *Close,* for example, would be family, friends, employers, and current teachers. *Medium* would be people you talk to and see frequently such as your dentist, attorney, or your UPS, FedEx, or mail delivery person. *Distant* would include people you talk to and see infrequently or those you have just met or have met just once or twice.

Here's an example.

It would be great to have a network full of people in the segment of law enforcement in which you hope to have your career. However,

Networking Worksheet

Name	Relationship/ Position	Type of Contact (Primary or Secondary)	Closeness of Contact (Close, Medium, or Distant)
Sam Hancock	College Advisor	Primary	Medium
Nancy Helms	Bank Teller	Primary	Distant
Bob	UPS Delivery Person	Primary	Medium
William Thomas	Newspaper Reporter	Secondary	Distant
Gina	Sister-in-law	Primary	Close
Dr. Sampson	Dentist	Primary	Medium
Allen Roberts	Attorney	Primary	Medium
Erica Jones	WOTO-TV Crime Reporter	Secondary	Distant
Sid Phillips	Criminal Procedure Professor	Primary	Medium

that may not be the case. That does not mean, however, that other people can't be helpful. Your network may include a variety of people from all walks of life. These may include:

◎ family members
◎ friends
◎ friends of friends
◎ coworkers and colleagues
◎ teachers or professors
◎ your doctor and dentist
◎ your pharmacist
◎ your mail carrier
◎ your hairstylist
◎ your personal trainer
◎ your priest, pastor, or rabbi
◎ members of your congregation
◎ UPS, FedEx, Airborne, or other delivery person
◎ your auto mechanic
◎ your attorney
◎ the server at the local diner or coffee shop
◎ bank tellers from your local bank
◎ your neighbors
◎ friends of your relatives
◎ your college advisor
◎ business associates of your relatives
◎ people you serve with on volunteer not-for-profit boards and civic groups
◎ a local police officer or sheriff's deputy
◎ a firefighter

Now look at your list. Do you see how large your network really is? Virtually everyone you come in contact with during the day can become part of your network. Just keep adding people to your list.

		Networking Worksheet	
Name	**Relationship/ Position**	**Type of Contact (Primary or Secondary)**	**Closeness of Contact (Close, Medium, or Distant)**

Expanding Your Network

How can you expand your network? There are a number of ways. Networking events are an excellent way to meet people. Industry networking events are, of course, the best, but don't count out nonindustry events too. For example, your local chamber of commerce may have specific networking programs designed to help people in the community meet and network.

How do you know if the people who are at the event have any possibility of being related to the area of law enforcement in which you're interested? You don't. But as we've discussed, you don't know who people know. People you meet may know others who *are* in the part of the industry you want to pursue.

Civic and other not-for-profit groups also have a variety of events that are great for networking. Whether you go to a regular meeting or you attend a charity auction, cocktail party, or large gala to benefit a not-for-profit, you will generally find people in the community you might not know. As an added bonus, many larger not-for profit events also have media coverage, meaning that you have the opportunity to add media people to your network.

A good way to meet people involved in law enforcement is to attend their events and fundraisers. Many PBAs, for example, sponsor fundraising concerts, dances, comedy nights, and so on. These events are well attended by department members of all local law enforcement agencies.

Once you're at an event, how do you meet people? How do you take advantage of opportunities? You might just walk around and network. Or you might want to volunteer to help with a fund-raiser or event so people start to know you and what you can do.

Those who take advantage of every opportunity to meet new people will have the largest networks. The idea in building a network is to go out of your comfort zone. If you just stay with people you know and are comfortable with, you won't have the opportunity to get to know others. You want to continually meet new people; after all, you never know who knows who.

Networking Savvy

You are now learning how to build your network. However, the largest network in the world will be useless unless you know how to take full advantage of it. So let's talk a little about how you're going to use the network you are building.

Previously we discussed the difference between skills and talents. Networking is a skill. You don't have to be born with it. You can acquire the skill to network, practice, and improve. What that means is that if you practice networking, you can get better at it, and it can pay off big in your career!

Get out. Go to new places. Meet new people. The trick here is when you're in a situation where there are new people, don't be afraid to walk up to them, shake their hand, and talk to them. People can't read your mind, so it's imperative to tell them about your career goals, dreams, and aspirations.

When you meet new people, listen to them. Focus on what they're saying. Ask questions. Be interested in what *they* are telling you. You can never tell when the next person you talk to is the one who will be able to help you open the door *or* vice versa.

If you're shy, even the thought of networking may be very difficult for you. However, it is essential to make yourself do it anyway. Successful networking can pay off big in your ca-

reer. In some situations it can mean the difference between getting a great job or not getting a job at all. It can also mean the difference between success and failure in your career. And that is worth the effort!

Just meeting people isn't enough. When you meet someone that you add to your network, the idea is to try to further develop the relationship. Just having a story to tell about who you know or who you met is not enough. Arrange a follow-up meeting, send a note, write a letter, or make a phone call. The more you take advantage of every opportunity, the closer you will be to getting what you want.

A good way to network is to volunteer. We just discussed attending not-for-profit events and civic meetings to expand your network, but how about volunteering to work with a not-for-profit or civic group? There are a ton of opportunities just waiting for you.

I can imagine you saying, "When? I'm so busy now, I don't have enough time to do anything."

Make the time. It will be worth it. Why?

People will see you on a different level. They won't see you as someone looking for a job or trying to succeed at some level. Generally, people talk about their volunteer work to friends, family, business associates, and other colleagues. What this means is that when someone is speaking to someone else, they might mention in passing that one of the people they are working with on their event or project is trying to get a job as a police officer, state police officer, or sheriff's deputy. They might mention that one of the people on their committee is looking for a position as a probation officer, parole officer, or corrections officer. They might mention that you are trying to locate a position handling communications duties at a large police department, trying to land a position as a crime reporter, or almost anything else.

Anyone these people mention you or your situation to is a potential secondary networking contact. Those people, in turn, may mention it to someone else. Eventually, someone involved in the area of law enforcement you are pursuing might hear about you.

Another reason to volunteer is so people will see that you have a good work ethic. Treat volunteer projects as you would work projects. Do what you say you are going to do and do it in a timely manner. Do your best at all times. Showcase your skills and your talents and do everything you do with a positive attitude and a smile.

Volunteering also gives you the opportunity to demonstrate skills and talents people might not otherwise know you have. Can you do publicity? Can your write? Do you have leadership skills? Are you good at organizing things? Do you get along well with others? What better way to illustrate your skills than utilizing them by putting together an event, publicizing it, or coordinating other volunteers?

Best of all, you can use these volunteer activities on your resume. While volunteer experiences don't take the place of work experience, they certainly can fill out a resume short of it.

Don't just go to meetings. Participate fully in the organization. That way you'll not only be helping others, you will be adding to your network.

Where can you volunteer? Pretty much any not-for-profit, community group, school, or civic organization is a possibility. The one thing to remember, however, is that you should only volunteer for organizations in whose cause you believe.

In order to make the most of every networking opportunity, it's essential for people to remember you. Keep a supply of your business or networking cards with you all the time. Don't be stingy with them. Give them out freely to everyone. That way your name and number will be close at hand if needed. Make sure you ask for cards in return. If people don't have them, be sure to ask for their contact information.

Try to keep in contact with people in your network on a regular basis. Of course, you can't call everyone every day, but try to set up a schedule of sorts to do some positive networking every day. For example, you might decide to call one person every day on your networking list. Depending on the situation, you can say you were calling to touch base, say hello, keep in contact, or see how they were doing. Ask how they have been or talk about something you might have in common or they might think is interesting. You might also decide that once a week you will try to call someone and set up a lunch or coffee date.

Be on the lookout for stories, articles, or other tidbits of information that might be of in-

Words from a Pro

Keep a scrapbook of articles, photos, programs, and other supporting material from volunteer events you have worked and participated in. It will be useful when putting together your career portfolio.

Tip from the Top

After you have worked on a volunteer project, ask the executive director or board president if he or she would mind writing you a letter of recommendation for your file.

terest to people in your network. Clip them out and send them with a short note saying you saw the story and thought they might be interested. If you hear of something they might be interested in, call them. The idea is to continue cultivating relationships by keeping in contact with people in your network and staying visible.

Keep track of the contacts in your network. You can use the sample sheet provided, a card file using index cards, or a database or contact software program on your computer. Include as much information as you have about each person. People like when you remember them and their interests. It makes you stand out.

Then use your networking contact list. For example, a few days before someone's birthday,

Tip from the Coach

Have you ever received a birthday card from someone who wasn't a close friend or relative, someone to whom you just happened to mention your upcoming birthday? Remember how it put a smile on your face when you opened that card and read who it was from? Remember thinking how nice the person who sent you the card was? Remember thinking about what you could do for them? You might not have known them well, but you probably won't forget them now. If you do the same type of thing for others, you will stand out as well.

send him or her a card. If you know someone collects old guitars, for example, and you see an article on old guitars, clip it out and send it. Don't be a pest, but keep in contact. People in sales have been using this technique for years. It works for them and it will help you in your career as well.

You might want to use some of the items here and then add more information as it comes up. You don't have to ask people for all this information the first time you meet them. Just add it when you get it.

Networking and Nerve

Successful networking will give you credibility and a rapport with people in and out of the industry. But networking sometimes takes nerve, especially if you're not naturally outgoing. You have to push yourself to get out and meet people, talk to them, tell them what you are interested in doing, and then stay in contact. On occasion, you may have to ask people if they will help you, ask for recommendations, ask for references, and so on. Don't let the fear of doing what you need to do stop you from doing it. Just remember that the end result of all this effort will be not only entry into a career you want but a shot at success.

As long as you're pleasant and not rude, there is nothing wrong with asking for help. Just remember that while people can help you get your foot in the door, you are going to have to sell yourself once you open it.

Networking Contact Information Sheet

Name
_____

Business Address
_____

Business Phone
_____

Home Address
_____

Home Phone
_____

E-mail Address
_____

Web Address
_____

Birthday
_____

Anniversary
_____

Where and When Met
_____

Spouse or Significant Other's Name
_____

Children's Name(s)
_____

Dog Breed and Name
_____

Cat Breed and Name
_____

Hobbies
_____

Interests
_____

Things Collected
_____

Honors
_____

Awards
_____

Interesting Facts

Networking is a two-way street. While it might be hard for you to imagine at this moment, someone might want you to help them in some segment of their career. Reciprocate and reciprocate graciously. As a matter of fact, if you see or know someone you might be able to help even in a small way, don't wait for them to ask, just offer your help.

Finding a Mentor or Advocate

Mentors and advocates can help guide and boost your career. A mentor or advocate in law enforcement can also often provide you with valuable contacts, which, as we know, are essential to your success. The best mentors and advocates are supportive individuals who help move your career to the next level. While having a mentor in some aspect of law enforcement would be ideal, that doesn't mean others from outside the industry might not be helpful.

Can't figure out why anyone would help you? Many people like to help others. It makes them feel good and makes them feel important.

Words from the Wise

It is not uncommon to run into someone who doesn't want to help you. This may be for any number of reasons, ranging from they really don't know how they can help, they don't have the time in their schedule, or they think that if they help you in your career, it puts their position at risk. If you do ask someone to be your mentor and he or she says no, just let it go. Look for someone else. The opposite of having a great mentor in your life is having someone who is sabotaging your career.

How do you find a mentor? Look for someone who is successful and ask. Sounds simple? It is simple. The difficult part is finding just the right person or persons.

Sometimes you don't even have to ask. In many cases, a person may see your potential and offer advice and assistance. It is not uncommon for a mentor to be a supervisor or former supervisor. He or she might hear of a better job or be on a search committee and recommend you. As your career goes on, the individual may follow you and your career, helping you along the way.

Time is a valuable commodity, especially to busy people. Be gracious when someone helps you or even tries to help. Make sure you say thank you to anyone and everyone who shares his or her time, expertise, or advice. And don't forget to ask them if there is any way you can return the favor.

No matter what area of law enforcement you are pursuing, getting your foot in the door is essential. Whether you need to open the door just a crack or you need it flung wide open to get you where you want to go, use every opportunity.

Tip from the Coach

If someone asks you to be their mentor or asks for your help and you can, say yes. As a matter of fact, if you see someone you might be able to help, do just that. You might think that you don't even have your own career on track or you don't have time. You might be tempted to say no. Think again. You are expecting someone to help you. Do the same for someone else. There is no better feeling than helping someone else. And while you shouldn't help someone for the sole purpose of helping yourself, remember that you can often open doors for yourself while opening them for someone else.

8

THE INTERVIEW

Getting the Interview

You can have the greatest credentials in the world, wonderful references, a stellar resume, graduate first in your class, and be the top scorer on your written exam, but if you don't know how to interview well, it's often difficult to land the job, especially if you're seeking a job in any aspect of law enforcement.

Whether your dream is to work in local, state, or federal law enforcement, in the administration or support segment of the industry, the business sector, or anywhere in between, the first step is always getting the job.

One of the keys to getting most jobs is generally the interview. Landing a job in law enforcement is no different. Let's take some time to discuss how to get that all-important meeting.

The interview is your chance to shine. During an interview you can show what can't be illustrated on paper. This is the time your personality, charisma, and talents can be showcased. This is where someone can see your demeanor, your energy level, your passion, and your attitude. Obtaining an interview and excelling in that very important meeting can help get you the job you want.

If you do it right, the interview can help make you irresistible. It is your chance to per-

suade the interviewer to hire you. It is your main shot at showing why *you* would be better than anyone else; why hiring *you* would benefit the agency, organization, or company and why *not* hiring *you* would be a major mistake.

There are many ways to land job interviews. Some of these include:

◎ Responding to advertisements.
◎ Responding to canvassing letters.
◎ Recommendations from friends, relatives, or colleagues.
◎ Making cold calls.
◎ Writing letters.
◎ Working with executive search firms, recruiters, or headhunters.
◎ Working with employment agencies.
◎ Attending job and career fairs.
◎ Finding jobs that have not been advertised (the hidden job market).
◎ Responding to civil service job postings.

The most common approach people generally take in obtaining a job interview is by responding to an advertisement or job posting. Where can you look for advertisements for jobs in law enforcement? Depending on the exact type of job you're looking for, you might find them in newspapers or trade journals.

Where else might you see openings advertised or listed?

◎ Association Web sites
◎ Law enforcement agency Web sites
◎ Local, state and federal agencies
◎ Police and other law enforcement equipment company Web sites
◎ Private security company Web sites
◎ Career-oriented Web sites
◎ Law enforcement–oriented Web sites
◎ County Web sites and bulletin boards
◎ State Web sites and bulletin boards
◎ Local municipality Web sites, bulletins, and announcements
◎ Civil service vacancy announcements

While landing interviews for positions in law enforcement is similar to doing so in other industries, there may be a number of differences. One thing to keep in mind is that depending on the specific position, before you even get to the interview process for many jobs in law enforcement, you often are required to take a written exam. If the job you are pursuing is a civil service position, for example, you may not only have to take an exam and pass it but score in the top percentage in order to be called. Similarly, if you're applying for a job in a police department, in many situations, you may be required to take the written police

The Inside Scoop

No matter where you live, you can usually view the classified ads for most of the major newspapers throughout the country online. Go to the newspaper's main Web site and look for "classifieds," "jobs," or "employment." Similarly, you can usually locate local, state, and federal openings on Web sites as well.

exam first. Every job search has its own set of circumstances.

Let's look at a scenario for a moment. Let's say you open up the paper and the job opening you've been hoping for is advertised in the classifieds. Once you see the ad, you get excited. You have been looking for a job just like the one in the advertisement. You can't wait to send your resume.

Want a reality check? There may be hundreds of other people who can't wait either. Here's the good news. With a little planning, you can increase your chances of getting an interview from the classified or display ad, and as we've just discussed, this is your key to the job.

Your resume and cover letter need to stand out. Your resume needs to generate an interview. Most importantly, in a broad sense, you want your resume to define you as the one *in* a million candidates an employer can't live without instead of one *of* the million others that are applying for a job.

In essence, it's essential that your resume and cover letter distinguish you from every other applicant going for the job. Why? Because if yours doesn't, someone else's will and he or she will be the one who gets the job.

Let's look at the journey a resume might take after you send it out in response to a classified ad. Where does it go? Who reads it? That depends. In smaller organizations, your resume and cover letter may go directly to the person who will be hiring you. It may also go to that person's receptionist, secretary, administrative assistant, or office manager. If you were applying for a job in a small police department, for example, your resume might go directly to the police chief.

In larger organizations, your resume and cover letter may go to a hiring manager or human

---

⭐ Tip from the Top

Here is what you need to know. The requirements set forth in an advertisement are the ideal requirements that the company would like, not necessarily what they are going to end up with. Yes, it would be great if they could find a candidate with every single requirement, but in reality, it doesn't always work like that. In many cases, while there may be a candidate who has all the qualifications, someone who is missing one or two stands out and ultimately is the one who lands the job.

---

resources director. This would probably occur if you are answering an ad for a position in a large police department; county, state or federal law enforcement agency; corporation; and so on.

If you are replying to an advertisement placed by an employment agency, your response will generally go to the person at the employment agency responsible for that client and job.

In any of these situations, however, your resume may take other paths. Depending on the specific job and organization, your response may go through executive recruiters, screening services, clerks, secretaries, or even receptionists. Whoever the original screener of resumes turns out to be, he or she will have the initial job of reviewing the information to make sure that it fits the profile of what is needed. But—and I repeat *but*—that doesn't mean that if you don't have the exact requirements you should not reply to a job.

For example, let's say you see an opening for a job in the district attorney's office that looks something like this:

ASSISTANT DISTRICT ATTORNEY – SOME COUNTY. Dedicated prosecutor with proven track record. Must have strong organization skills and excellent verbal and writing skills and six years prosecuting experience; graduate of accredited law school; licensed to practice in Some State. Resident of Some County. Sincere interest in public service.

Now let's say that while you are a dedicated prosecutor with strong organizational skills and excellent verbal and writing sills, you don't have six years of experience prosecuting. Instead, you only have three years of experience. You do, however, also have three years of experience as a defender. You also are not a current resident of Some County. Should you not apply for the job? If you want it, I say go for it.

Here is what you need to know. In addition to tailoring your resume as closely as possible to the specific job requirements, there are some other things you can do. Stress what you have done successfully, not what you haven't done. Use your cover letter to help showcase these accomplishments.

No matter who your resume and cover letter go to, your goal is to increase your chances of it ending up in the pile that ultimately gets called for an interview. Whoever the screener of the resumes is, he or she will probably pass over anything that doesn't look neat and well thought out or anything where there are obvious errors.

What can you do? First, go over your resume. Make sure it is perfect. Make sure it is perfectly tailored to the job you are going after. Make sure it is neat, not wrinkled, crumpled, or stained. If you are going to mail it, make sure it's printed on good paper.

Human resources and personnel departments often receive hundreds of responses to ads. While most people use white paper, consider using off-white or even a different color such as light blue or light mauve. You want your resume to look sophisticated and classy but still stand out. Of course, the color of the paper will not change what is in your resume, but it will at least help your resume get noticed in the first place.

If the advertisement directs you in a specific method of responding to the ad, use that method. For example, if the ad instructs applicants to fax their resumes, fax it. If it says e-mail your resume, use e-mail and pay attention to whether the ad specifies sending the file as an attachment or in the body of your e-mail. The organization may have a procedure for screening job applicants. Not following their demands may delay your resume being seen.

If given the option of methods of responding, which should you use? Each method has its pros and cons.

◎ E-mail
  ▫ On the pro side, e-mail is one of the quickest methods of responding to ads. Many companies utilize the e-mail method.
  ▫ On the con side, you are really never assured someone gets what you sent and even if they do, you're not sure that it won't be inadvertently deleted. Another concern is making sure that the resume you sent reaches the recipient in the form in which you sent it. If you are using a common word processing program and the

same platform (Mac or PC) as the recipient, you probably won't have a problem. If you are using a Mac and the recipient is using a PC or you are using different word processing programs, you might have a problem.

◎ Fax
  ▫ On the pro side, faxing can get your resume where it's going almost instantaneously.
  ▫ On the con side, if the recipient is using an old-fashioned fax, the paper quality might not be great. The good news is that most companies now are using plain paper faxes.

◎ Mailing or shipping (USPS, FedEx, Airborne, UPS, and so on)
  ▫ On the pro side, you can send your resume on good paper so you know what it is going to look like when it arrives. You can also send any supporting materials that might help you get the coveted interview. You can send it with an option to have someone sign for it when it arrives so you definitely know if and when it arrived.
  ▫ On the con side, it may take time to arrive by mail. One of the ways to get past this problem is to send it "overnight" or two-day express. It will

cost more, but you will have control over when your package arrives.

When is the best time to send your response to an ad in order to have the best chance at getting an interview? If you send your resume right away, it might arrive with a pile of hundreds of others, yet, if you wait too long, the company might have already "found" the right candidate and stopped seriously looking at new resumes.

Many people procrastinate, so if you can send your response immediately, such as the day the ad is published or the very next morning, it will probably be one of the first ones in. At that time the screener will be reading through just a few responses. If yours stands out, it stands a good chance of being put into the "initial interview pile."

If you can't respond immediately, then wait two or three days so your resume doesn't arrive with the big pile of other responses. Once again, your goal is to increase your chances of your resume not being passed over.

When you are trying to land an interview through a recommendation from friends or colleagues, cold calls, letters, executive search firms, recruiters, headhunters, employment agencies, people you met at job fairs, through other networking events, or any aspect of the hidden job market, the timing of sending a resume is essential. In these cases you want the people receiving your information to remember

> ### Tip from the Coach
> Don't be in such a rush to get your resume out that you make errors or don't produce a neat and tailored resume. If you're not ready, send your information out in a few days instead.

> ### Tip from the Coach
> If mailing your resume and cover letter, use an envelope large enough to fit the paper and any supporting materials, so you don't have to fold it. That way it comes in flat and looks neat when it arrives.

that someone said it was coming, so send it as soon as possible. This is not the time to procrastinate. If you do, you might lose the opportunity to set up that all-important meeting.

Persistence is the word to remember when trying to get an interview. If you are responding to an advertisement and you don't hear back within a week or two, call to see what is happening. If after you call the first time you don't hear back after another week or so (unless you've been specifically given a time frame), call back again. Don't be obnoxious and don't be a pain, but call.

If you're shy, you're going to have to get over it. Write a script ahead of time to help you. Don't read directly from the script, but practice, so it becomes second nature. For example: "Hello, this is Ellen Gray. I replied to an advertisement you placed in the newspaper for the security officer. I was wondering who I could speak with to find out about the status of the position?"

When you get to the correct person, you might have to reiterate your purpose in calling. Then you might ask, "Do you know when interviewing is starting? Will all applicants be notified one way or the other? Is it possible to tell me whether I'm on the list to be contacted?" Don't be afraid to try to get as much information as possible, once again making sure you are being pleasant.

You want to be friendly with the secretary or receptionist. These people are on the inside and can provide you with a wealth of information.

Be aware that there is a way that you can get your resume looked at, obtain an interview, and beat the competition out of the dream job you want. Remember we discussed the hidden job market? Following this theory, all you have to do is contact a company and land the job you want *before* it is advertised.

While many of the positions in law enforcement, most notably those classified as civil service, are advertised or posted, we know that there are other jobs that are not. If you are pursuing a career in one of these noncivil service areas, contacting a company before anyone else knows of a job can give you a tremendous edge.

"How?" you ask.

Take a chance. Make a call or write a letter and ask. You might even stop in and talk to the human resources department or one of the department heads. There is nothing that says you have to wait to see an ad in the paper. Call up and ask to speak to the human resources department, recruitment services, or hiring manager. Once again, write out a script ahead of time so you know exactly what you want to say. Ask for the hiring manager or human resources department. Ask about job openings. Make sure you have an idea of what you want to do and convey it to the person you are talking to.

If you are told there are no openings or that the company or organization doesn't speak to people regarding employment unsolicited, be pleasant yet persistent. Ask if you can forward a resume to keep on file. In many cases, they will agree just to get you off the phone. Ask for the name of the person to direct your resume; then ask for the address to send it *and* the fax number. Thank the person you spoke with and make sure you get his or her name.

Now here's a neat trick. Fax your resume. Send it with a cover letter that states that a hard copy will be coming via mail. Why fax it?

Did you know that when you fax documents to a company they generally are delivered directly to the desk of the person you are sending it to? They don't go through the mailroom where they might be dumped into a general inbox. They don't sit around for a day. They are generally delivered immediately.

Now that your resume is in the hands of the powers that be, it's your job to call up, make sure they got it, and try as hard as you can to set up an interview. The individual's secretary might try to put you off. Don't be deterred. Thank him or her and say you understand his or her position. Say you're going to call in a week or so after the boss has had a chance to review your material. Send your information out in hard copy immediately. Wait a week or so and call back. Remember that persistence pays off.

Depending on the job, you sometimes might reach someone who tells you that "if I weren't so busy I would be glad to meet with you." They might tell you when their workload lightens or a project is done they will schedule an interview. You could say thank you and let it go. Or you could tell them that you understand that they're busy. All you are asking for is 10 minutes and not a minute longer. You'll even bring a stopwatch and coffee if they want. Guarantee them that 10 minutes after you get in the door, you will stand up to leave.

If you're convincing, you might land an interview. If you do, remember to *bring* that stopwatch. Introduce yourself, put the stopwatch down on the desk in front of you, and present your skills. It's essential that you practice this before you get there. Give the highlights of your resume and how hiring you would benefit the company. When your 10 minutes are up, thank the person you are meeting for his or her time and give him or her your resume, any supporting materials you have brought with you, and your business card. Then leave. If you are asked to stay, by all means, stay and continue the meeting. One way or the other, write a note thanking them for their time.

If you have sold yourself or your idea for a position, someone may just get back to you. Once again, remember to follow up with a call after a week or two.

⭐ Tip from the Coach

While the following incident occurred when I was first trying to enter the music business, I think the concept illustrates how persistence can pay off in any industry. At that time, I got to know a young man who was a comedian. He wasn't a very good comedian, but he said he was a comedian and did have a good number of jobs and bookings, so I guess he was a comedian.

During this time, I was trying to land interviews with everyone I could so I could get my own dream job in the music industry.

I made a contact with a booking agent whom I called and developed a business relationship. Every week, I'd call, and every week he would tell me to call him back. It wasn't going anywhere, but at least someone was taking my call. This went on for about three or four months.

One day when I called, the owner got on the phone and said, "Do you know Joe Black (not his real name)? He said he has worked in your area?"

I said, "Yes, he works as a comedian."

"What do you know about him?" he asked.

"He's very nice," I answered.

"But what do you know about him," the agent asked again? "Is he any good?"

"Well, he's not a great comedian, but he seems to keep getting jobs. He's booking himself," I replied.

"That's interesting," he said. "He has called me over 25 times looking for a job as an agent. What do you think?"

I was wondering why he was asking my opinion, because I had yet to get into his office myself. "If he can book himself, he can probably do a great job for your agency," I said. "You have great clients. I bet he would do a great job."

"Thanks," he said, "I might give him a call."

"What about me?" I asked.

"I still can't think of where you might fit in," he said. "Why don't you give me a call in a couple of weeks."

I waited a couple of weeks, called back, and asked to speak to the owner.

"Hello," he said. "Guess who's standing next to me?"

He had hired Joe Black the comedian to work as an agent in his office.

"He had no experience outside of booking himself," the agent said. "But I figured if he was as persistent making calls for our clients as he was trying to get a job, he'd work out for us. Why don't you come in and talk when you have a chance. I don't have anything, but maybe I can give you some ideas."

I immediately said that I had been planning a trip to the booking agent's city the next week. We set up an appointment.

Did the agent ever have a job for me? No, but while in his office, he introduced me to some of the clients he was booking, who introduced me to some other people, who later turned out to be clients of mine when I opened up my public relations company.

No matter what industry you want a job in, the moral of the story is the same: Networking and persistence always pay off.

> ### ★ Tip from the Top
> Depending on the area of law enforcement you are pursuing, you might land an interview soon after you respond to an advertisement, after you fill in an application, or after you have taken a civil service or police exam.

What kinds of positions might not be advertised? A variety of noncivil service jobs might fall into this category. For example, positions as the director of legal aid agencies may or may not be advertised. Positions as attorneys may not be advertised. Jobs as sketch artists, newspaper crime reporters, television crime reporters, or authors of test-prep books might not be advertised. Sales representatives for police or law enforcement equipment may not be advertised. Similarly, jobs as security guards, bodyguards, theft prevention specialists, private investigators, and so on might not be advertised either.

"Can you really land a job like that?" you ask.

Absolutely! While openings for any of these or hundreds of other positions might be advertised, they might not. And that is good news for you if you are job hunting because you can gain an edge. Many others have been successful in this technique and you are no exception.

The Interview Process

You landed an interview. Now what? The interview is an integral part of getting the job you want. Use it to your advantage.

There are a number of different types of interviews. Depending on the specific organization, company, and position, you might be asked to go on one or more interviews ranging from initial or screening interviews to interviews with department heads or supervisors with whom you will be working.

Things to Bring

Once you get the call for an interview, what's your next step? Let's start with what you should bring with you to the interview.

◎ Copies of your resume
  ▫ While they probably have copies of your resume, they might have misplaced it or you might want to refer to it.
◎ Letters of reference
  ▫ Bring your letters of reference, even if you have sent them in with your application and resume. Additionally, even though people have given you their letters of reference, make sure you let them know you are using them.
◎ References
  ▫ When interviewing for jobs, you often need to fill in job applications that ask for both professional and personal references. Ask before you use people as references. Make sure they are prepared to give you a good reference. Then when you go for an interview, call the people on your reference list and give them the heads up on your job-hunting activities. Once again, bring these with you, even if you have provided them previously.
◎ A portfolio of your achievements and other work
  ▫ Refer to Chapter 6 to learn how to develop your professional portfolio.
◎ Business or networking cards
  ▫ Refer to Chapter 6 to learn more about business and networking cards.
◎ Other supporting materials

▫ This might include a variety of materials, including copies of certifications, licenses, and so on.

You want to look as professional as possible, so don't throw your materials into a paper bag or a sloppy knapsack. A professional-looking briefcase or portfolio is the best way to hold your information. If you don't have that, at the very least put your information into a new envelope or folder to carry into the interview.

Your Interviewing Wardrobe

You've landed an interview, but what do you wear? It's essential that you dress professionally so that interviewers will see you as a professional, no matter what level you currently are in your career.

First let's start with a list of what not to wear:

◎ Sneakers
◎ Flip-flops
◎ Sandals
◎ Micro-mini skirts or dresses
◎ Very tight or very low dresses or tops
◎ Jeans of any kind
◎ Midriff tops
◎ Skin-tight pants or leggings
◎ Very baggy pants
◎ Sweatshirts
◎ Work-out clothes
◎ T-shirts
◎ Heavy perfume, men's cologne, or aftershave lotion
◎ Very heavy makeup
◎ Flashy jewelry (this includes nose rings, lip rings, and other flamboyant piercings)
◎ Tattoos (If you have large, visible tattoos, cover them with either clothing or some type of cover-up or makeup.)

Now let's talk about what you should wear:

Men
◎ Dark suit
◎ Dark sports jacket, white or light colored button down shirt, tie, and dress trousers
◎ Clean, polished shoes
◎ Socks

Women
◎ Suit
◎ Dress with jacket
◎ Skirt with blouse and jacket
◎ Pumps or other closed-toe shoes
◎ Hose

Interview Environments

In most cases interviews are held in office environments. If you are asked if you want coffee, tea, soda, or any type of food, my advice is to abstain. This is not the time you want to accidentally spill coffee, inadvertently make a weird noise drinking soda, or get sugar from a donut on your fingers when you need to shake hands.

With that said, in some cases, however, you may be interviewed over a meal. In these situations you are going to have to eat. Whether it is breakfast, lunch, or dinner, it is usually best to order something simple and light. This is not the time to order anything that can slurp, slide, or otherwise mess you up. Soups, messy sauces, spaghetti, lobster, fried chicken, ribs, cheese sticks, or anything that you have to pick up with your hands would be bad choices. Nothing can ruin your confidence during an interview worse than a big blob of sauce accidentally dropping on your shirt—except if you cut into something and it splashes on to your interviewer's suit. Eating should be your last priority. Use this time to tell your story, present your attributes, and ask intelligent questions.

This is also not the time to order alcoholic beverages. Even if the interviewer orders a drink, abstain. You want to be at the top of your game.

If the interviewer orders dessert and coffee or tea, do so as well. That way he or she isn't eating alone and you have a few more minutes to make yourself shine.

When might you be required to go to a meal interview instead of the traditional office interview? These generally are not the first interviews you are asked to attend. You may need to go on a meal interview if you are being interviewed by a recruiter or headhunter. You might also be invited on a meal interview if you are pursuing an upper-level position in the business or administrative segment of law enforcement. I mention meal interviews here so you will be prepared in the event you are invited to participate in one.

In some cases, a company may invite you to participate in a meal interview to see how you will act in social situations. They might want to check out your table manners, whether you keep your elbows on the table or talk with your mouth full. They might want to see whether you drink to excess or how you make conversation. They might want to know if you will embarrass

Words from the Wise

In your effort to tell people about your accomplishments, try not to monopolize the conversation talking solely about *you*. Before you go to an interview, especially a meal interview, read up on the news of the day in case someone at the table asks your opinion about the day's happenings. You want to appear as well rounded as possible.

them, if you can handle pressure, or how you interact with others. They might want you to get comfortable so they can see the true you. If you are prepared ahead of time, you will do fine. Just remember that this is not a social meal. You are being scrutinized. Be on your toes.

How can you increase your chances of this specific type of interview going well? During the meal, pepper the conversation with questions about the organization or company and the job. Don't be afraid to say you're excited about the possibility of working with them or that you think you would be an asset to the organization and you hope they agree.

Make eye contact with those at the table throughout the meal. Genuinely listen with interest to what others are saying.

When the interviewer stands up after the meal, the interview is generally over. Stand up, thank the interviewer or interviewers for the

Voice of Experience

Never ask for a doggie bag at an interview meal. I don't care how good the meal was, how much you have left over, or how much you've had it drummed into your head that you shouldn't waste food. I don't care if the interviewer asks for a doggie bag. In case you're missing the message, do not ask for a doggie bag! I've seen it happen and I've heard the interviewers talking about it in a negative manner weeks later.

Tip from the Coach

Everyone has their own opinions on politics and religion. During an interview, stay clear of conversations involving either subject as well as any other controversial issues.

> ### ★ The Inside Scoop
>
> If you have been invited to a meal interview, generally the interviewer will pay the tab and tip. At the end of the meal, when you are leaving, thank the person who paid the check and tell him or her how much you enjoyed the meal and the company.

meal, tell them you look forward to hearing from them, shake everyone's hand, and leave.

Many organizations today pre-interview or do partial interviews on the phone. This might be to pre-screen people without bringing them into the office. It also might come about if the employer is interested in a candidate and that individual lives in a different geographic location.

Whatever the reason, be prepared. If the company has scheduled a phone interview ahead of time, make sure your "space" is prepared so you can do your best.

Here are some ideas.

◎ Have your phone in a quiet location. People yelling, a loud television, or music in the background is not helpful in this situation.

◎ Have a pad of paper and a few pens to write down the name of the people you are speaking to, notes, and to jot down questions as you think of them.

◎ Have a copy of your resume near you. Your interviewer may refer to information on your resume. If it's close you won't have to fumble for words.

◎ Prepare questions to ask in case you are asked if you have any questions.

◎ Prepare answers for questions that you might be asked. For example:

☐ Why do you want to work for us?

☐ What can you bring to the department [organization, company]?

☐ What type of experience do you have?

☐ Why are you the best candidate?

☐ Where do you see yourself in five years?

☐ Why did you leave your last job?

☐ Did you get along with your last boss?

☐ What are you best at?

☐ What is your greatest strength?

☐ What is your greatest weakness?

Preparing for these questions is essential. While I can't guarantee what an interviewer might ask, I can pretty much guarantee that he or she probably will ask at least one of those questions or something similar.

Other Types of Interview Scenarios

When you think of an interviewing situation, you generally think of the one-on-one scenario where the interviewer is on one side of the desk and you are on the other. At some time during your career, you may be faced with other types of interviews. Two of the more common ones you may run into are group interviews and panel interviews. What's the difference?

A group interview is a situation where an organization brings a group of people together to tell them about the company and job opportunities. There may be open discussions and a question-and-answer period. During this time, one-on-one interviews may be scheduled.

Organizations use these types of situations not only to bring a group of potential employees together but to screen potential employees. What do you need to know? Remember that while this may not be the traditional interview setting you are used to, this is still an interview.

The Inside Scoop

I frequently receive calls from individuals who are distraught after going on a particular interview. It seems while they prepared for answering every question they can possibly think an interviewer might ask about the job they are applying for, they hadn't prepared for the unexpected.

"I prepared for answering every question," a man told me. "And then the interviewer threw me for a loop. He started asking me all kinds of questions that had nothing to do with the job I was applying for. I just couldn't come up with answers that made sense."

"What did he ask?" I questioned.

"He asked me what my favorite book was when I was a child. He asked me what I wanted to be when I was little. He asked me what my greatest strength was in my last job. Then he asked me what my biggest mistake was in my last job. I couldn't think of anything to say that quickly."

Interviewers often come up with questions like this for a variety of reasons. They may want to see how you react to nontraditional questions. They may want to see how well rounded you are. On occasion, they might just be thinking about something at the time they were interviewing you and the questions just popped out of their mouth.

If this has happened to you in the past, instead of beating yourself up about not coming up with what you consider a *good* answer, prepare for next time. Know there generally isn't any right or wrong answer. When an interviewer asks you a question, it's okay to take a moment to compose yourself and think about the answer you want to give.

From the minute you walk in the door in these settings, the potential employer is watching your demeanor and your body language. He or she is listening to what you say and any questions you might ask. He or she is watching you to see how you interact with others and how you might fit into the company.

How can you increase your chances of being asked to a one-on-one interview?

- Actively participate in conversations and activities.
- Be a leader, not a follower.
- Ask meaningful questions.

Panel Interviews

Basically, a panel interview is one in which you are interviewed by a group of people at the same time. This type of interview is often utilized for higher-level positions. You might, for example, go through a panel interview if you are pursuing a position as police chief. You might also go through a panel interview if you are pursuing a position such as the director of campus security. You might also go through a panel interview if you were going for a position as the director of media relations for a large police department. Some police departments also utilize panel interviews where a professional panel consisting of members of the department is set up to interview individuals pursuing positions as police officers.

Why do employers use panel interviews? There are a number of reasons. Every member of the panel brings something different to the table. Everyone has a different set of skills and experience. Many employers feel that a panel can increase the chance of finding the perfect applicant for the job. It also is sometimes easier to bring everyone involved together for one interview instead of scheduling separate interviews.

While there are exceptions, the panel interview is usually not the first interview you go

Tip from the Coach

If the thought of participating in a panel interview stresses you out, think of it this way. You have more than one chance to impress interviewers. While one member of the panel may not be impressed by your credentials, another may think you are the perfect candidate and after the interview be your cheerleader.

Tip from the Top

If you have an extreme emergency and absolutely must be late, call and try to reschedule your appointment. Do not see if you can get there late and come up with an excuse when you get there.

through. Generally, after going on one or more one-on-one interviews, if you become one of the finalists, you will be asked to attend a panel interview.

Who is there? It can be any mixture of people, depending on the job. If you are pursuing a job as a chief of police, for example, the panel might include the village, town, or city manager; human resources or personnel director; board members; and perhaps someone from the police department. Depending on the situation, there might also be members of search committees. It all depends on the specific job.

How can you succeed in a panel interview? Start by relaxing. Looking *or* feeling stressed will not help in this situation. When you walk into the interview, smile sincerely and make sure you shake each person's hand firmly. You want each person to feel equally important.

Voice of Experience

Always prepare a response for the beginning of the interview when someone on an interview panel says, "Tell us about yourself." Have a long and short version of your response. Don't say, "I don't know what to tell you." Or, "Where should I start?" Begin with your short version and ask if they would like you to go into more detail.

Prepare ahead of time. Know what is on your resume or CV. It sounds simple, but believe it or not, when you're on the hot seat, it is very easy to get confused. You want to be able to answer every question about your background without skipping a beat.

Research the law enforcement agency, organization, or company. Have some questions prepared so you can show a true interest in the position for which you are interviewing. Instead of referring to notes you have written, try to have your questions seem part of the conversation.

One of the important things to remember when participating in a panel interview is to make eye contact with everyone. Start by looking at the person who asks you the question. Then as you're answering, glance at the other people sitting around the table, making contact with each of them. You want everyone there to feel that you are talking to them.

Timing is everything in an interview. Whatever you do, don't be late. If you can't get to an interview on time, chances are you won't get to a job on time. On the other hand, you don't want to show up an hour early either.

Try to time your arrival so you get there about 15 minutes before your scheduled interview time. Walk in and tell the receptionist your name and who your appointment is with. When you are directed to go into the interview, walk in, smile sincerely, and shake hands with the interviewer or interviewers and sit down. Look

---

Tip from the Coach

Anyone can get stumped by a question an interviewer asks. The trick is, instead of stammering and stumbling and then saying something that you wish you could suck back into your mouth, take a moment to compose yourself and think about the best answer. If you do this, you will appear poised and confident.

---

around the office. Does the interviewer have a photo on the desk of children? Is there any personalization in the office? Does it look like the interviewer is into golf or fishing or basketball or some other hobby? Do you have something in common? You might say something like:

"What beautiful children."

"Is golf one of your passions too?"

"Do you go deep-sea fishing?"

"Those are amazing orchids. How long have you had them?"

"What an incredible antique desk. Do you collect antique furniture?"

Try to make the interviewer comfortable with you before his or her questions begin.

What might you be asked? You will probably be asked a slew of general questions and then, depending on the job, some questions specific to your skills and talents.

◎ Why should we hire you?

  ▫ This is a common question. Think about the answers ahead of time. Practice saying them out loud so you feel comfortable. For example, "I believe I would be an asset to your department (agency, facility, company, or organization.) I have the qualifications. I'm a team player and this is the type of career I've

always wanted to pursue. I'm a hard worker, a quick study, I have a positive attitude, and I'll help you achieve your goals."

  ▫ You can then go on to explain one or two specifics. For example, "While I was in college during an internship, I helped develop a couple of pilot programs. One was a community-based program that involved parents teaching kids how to deal with potential child predators. It involved teaching kids what to do if they were approached. A couple months after we instituted the program, amazingly enough a little boy was approached and remembered what his parents taught him during the program and got away. The man was arrested shortly after that. I would love the opportunity and challenge to keep other people safe."

◎ What are your qualifications for this job?

  ▫ This is a common question asked during any job interview. When asked, be ready to go over some of the specific qualifications you have for the job.

◎ What makes you more qualified than other candidates?

  ▫ This is another common question. Depending on the situation, you might say something like, "I believe my experience first working as a police officer in a small community and then as an undercover officer in a metropolitan city has prepared me for this opportunity."

◎ Where do you see yourself in five years?

  ▫ Do not say, "Sitting in your chair" or "In your job." People in every job and every business are paranoid that someone is going to take their job, so don't even joke about it. Instead, think about the question ahead of time. It's meant to find out what your aspirations are and if you have direction?

- ⊡ Depending on your situation, one answer might be, "I hope to be a seasoned agent with the DEA. This agency is such an important part of law enforcement. I would love to think that I can have a long career here."

◎ What are your strengths?

- ⊡ Be confident but not cocky when answering this one. Toot your horn, but don't be boastful. Practice ahead of time communicating your greatest strengths, talents, and skills. "I'm passionate about what I do. I love working at something I'm passionate about. That's one of the main reasons I applied for this position. I am really good at thinking outside of the box. I'm a skilled investigator. I'm multilingual and I have a lot of resources both in law enforcement and the community. I'm also a people person and a really good communicator. I pride myself on being able to solve problems quickly, efficiently, and successfully."

◎ Where are your weaknesses?

- ⊡ We all have weaknesses. This is not the time to share them. Be creative. "My greatest weakness is also one of my strengths. I'm a workaholic. I don't like leaving a project undone. I have a hard time understanding how

someone cannot do a great job when they love what they do."

◎ Why did you leave your last job?

- ⊡ Be careful answering this one. If you were fired, simply say you were let go. Don't go into the politics. Don't say anything bad about your former job, company, or boss. If you were laid off, simply say you were laid off, or, if it's true, that you were one of the newer employees and unfortunately, that's how the layoff process worked. You might add that you were very sorry to leave because you really enjoyed working there, but on the positive side, you are free to apply for this position. If you quit, simply say the job was not challenging and you wanted to work in a position where you could create a career.

  Never lie. Don't even try to stretch the truth. As I've mentioned before, this is a transient society. People move around. You can never tell when your former boss knows the person interviewing you. In the same vein, never say anything during an interview that is derogatory about anyone or any other law enforcement agency, organization, facility, or company. The supervisor you had yesterday might just be transferred to your new company and end up being your new boss. It is not unheard of in the industry.

◎ What have you done to prepare yourself for the position as a police officer (sheriff's deputy, state police officer, DEA agent, police chief, corrections officer, attorney, probation officer, parole officer, and so on)?

- This is your chance to tell the interviewer some of the things you have done to prepare for the position for which you are applying. Have you attended college? Completed your degree? Taken training? Gone though an internship? Shadowed an officer?
- Why do you want to work in law enforcement? (Depending on the specific area of the industry, the question might be, "Why do you want to work as a police officer?" "Why do you want to work as a corrections officer?" "Why do you want to work in the DEA?" "Why do you want to be a special agent with the FBI?")
  - Think about it ahead of time and be sure to have an answer ready for this question. Don't just come up with a stock answer. Show your passion.

Depending on the position you are pursuing, the interviewer may ask more industry-specific questions.

- What do you think is the biggest problem in law enforcement at this time?
- What is your philosophy of law enforcement?
- What is your philosophy of the manner in which the correctional department should work?
- If you had to pick the most important new advancement in law enforcement, what would it be?
- What would you do if you witnessed a crime in progress right now?
- Under what circumstances, do you believe deadly force is justified within the scope of law enforcement?

- When did you decide you wanted to work in law enforcement?
  - Think about questions like this ahead of time and come up with answers. There is no right or wrong answer for these types of questions. You just want to be able to come up with answers without saying, "Uh, let me think. Well, I'm not sure."
- Are you a team player?
  - Whether you're working in a local police department, a state or federal law enforcement agency, a correctional facility, in the business segment of the industry, the support segment, the peripherals, or anywhere in between, the answer is, "Yes, it's one of my strengths."
- Do you need supervision?
  - You want to appear as confident and capable as possible. Depending on the specific job and responsibilities, you might say, "Once I know my responsibilities, I have always been able to fulfill them. I look forward to doing the same here."
- Do you get along well with others?
  - The answer they are looking for is, "Yes, I'm a real people person." Do not give any stories about times when you weren't. Do not say anything like, "I get along better with women" or "I relate better to men." Even if it's true, don't make any type of comment that can come back to haunt you later.

Every now and then, you get a weird question or a question that you just don't expect. If you could be a car, what type of car would you be and why? If you were an animal, what animal would you be? If you could have dinner with anyone alive or dead, who would it be? These questions generally are just meant to throw you off balance and see how you react. Stay calm and focused. Be creative but try not to come up with any answer that is too weird.

An interviewer might ask you about the last book you read, what newspapers you read, or what television shows are your favorites.

Be honest, but try not to say things like, "I don't have time to read." "I don't like reading." You want to appear well rounded.

- ◎ How do you deal with stress?
  - ▫ Stress is a major factor in many areas of law enforcement. The interviewer does not want to hear that you are stressed to the max. What he or she wants to hear is that you deal well with stress and you find healthy and constructive ways to manage it.
- ◎ Do you deal well with people? Have you had any experience dealing with the public?
  - ▫ The answer they are looking for is, "Yes. I deal well with others." You might then give some examples of dealing with the public (if you have).
- ◎ What type of salary are you looking for?
  - ▫ Depending on the area of law enforcement you are pursuing, this may or may not come up at the first interview. Salary is going to be discussed in more detail in a moment, but what you should know now is that this is an important matter. You don't want to get locked into a number before you know exactly what your responsibilities are. If asked, you might say

> ### Tip from the Top
> Try not to discuss salary at the beginning of the interview. Instead, wait until you hear all the particulars about the job and you have given them a chance to see how great you are.

something to the effect of, "I'm looking for a fair salary for the job. I really would like to know more about the responsibilities before I come up with a range. What is the range, by the way?" You might also turn the tables and say something like, "I was interested in knowing what the salary range was for this position." This turns the question back to the interviewer.

Depending on the specific type of job you are pursuing, interviewers may ask you one or more questions designed to see if you have integrity or what type of judgment you have.

If you are asked a question like this, take a moment to formulate your answer in your mind. What the interviewer is trying to do is get inside your head and see how you will react to certain situations.

What Can't They Ask You?

There are questions that are illegal for interviewers to ask. For example, they aren't permitted to ask you about age unless they are making sure you are over the minimum age required for the job and under the maximum age.

They aren't supposed to ask you about whether you are married, have children, or are in a relationship. Interviewers are not supposed to ask you about your race, color, religion, national origin, or sexual preference.

If an interviewer does ask an illegal question, in most cases it is not on purpose. He or she just might not know that it shouldn't be asked.

Your demeanor in responding to such questions can affect the direction of the interview. If you don't mind answering, then by all means, do so. If answering bothers you, try to point the questions in another direction, such as back to your skills and talents. If you are unable to do so, simply indicate in a nonthreatening, nonconfrontational manner that those types of questions are not supposed to be asked in interviews.

What You Might Want to Ask

Just because you're the one being interviewed doesn't mean you shouldn't ask questions. You want to appear confident. You want to portray someone who can fit in with others comfortably. You want to ask great questions. Depending on the specific job, here are some ideas.

◎ What happened to the last person who held this job? Was he or she promoted or did he or she leave the organization?
  ▫ You want to know whose shoes you're filling.
◎ What is the longevity of employees here?
  ▫ Employees who stay for a length of time generally are happy with the organization.
◎ Does the company (agency or department) promote from within as a rule or look outside?
  ▫ This is important because companies that promote from within are good organizations with which to build a career.
◎ Are there opportunities to advance in the department? Will I be able to take my skills and career to the next level?

  ▫ You are continuing to look for answers about building a career.
◎ Is there a lot of laughing in the workplace? Are people happy here?
  ▫ If there is, it means it is a less-stressed environment.
◎ Is there a probationary period? How long is that period?
  ▫ You want to know how long you will be a provisional employee.
◎ How will I be evaluated? Are there periodic reviews?
  ▫ You want to know how and when you will know if you are doing well in your supervisor's eyes.
◎ How do your measure success on the job? By that I mean how can I do a great job for you?
  ▫ You want to know what your employer expects from employees.
◎ What are the options for advancement in this position?
  ▫ This illustrates that you are interested in staying with the organization.
◎ Who will I report to? What will my general responsibilities be?
  ▫ You want to know what your work experience and duties will be like.
◎ What are some of the challenges of this job?
  ▫ An interviewer, may say, for example, "Some feel the job is stressful" or "There is never enough funding to have as many officers in the field as we need." Whatever he or she says, do not respond with something to the effect of, "Oh, I don't know if I can deal with that."

Feel free to ask any questions you want answered. While it is perfectly acceptable to ask questions, don't chatter incessantly out of nervousness. You want to give the interviewer time to ask you questions and see how you shine.

It's normal to be nervous during an interview. Relax as much as you can. If you go in prepared and answer the questions you're asked, you should do fine. Somewhere during the interview, if things are going well, salary will come up.

Salary and Compensation

No matter how much you want a job, unless you are doing an internship, the good news is, you're not going to be working for free. Compensation may be discussed in a general manner during your interview or may be discussed in full. In some cases, it might not be discussed at all until you are offered the position. A lot has to do with the specific job. Unless your interviewer brings up salary at the beginning of an interview, you should not. If you feel an interview is close to ending and another interview has not been scheduled, feel free to bring up salary when asked if you have any questions.

A simple question such as "What is the salary range for the job?" will usually start the ball rolling. Depending on the specific job, your interviewer may tell you exactly what the salary and benefits are or may just give you a range. In many cases, salary and compensation packages are only ironed out after the actual job offer is made.

Let's say you are offered a job and a compensation package. What do you do if you're not happy with the salary? What about the benefits? Can you negotiate? That depends on the job. If

it is a civil service job, the answer probably is no. If not, you certainly can try. Sometimes you can negotiate better terms as far as salary, sometimes better benefits, and sometimes both. Sometimes you might be offered a signing bonus. A lot of it depends on how much they want you, how much of an asset you will be, and what the organization can afford.

When negotiating, speak in a calm, well-modulated voice. Do not make threats. State your case and see if you can meet in the middle. If you can't negotiate a higher salary, perhaps you can negotiate extra vacation days. Depending on the company and specific job, compensation may include salary, vacation days, sick days, health insurance, stock options, pension plans, or a variety of other things. When negotiating, look at the whole package.

You might do some research ahead of time to see what similar types of jobs are paying. Depending on the specific job, information on compensation may also have been in the original advertisement you answered.

Over the years I have seen many people who are so desperate to get the job of their dreams that once offered the job, they will take it for almost anything. Often, when questioned about salary, they ask for salary requirements far be-

> ### The Inside Scoop
> Many jobs in law enforcement require overtime, which can increase earnings dramatically. Federal laws provide special salary rates to federal employees who serve in law enforcement. Federal special agents and inspectors, for example, receive law enforcement availability pay known as LEAP. Currently, this is equal to 25 percent of the agent's grade and step.

low what might have been offered. Whatever you do, don't undersell yourself.

Accepting a job offer below your perceived salary "comfort level" often results in you resenting your company and coworkers. Even worse, it whittles away at your self-worth.

If you want to, feel free to ask for a day or two to consider an offer. Simply say something like, "I appreciate your confidence in me. I'd like to think about it overnight if that's okay with you. Can I give you a call tomorrow afternoon?"

There are a number of things to keep in mind regarding compensation in jobs in law enforcement. First of all, you should be aware that many jobs in law enforcement are unionized. What that means in regard to salary is that minimum earnings (as well as working conditions) are negotiated and set by a specific union.

Another area to keep in mind is that salaries for civil service positions are governed by laws and regulations and therefore your wages would be set by those limitations based on your grade and step.

Things to Remember

In order to give yourself every advantage in acing the interview, there are a few things you

should know. First of all, practice ahead of time. Ask friends or family members for their help in setting up practice interviews. You want to get comfortable answering questions without sounding like you're reading from a script.

Here are some other things to remember to help you land an offer.

◎ If you don't have confidence in yourself, neither will anyone else. No matter how nervous you are, project a confident and positive attitude.

◎ The one who looks and sounds most qualified has the best chance of getting the job. Don't answer questions in monosyllables. Explain your answers using relevant experiences. Use your experiences in both your work and personal life to reinforce your skills, talents, and abilities when answering questions.

◎ Try to develop a rapport with your interviewer. If your interviewer "likes" you, he or she will often overlook less than perfect skills because you "seem" like a better candidate.

◎ Smile and make sure you have good posture. It makes you look more successful.

◎ Be attentive. Listen to what the interviewer is saying. If he or she asks a question that you don't understand, politely ask for an explanation.

◎ Be pleasant and positive. People will want to be around you.

◎ Turn off your cell phone and beeper *before* you go into the interview.

◎ Be 100 percent truthful and honest during your interview.

◎ When you see the interview coming to a close, make sure you ask when a decision will be made and if you will be contacted either way.

- When the interview comes to a close, stand up, thank the interviewer, shake his or her hand, and then leave.

Here are some things you should not do:

- Don't smoke before you go into your interview.
- Don't chew gum during your interview.
- Don't be late.
- Don't talk negatively about past bosses, jobs, or companies.
- Don't say "ain't," "heh," "uh-huh," "don't know," "got me," or other similar things. It doesn't sound professional and suggests that you have poor communication skills.
- Don't wear heavy perfume or men's cologne before going on an interview. You can never tell if the interviewer is allergic to various odors.
- Don't interrupt the interviewer.
- While you certainly can ask questions, don't try to dominate the conversation to try to "look smart."
- Don't swear, curse, or use off-color language.
- Don't make sexist or racist remarks.

Thank-You Notes

It's always a good idea to send a note thanking the person who interviewed you for his or her time. Think a thank-you note is useless? Think again. Take a look at some of the things a thank-you note can do for you.

A thank-you note after an interview can:

- Show that you are courteous and well mannered
- Show that you are professional

- Give you one more shot at reminding the interviewer who you were
- Show that you are truly interested in the job
- Illustrate that you have written communication skills
- Give you a chance to briefly discuss something that you thought was important yet forgot to bring up during the interview
- Help you stand out from other job applicants who didn't send a thank-you note

Try to send thank-you notes within 24 hours of your interview. You can hand write or type them. While it's acceptable to e-mail or fax them, I suggest mailing.

What should the letter say? It can simply say thank you for taking the time to interview you, or it can be longer, touching on a point you discussed in the interview or adding something you may have forgotten.

Waiting for an Answer

You've gone through the interview for the job you want. You've done everything you can do. Now what? Well, unfortunately, now you have to wait for an answer. Are you the candidate who was chosen? Hopefully, you are!

What now? That depends on the specific job. In some cases, the interview was only one portion of the selection process. Depending on the situation, you may still need to go through a physical agility test, a psychological evaluation, background check, and a physical and a urinalysis to check for drug usage before you are offered a position.

In other situations, you might be offered a job on the spot. In still others, interviewers may want to interview other candidates before they make a decision.

If you haven't heard back in a week or so (unless you were given a specific date when an applicant would be chosen), call and ask the status of the job. If you are told that they haven't made a decision, ask when a good time to call back would be.

If you are told that a decision has been made and it's not you, thank them and say how you appreciated the consideration. Request that your resume be kept on file for the future. You might just get a call before you know it. If the organization or agency is a large one, ask if there are other positions available and how you should go about applying for them if you are interested.

If your phone rings and you got the job, congratulations! Once you get that call telling you that you are the candidate they want, depending on the situation, they will either make an offer on the phone or you will have to go in to discuss your compensation package. If an offer is made on the phone, as we previously discussed, you have every right to ask if you can think about it and get back to them in 24 hours. If you are satisfied with the offer as it is, you can accept it.

Depending on the job, you may be required to sign an employment contract. Read the agreement thoroughly and make sure that you are comfortable signing it. If there is anything you don't understand, ask. Do not just sign without reading. You want to know what you are agreeing to.

Interviewing for jobs is a skill. Practice until you feel comfortable answering every type of

question and being in a variety situations. The more prepared you are ahead of time, the better you'll usually do. The more you do it, the more comfortable you'll be going through the process.

Mastering the art of interviewing can make a huge difference in your interview. Remember the intangible essentials that can help you win the job:

◎ Enthusiasm
◎ Excitement
◎ Passion
◎ Interest
◎ Confidence

Let's discuss these areas for a moment. Enthusiasm is key when interviewing for a job. You want to be enthusiastic at the interview.

"But I don't want them to think I'm desperate," people always tell me.

My response is always the same: You don't want to appear desperate, but you don't want there to be a question in your interviewer's mind that you want the job.

What else? You want to be excited about the possibility of working at the job for which you are interviewing.

Passion is essential. Make sure you let your passion shine. It can make the difference between you getting the job or someone else.

Anything else? You definitely want to appear interested. What does that mean? You want your interviewer to know without a shadow of a doubt that you are interested not only in the job but in the concept of working at that particular job.

And finally, you want to appear confident. As we have already discussed, if you don't believe you are the best, neither will anyone else.

With some thought, planning, and effort, you can master job interview skills to tip the scale in your favor and land the job you are going after.

⭐ Tip from the Coach

Take every interview seriously. Don't waste any opportunity to sell yourself.

9

MARKETING YOURSELF FOR SUCCESS

What Marketing Can Do for You

Who hasn't heard of Nabisco, Pepperidge Farm, and Bird's Eye? How about Coca-Cola, Pepsi, and Dr Pepper? What about McDonald's, Burger King, and Wendy's? Here's a question. Do you know what those companies have in common with Las Vegas, Disney World, the Rolling Stones, Elvis Presley and every other successful corporation and person? It's the same thing that hot trends, major sports events, blockbuster movies, top television shows, hot CDs, megasuperstars, and even hot new toys have in common. Do you know what it is yet?

Here's the answer. Every one of them utilizes marketing. Do you want to know the inside track on becoming successful and getting what you want no matter what segment of law enforcement you're interested in pursuing? It's simple: All you have to do is utilize marketing yourself.

Many people think that marketing techniques are reserved for businesses, products, or celebrities. Here's something to think about. From the moment you begin your career until you ultimately retire, you are a product. It doesn't matter what direction your career is going, what level you're at, or what area you want to pursue.

There are thousands of people who want to work in various segments of law enforcement. Some make it and some don't. Is it all talent? A lot of it has to do with talent, but that is not everything. We all have heard of talented individuals who haven't made it in their chosen field. Is it skills? We have all heard of people who are skilled yet don't make it either. Is it that one individual has more education or training than another?

So if it isn't just talent or skills, what is the answer? What is the key to success? A lot of it is related to working hard and having a strong passion. As we've discussed previously, probably a lot of it may also have to do with luck and being in the right place at the right time. One of the important factors that appears to be related to success, however, is also how one individual sets him- or herself apart from another in the way they were marketed or conversely marketed themselves.

Here's something you should know. When major corporations want to turn a new product into a hot commodity, they develop and implement a successful marketing plan. When record executives want to turn a CD and an artist into a hot commodity, they develop and implement a successful marketing plan. When book publishers want to turn a new book into a hot commodity, they develop and implement a successful marketing plan.

What does this mean to you? No matter which segment of law enforcement in which you want to work and succeed, marketing can help *you* become one of the hottest commodities around.

While most people can understand how marketing can help a product succeed, a celebrity become more popular, or a book become a best-seller, they often don't think about the possibility of marketing themselves if they are pursuing a career in an industry such as law enforcement.

When I give seminars and we start discussing this area, there are always a number of attendees who inevitably ask, "Does this relate to me?" "Can't I just look for a job, interview, get it, and forget it," they ask? "Do I need to go through this extra process? Why do I have to market myself?"

Here's the answer in a nutshell. If you aren't marketing yourself and someone else is, they will have an advantage over you. One of the tricks to success is taking advantage of every opportunity. Marketing yourself is an opportunity you just can't afford to miss.

What is marketing? On the most basic level, marketing is finding markets and avenues to sell products or services. In this case, you are the product. The buyers are employers.

To be successful, you not only want to be the product; you want to be the *brand*. Look at Nabisco, Kellogg's, McDonald's, Coke, Pepsi, and Disney. Look at Orange County Choppers, Martha Stewart, NASCAR, *American Idol,* and Michael Jordan.

Look at Donald Trump. One of the most successful people in branding, Trump, a master marketer, believes so strongly in this concept that he successfully branded himself. While he made his mark in real estate, in addition to having a number of successful television shows under his belt, Trump has a successful line of hotels, casinos, clothing, water, ice-cream, meats, books, seminars, and even a Trump University. He continues to illustrate to people how he can fill *their needs.* Then he finds new needs he can fill. If you're savvy, you can do the same.

"Even if I want to work in law enforcement?" you ask.

Absolutely! If you know or can determine what you can do for an employer or what can help them, you can market yourself to illustrate how you can fill those needs. If you can sell and market yourself effectively, you can succeed in your career; you can push yourself to the next level and you can get what you want.

Is there a secret to this? No, there really isn't a secret, but it does take some work. In the end, however, the payoff will be worth it.

Do you want to be the one who gets the job? Marketing can help. Want to make yourself visible so potential employers will see you as desirable? Marketing can help. Do you want to set yourself apart from other job candidates? Guess what? Marketing can help. It can also distinguish you from other employees. If you have marketed yourself effectively, when possible promotions, raises, or in-house openings are on the horizon, your name will come up. Marketing can give you credibility and open the door to new opportunities.

Do you want to stand out from others in your specific area of law enforcement? Do you want to set yourself apart from other law enforcement officers? Do you want to set yourself apart from other police chiefs or police commissioners? Do you want to set yourself apart from other federal law enforcement special agents? Do you want to set yourself apart from other parole officers? Other probation officers? Other district attorneys or prosecutors? Do you want to set yourself apart from every other person in your field? You know what you have to do. Market yourself!

Do you want to become more visible? Get the attention of the media? Do you want to get the attention of recruiters, headhunters, industry insiders, and other important people? Do you want to open the door to new opportunities? Do you want to catch the eye of board members, human resources directors, or personnel officers of municipal, county, state, or federal governmental law enforcement agencies who want you to be part of their team? Market yourself!

"Okay," you're saying. "I get it. I need to market myself. But how?"

That's what we're going to talk about now. To begin with, understand that in order to market yourself effectively, you are going to have to do what every good marketer does: You're going to have to develop your product, perform market research, and assess the product and the marketplace.

Are there going to be differences between marketing yourself for a career in local law enforcement and federal law enforcement? What

---

Tip from the Coach

If you want to market yourself effectively, find ways to set yourself apart. One of the ways you can do this is by doing more than is expected of you. If you see something that needs to be done, don't wait for someone to tell you to do it; be proactive and offer to help. If things aren't busy at work, look for something to do. Your extra efforts will not go unnoticed.

Tip from the Top

Effective marketing focuses on the needs of the customer (in this case, the employer.) You want to show employers how you can fill their needs, not what they can do for you. What does this mean to you? You not only want to show potential employers how good you are but how your skills, talents, and package can help them.

---

about differences in marketing yourself for a career working hands on in law enforcement or working in one of the peripherals? Yes, of course there may be some differences, but in general, you're going to use a lot of the same techniques.

Read this section and see which techniques and ideas work best for you. As long as you are marketing yourself in a positive manner, you are on the right track.

The Five Ps of Marketing and How They Relate to Your Career

There are five Ps to marketing, whether you're marketing your career, a hot new restaurant, a new product, a brand new book, a CD or anything else. They are:

◎ Product
◎ Price
◎ Positioning
◎ Promotion
◎ Packaging

Let's look at how these Ps relate to your career.

Product: In this case, as we just mentioned, the product is *you*. "Me," you say. "How am I a product?" *You* are a package complete with your physical self, skills, ideas, and talents.

Price: Price is the compensation you receive for your work. One of your goals in marketing yourself is to sell your talents, skills, and anything else you have to offer for the best possible compensation.

Positioning: What positioning means in this context is developing and creating innovative methods to fill the needs of one or more employers or potential clients. It also means differentiating yourself and/or your talent and skills from other competitors. Depending on your career area, this might mean differentiating yourself from other employees, administrators, businesspeople, and so on.

Promotion: Promotion is the creation and implementation of promotional methods that make you visible in a positive manner.

Packaging: Packaging is the way you present yourself.

Putting Together Your Package

Now that we know how the five Ps of marketing are related to your career, let's discuss a little more about putting together your package.

The more you know about your product (*you*), the easier it is to market and sell it. It's also essential to know as much as possible about the markets to which you are trying to sell. What do you have to offer that a potential buyer (employer) needs? If you can illustrate to a market (employer) that you are the package that can fill their needs, you stand a good chance to turn the market into a buyer.

Assess what you have to offer as well as what you think an employer needs. We've already discussed self-assessment in a prior chapter. Now review your skills and your talents to help you determine how they can be used to fill the needs of your target markets.

While all the Ps of marketing are important, packaging is one of the easiest to change. It's something you have control over.

★ Tip from the Coach

While you can't tell a book by its cover, it is human nature to at least look at the book with an interesting cover first. You might put it back after looking at it, but you at least gave it a first shot. That is why it is so important to package yourself as well as you possibly can.

How important is packaging? Very! Good packaging can make a product more appealing, more enticing, and make *you* want it. Not convinced? Think about the last time you went to the store. Did you reach for the name-brand products more often than the bargain brands?

Still not convinced? How many times have you been in a bakery or restaurant and chosen the beautifully decorated desserts over the simple un-iced cakes? Packaging can make a difference—a big difference—in your career. If you package yourself effectively, people will want your package.

Want to know a secret? Many job candidates in every industry are passed over before they get very far in the process because they simply don't understand how to package themselves. What does this mean to you?

It means that if you can grasp the concept, you're ahead of the game. In a competitive world, this one thing can give you the edge. Knowing that a marketing campaign utilizes packaging to help sell products means that you will want to package yourself as well as you can. You want potential employers, recruiters, headhunters, board members, and others to see you in the most positive manner possible. You want to illustrate that you have what it takes to fill *their* needs.

So what does your personal package include?

⭐ Tip from the Top

Make sure you have mints or breath strips with you when you go to interviews, meetings, or even work. Nothing can turn off people faster than someone breathing funky breath in their face.

People base their first impression of you largely on your appearance. Whether you are going for an interview for a hot job or currently working and trying to move up the ladder of success, appearance is always important.

It might seem elementary, but let's go over the elements of your appearance. Personal grooming is essential. What does that mean?

◎ Your hair should be clean and neatly styled.
◎ You should be showered with no body odor.
◎ Your nails should be clean. If you polish them, make sure that your polish isn't chipped.
◎ If you are a man, you should be freshly shaved and mustaches and beards should be neatly styled. (Keep in mind that in some law enforcement agencies facial hair is against policy.)

◎ If you are a woman, your makeup should look natural and not overdone.
◎ Your breath should be clean and fresh.

Good grooming is important no matter what segment of the industry you are pursuing.

Now let's discuss your attire. Whether you're going on interviews, are in a networking situation, or are already on the job, it's important to dress appropriately. What's appropriate? Good question.

Appropriateness to a great extent depends on what area of the industry you're involved and your specific job. If you are working in a position that utilizes uniforms, such as a police officer, corrections officer, state police officer, and so on, you will, of course, be wearing a uniform while on duty. Make sure if you are wearing a uniform that it is clean and pressed and that your grooming is immaculate.

As all positions in law enforcement are not uniformed, it is important to remember that dressing professionally can help your career in a number of ways, from establishing credibility to maintaining respect, to establishing yourself as an authority figure.

Always dress to impress. Employers want to see that you will not only fit in but that you will not embarrass them when representing the agency, company, department, or organization. So what should you do? What should you wear?

⭐ Words from the Wise

Strong perfume, cologne, and after-shave often make people *not* want to be near you. Many people are allergic to strong odors. Many just can't stand the smell. You don't want to be known as the one who wears that stinky stuff. If you wear scents, go light.

⭐ Words from a Pro

Even if you are interviewing for an entry-level job, dress professionally. You want your interviewer to see that you are looking for a *career,* not just a job.

If you are going on an interview, dress professionally. While we discussed interviewing attire in a previous chapter, let's touch on it again. If you're a man, you can never go wrong in a suit and tie or a pair of dress slacks with a sports jacket, dress shirt, and tie. Women might wear a suit, a professional-looking dress, a skirt and jacket, skirt and blouse, or perhaps a pantsuit. Once you're hired, learn the company dress policy. It's okay to ask. No matter what the policy is, observe what everyone else is wearing. If the policy is casual and everyone is still dressed in business attire, dress in business attire.

"But what if I'm a probation officer [or whatever other job you hold]?" you ask. "Why would I get dressed up? None of the other probation officers in the office get dressed up? As a matter of fact, a number of them wear jeans to work."

The answer is simple. You want to make a good impression. You want to look like you care and you want to look like you're serious about your career. You want to look professional. You also want to illustrate that you have respect for the interviewer and the interview process.

You might also want to think about your image when you're *not* working. Why is this important? If you project an unprofessional image off the job, it might affect your career in a negative manner.

This isn't to say that you have to wear a suit all the time or even be dressed up. What it means is that you never want to be in a position where you leave home looking sloppy and then run into someone who could be helpful to your career.

Communication Skills

Your communication skills, both verbal and written, are yet another part of your package. What you say and how you say it can mean the difference between success and failure in getting a job or succeeding at one you already have. You want to sound articulate, polished, strong, and confident.

Do you ever wonder how others hear you? Consider using a tape recorder, recording yourself speaking, and then playing it back.

Is this scary? It can be if you have never heard yourself. Here's what you need to remember. No matter what you think you sound like, it probably isn't that bad. If you are like most people, you are probably your own worst critic.

When you play back your voice, listen to your speech pattern. You might, for example, find that you are constantly saying "uh" or "uh-huh." You might find that your voice sounds nasal or high pitched or that you talk too quickly. If you're not happy with the way you sound, there are exercises you can do to practice to change your pitch, modulation, and speech pattern.

Because you can't take words back into your mouth after you say them, here are some *don'ts* to follow when speaking.

◎ Don't use off-color language.
◎ Don't swear or curse.
◎ Don't tell jokes or stories that have sexual, ethnic, or racial undertones or innuendoes.
◎ Don't interrupt others when they are speaking.
◎ Don't use poor grammar or slang.
◎ Don't talk about people.

We've discussed your verbal communication skills; now let's discuss the importance of your written communication skills. Here's the deal. Written communication skills are important in every aspect of law enforcement. At the very least, you will need the ability to write reports and simple letters.

If you are uncomfortable with your writing skills, you have a couple of choices. You might

---

★ Words from the Wise

Don't say words like *ain't*. It makes you sound stupid even if you're not.

---

pick up a book to help improve your skills or perhaps take a writing class at a local school or college.

Your body language can tell people a lot about you. The way you carry yourself can show others how you feel about yourself. We've all seen people in passing that were hunched over or who looked uninterested or just looked like they didn't care.

Would you want someone like that prosecuting a case? Would you want someone like that working on the police force? What about protecting the president or first family? Would you like someone like that handling inmates? How about representing the department or agency? Would you like someone that looked like that working for *you?* Well generally, neither do most employers.

What does your body language illustrate? Does it show that you are confident? That you are happy to be where you are? Do you make eye contact when you're speaking to someone? What about your demeanor? Common courtesy is mandatory in your life and your career. Polite expressions such as "please," "thank you," "excuse me," and "pardon me" will not go unnoticed.

Your personality traits are another part of your package. No one wants to be around a whiner, a sad sack, or people who complain constantly. You want to illustrate that you are calm, happy, well balanced, and have a positive attitude.

You want to show that you can deal effectively with others, are a team player, and can

---

★ Voice of Experience

Don't speak negatively about coworkers or superiors to other coworkers. Similarly, don't speak negatively about coworkers or superiors to people outside of your workplace.

deal with problems and stress effectively. You might be surprised to know that in many cases employers will lean toward hiring someone with a positive and energetic personality over someone with better skills who seems negative and less well balanced.

Remember that the education you have is an important part of your package. Get the best education you can. Don't stop at the minimum requirements. Continue learning throughout your career. Education, both formal and informal, not only helps you increase knowledge and build new skill sets but helps you make new contacts and build your network.

Last but not least in your package are your skills and talents. These are the things that make *you* special. What's the difference between skills and talents?

Skills can be learned or acquired. Talents are things that you are born with and can be embellished. Your personal package includes both.

What you need to do is package the product so the buyer wants it. In this case, as we have discussed, the product is you and the buyer might be a potential employer, recruiter, headhunter, human resources director, and so on.

Now that you know what goes into your package, and you are working on putting together your best possible package, what's next?

Marketing Yourself Like a Pro and Making Yourself Visible

How can you market yourself? If you're like many people, you might be embarrassed to promote yourself, embarrassed to talk about your accomplishments, and embarrassed to bring them to the attention of others. This feeling probably comes from childhood when you were taught "it wasn't nice to brag."

Tip from the Coach

Be positive about yourself and never be self-deprecating, even in a joking manner. The truth is when you're self-deprecating, you will start believing it and so will the people with whom you are speaking.

It's time to change your thinking. It's time to toot your own horn! Done correctly, you won't be bragging. Done correctly, you are simply taking a step to make yourself visible. You are taking a step to help let potential employers know that you are the one who can fill their needs.

Want to know the payoff to doing this? You can move your career in a positive direction quicker. Career success can be yours, but you need to work at it.

Visibility can help. Visibility is important in climbing the career ladder in every industry and law enforcement is no exception. No matter the segment of law enforcement in which you want to succeed, visibility can assist you in attaining your goals.

How? To begin with, it can help set you apart from others who might have similar skills and talents.

How can you make yourself visible?

◎ Tell people what you are doing.
◎ Tell people what you are *trying* to do.
◎ Share your dreams.
◎ Live your dreams.
◎ Toot your own horn.
◎ Get into the media.
◎ Get involved in the community.
◎ Do more than is expected of you.
◎ Make it happen.

When you make yourself visible, you will gain visibility in the workplace, the community, and more. This is essential to getting what you want and deserve in your career, whether it's the brand-new job or a promotion pushing you up the career ladder.

We'll discuss how you can you tell people what you're doing without bragging later, but first, let's discuss when it's appropriate to toot your own horn. Here are some situations.

◎ When you get a new job.
◎ When you get a promotion.
◎ When you are giving a speech.
◎ When you are giving a presentation.
◎ When you are going to be (or have already appeared) on television or radio.
◎ When you have a major accomplishment.
◎ When you receive an honor or an award.
◎ When you chair an event.
◎ When you graduate from school, college, the police academy, law school, or a training program.
◎ When you obtain professional certification.
◎ When you work with a not-for profit or charity organization on a project (as a volunteer).

And the list goes on. The idea isn't only to make people aware of your accomplishments but to make yourself visible in a positive manner.

Tip from the Top

A press release is not an ad. Ads cost money. There is no charge to send press releases to the media. Press releases are used by the media to develop stories or are edited slightly or published as is.

Words from a Pro

Many of the stories you read in newspapers and magazines or hear on the radio or television are the direct result of press releases. Don't make the mistake of not sending out press releases because you *think* the media won't be interested or your story is not noteworthy.

How do you do it? Well, you could shout your news from a rooftop or walk around with a sign, but that probably wouldn't be very effective.

One of the best ways to get the most bang for your buck is by utilizing the media.

"I don't have money for an ad," you say.

"Here is the good news. You don't have to take out an ad. You can use publicity and publicity is free. Newspapers, magazines, and periodicals *need* stories to fill their pages. Similarly, television and radio need to fill airspace as well. If you do it right, your story can be one of the ones filling that space and it won't cost you anything.

How do you get your news to the media? The easiest way is by sending out press or news releases.

How do you write a news release? It really isn't that difficult once you get the basics down. You can always ask a professional publicist for some pointers. You also might ask the publicity chairperson from a local not-for-profit organization if he or she would mind giving you the basics on developing press releases. Local community colleges and schools often offer noncredit classes, seminars, and workshops that can help you learn how to write news releases effectively.

Basically, however, if you want to get started, you should know that news releases are developed by answering the five Ws. These are

◎ Who?
  ▫ Who are you writing about?
◎ What?
  ▫ What is happening or has happened?
◎ When?
  ▫ When did it happen or is it happening?
◎ Where?
  ▫ Where is it happening or has it happened?
◎ Why?
  ▫ Why is it happening or why is it noteworthy or relevant?

While it would be nice for everyone to have their own personal press agent or publicist, this is not generally the case, especially for those pursuing a career in law enforcement. So, until you have one, you are going to have to be your own publicist. You're going to have to develop your own personal publicity and marketing plan.

How do you do this? In order to market yourself, you are going to have to find opportunities to issue press releases, develop them, and then send them out. You want your name to be visible in a positive manner as often as possible.

Let's look at a possible scenario. Let's say Zack Dickson just received his degree in criminal justice with a minor in communications. He hasn't yet found a job.

Dickson was watching television one night when he heard a story that noted that not only were a great many teenagers in the local area joining gangs, but they couldn't find a way out.

Dickson thought about that story. It bothered him and he wanted to do something about it. Coincidentally, while he was in college, he had done a paper and special project on youngsters getting involved in gangs because they wanted to feel like they were part of a group.

Dickson had been volunteering with a local program, Paws for Assistance, which helped train assistance dogs. As he thought about it, he developed an idea.

He went in to see the executive director of the program and told him about it. He explained the story he had seen on the news a few days prior regarding gang activity. He also discussed the paper and project he worked on during college.

Dickson asked the executive director what he thought about starting a program for youngsters on the verge of joining gangs to give them the opportunity to help train the assistance dogs. He had read about a similar program that was very successful in a prison.

"What would happen," he asked, "if we put together a program where young people would feel that they were part of a group? Instead of the gang, they would be part of something else. Something positive. We could call the program 'Leaders of the Pack'—it's a cool and intriguing name for potential participants and it shows an understanding of animal behavior. They would be doing something special and we would make sure that we made them feel special too.

"We cold teach the kids how to train the dogs and make them responsible for caring for them. Because they're assistance dogs, we probably could work out something so the dogs could live with the kids until they were trained. We could even get one of the local police agencies involved. Maybe they could help us zero in on some kids who might be good for the program."

The director thought it was a great idea. He even thought he could get a grant to help fund the program. He excitedly asked Dickson to try to set up a meeting with the local police chief. Before long, Leaders of the Pack became a reality, with 25 kids involved in the pilot program.

Dickson acted as a liaison coordinator between the Leaders of the Pack, the trainers, Paws for Assistance, and the police department. He went into areas where there were large numbers of at-risk teens to talk about the program and try to pique their interest. He also spoke to kids who were arrested on their first offense, intervening by diverting them into the program instead of doing jail time. He spoke to judges, probation officers, civic groups, and the media, garnering interest in the program.

The youngsters in the program were given a lot of positive reinforcement. Dickson made sure the program structured activities to bring the youngsters together in a number of areas. He wanted them to both learn responsibility and understand that they were an important part of the program. He wanted them to feel like they were in a very special group.

Dickson realized he couldn't reach every youth but could impact many, both the participants as well as the people who would eventually be the beneficiaries of the assistance animals.

In between all this, Dickson studied for and took the police test. Unfortunately, he was not the top scorer, yet he was in the top five. Dickson, who now was well known and respected by the police department, was called into to an in-

terview and landed the job despite the stiff competition. Because of his involvement and commitment to the program, he was also assigned to work on special projects in the juvenile and gang units.

In this scenario, Dickson was gaining visibility in a number ways. Not only was he gaining visibility in the police department—he was gaining visibility in the community from people who might not have otherwise known him. He was also gaining the respect of many of the young people in the community. These people were a valuable resource when Dickson became a police officer.

When a promotion became available, Dickson would also stand out among others seeking the job. Dickson would already have something that other candidates wouldn't have on their resume.

Think it can't happen this way? Well, it can! While you might not live this exact scenario, you can potentially create your own scenario with a similar outcome if you are creative and think outside of the box.

Here's an example of a press release that Dickson might send out to further market the project. Note that in marketing the project, the press release is also helping market Dickson himself.

⭐ Tip from the Coach

Contacts are an important part of your career. Once you make them, don't risk losing your relationships. Stay in contact by periodically sending e-mails, cards, and letters, making periodic calls, and arranging to meet for lunch, coffee, or just to get together and talk.

Sample Press Release

NEWS FROM LEADERS OF THE PACK

P.O. Box 3033
Some City, NY 11111
Media: For additional information, contact:
Zach Dickson, 111-888-8888

For Immediate Release:

Zack Dickson of Some City, NY will be a guest on WRAN's popular talk show *Life Lessons* on Tuesday, May 18 at 8:00 p.m. He will be discussing Leaders of the Pack, a group of teens who train assistance dogs that are then given to individuals with special needs.

The organization was set up to help give teens a positive alternative to being part of a group without joining a gang. Leaders of the Pack works under the auspices of Paws for Assistance.

When Dickson, a graduate of State University with a major in criminal justice and a minor in communications, saw a news story on WSTE TV discussing the prevalence of teens joining gangs in the area, he wanted to do something. While Dickson was in college, he had written a paper and done a special project on youngsters joining gangs because they needed to be part of a group. After thinking about it, he came up with an idea.

Dickson wanted to give youngsters a positive alternative to joining the gangs so prevalent in Some City as well as all over the country today. He spoke to Marty Donato, executive director of Paws for Assistance, where he was volunteering training an assistance dog himself.

"Zack came to me and asked what I thought of the idea of putting together a program where we could help a few different segments of the community," noted Donato. "He wanted to give young people an alternative to joining gangs and knew we wanted to find more people to train dogs. It was a great idea. Everyone would benefit."

According to Dickson, he chose the name Leaders of the Pack because he was hoping the kids would think it was cool and intriguing and want to get involved. The program was designed to help young people feel that they were part of a special group.

Once involved in the program, young people are each assigned a puppy and a mentor who teaches them how to train assistance animals. Each volunteer is responsible for caring for his or her dog. Most participants take the puppies home with them, integrating the dog into their daily life. In addition to working with the dogs, participants are urged to take advantage of other activities the group coordinates, including a variety of workshops, career counseling, and social events.

The program started with 25 young people. Another group of 25 are currently going through the screening process, eager to be assigned their dogs. Young people must sign a document stating they will not join a gang and have no current gang affiliation. While not a requirement, participants are urged to stay in school or get their GED.

(continues)

Sample Press Release, continued

Dickson, who began this program when he completed college, has since achieved his own goal of becoming a police officer with the Some City Police Department.

"I know I can't save every teen from joining a gang," said Dickson, "but I am hoping this program makes an impact on some. I'm so excited to be part of a project that not only impacts the kids and our community but improves the lives of people who eventually benefit from having an assistance animal. I can't wait to see how the program progresses."

Individuals interested in joining Leaders of the Pack can contact Dickson by calling (111) 888-8888 and leaving a message.

-30-

What does this press release do? In addition to publicizing Dickson's radio appearance, it gets his name in the news. It gets his message out. It exposes his career accomplishments and helps keep him in the public eye in a positive way. By Dickson using this avenue to market himself, he is putting himself in a different light from those who are not doing so.

"Well, that's a nice story," I can hear you saying. "But in the real world, does *that* kind of thing happen?"

You might not hear about it all the time, but those situations do happen and they can happen to you. The key here is that in order for them to occur, you're going to have to start thinking outside of the box.

Make sure your press releases look professional by printing them on press or news release stationary. This can easily be created on your

⭐ Voice of Experience

It's difficult to proofread your own press releases to catch errors. Always have someone else read them not only for errors but to make sure they make sense.

⭐ The Inside Scoop

Always be ready for the media. Keep stock paragraphs on your computer so you can turn out press releases quickly when needed. As a matter of fact, you might want to keep stock press releases and bios on hand so you're always ready when the media calls.

⭐ Tip from the Top

When working on your basic media database, make sure you find out the publication's deadline. The deadline is the day you need to get the information to the publication so that your news can be considered for the next issue.

Words from the Wise

Remember that just because you send a press release doesn't mean it will get into the publication. Small local publications are likely to eventually use your press releases. Larger publications are more discriminatory. Do not call up media and insist that they use your release. This will make you look like an amateur and they will probably ignore your releases from that day forward.

Tip from the Coach

Send your press releases to all applicable publications and stations. The idea with press releases is to send them consistently. Keep in mind that while you don't want to write a press release about *nothing,* anytime you have *anything* noteworthy to send out a press release, you should.

computer. Have the words "News" or "News From" or something to that effect someplace on the stationary so the media is aware it is a press release. Also make sure to include your contact information. This is essential in case the media wants to call to ask questions about your release. In many instances, the media just uses the press release as a beginning for an article. Once you pique their interest, they use the press release as background and write their own story.

You've developed a press release. Now what? Whether it's about getting a promotion, being named employee of the month, or anything else, developing and writing a great press release is just the first step. Once that's done, you have to get the releases to the media.

How do you do this? You have a few options. You can print the press releases and then send or fax them to the media or you can e-mail them. Either way it's essential to put together a media list so you can reach the correct people. Look around your area. Get the names of your local media. Then find regional media. If your stories warrant it, national or trade media should also be included. Don't forget any online publications.

Call up each media outlet and ask to whom press releases should be directed. Sometimes it may just be "News Editor" or "Business Editor." Sometimes it will be a specific person. Get their contact information. Put together a database consisting of the name of the publication or station, contact name or names, address, phone, fax numbers, e-mail, and any other pertinent information.

Words from a Pro

Make it easier to issue press releases by setting up sheets of labels. That way when you're ready to send out a mailing, you need only to place the labels on envelopes.

Tip from the Top

If you're e-mailing press releases, find out what format publications accept *ahead* of time. If you're sending out printed press releases, you might also call to find out what font is preferred. Many smaller publications just scan your release and certain fonts scan better than others.

Becoming an Expert

Want another idea to make yourself visible? Become an expert. You probably already are an expert in one or more areas either in or out of law enforcement. Now it's time for you to exploit it.

Many people are so used to the things they do well that they don't give enough credence to being great at them. It's time to forget that type of thinking!

One of the wonderful things about being an expert in any given area is that people will seek you out. Everyone knows how to do something better than others. What you have to do is figure out what it is that you do.

"Okay," you say. "You're right. Let's say I'm a gourmet chef. But what does that have to do with law enforcement?"

Well, it might have nothing to do with law enforcement on the surface. However, if it can help you gain some positive attention and visibility, it will give you another avenue to get your story out. This will help you achieve the career success you desire. So with that in mind, it has everything to do with it.

"How could that happen?" you ask.

In any number of ways. You might, for example, be a detective at a municipal police department. You entered a recipe contest and won the grand prize. The contest sponsor put a press release in the local paper about the promotion and your winning recipe. It also mentioned a bit about your career, including some of your accomplishments. The local news came over and interviewed you as well. They, too, mentioned some of your accomplishments.

Coincidentally, a new sheriff has just been elected. He is looking for an under-sheriff. And guess what? The press from your winning recipe reminded the sheriff of all your accomplishments in law enforcement. He called you up and asked would you be interested in applying for the job. Once again, your scenario might be different, but you can end up with a similar result.

Let's begin by determining where your expertise is. Sit down with a piece of paper and spend some time thinking about what you can do better than anyone else in or out of law enforcement. What subject or area do you know more about than most? Do you volunteer in an interesting area? Are you a gourmet chef? Can you teach almost anyone how to pitch a ball? Can you teach senior citizens how to use a computer? Can you spell words backwards?

Need some help? Can't think of what you're expertise is? Here are some ideas to get you started.

◎ Are you a gourmet cook?
◎ Do you bake the best brownies?
◎ Are you a sports trivia expert?
◎ Are you a master gardener?
◎ Do you design jewelry?
◎ Are you a trivia buff?
◎ Can you speak more than one language fluently?
◎ Do you love to shop?
◎ Do you know how to coordinate just the right outfit?
◎ Do you know how to write great songs?
◎ Can you put together events with ease?
◎ Do you know how to write great press releases?
◎ Do you know how to pack a suitcase better than most people?
◎ Are you an expert organizer?
◎ Do you know how to arrange flowers?
◎ Are you an expert in building things?
◎ Are you an expert wood carver?
◎ Do you know everything there is to know about trees?

- Are you a marathon runner?
- Were you a golden gloves champ?
- Are you a great fund-raiser?
- Have you set a world record doing something?
- Do you volunteer teaching people to read?
- Do you know about helping children with special needs?
- Do you volunteer reading books for the blind?
- Do you have special skills or talents that others don't?

Are you getting the idea? You can be an expert in almost area. It's the way in which you exploit it that can make a difference in your career.

You want to get your name out there. You want to draw positive attention to yourself. You want others to know what you can do. That way you can market yourself in the areas in which you are interested.

How do you get your name and story out there? Developing and sending out press releases is one way, but what else can you do?

You can become known for your expertise by talking about it. How? Most areas have civic or other not-for-profit groups that hold meetings. These groups often look for people to speak at their meetings. You can contact the president of the board or the executive director to find out who sets up the meeting speakers. In some areas, the chamber of commerce also puts together speaker lists.

You might be asking yourself, "Unless I'm a rocket scientist, why would any group want to hear me speak about anything? Why would anyone want to know about me knowing how to pack a suitcase?" or "Why would anyone be interested in my organizing ability?" or "Why

would anyone want to hear me talk about keeping their home safe? I'm not famous."

Here's the answer: They might not, *unless* you tailor your presentations to their needs. If you create a presentation from which others can learn something useful or interesting, they usually will. For example, if you're speaking to a group of businesspeople, you might do a presentation about "The Stress-Free Bag: Packing Easily for Business Trips," "Organize Your Career, Organize Your Life," "Helping Children Feel Good About Themselves Through Sports," "Using Cooking to Build Teamwork," or "Keeping Your Home Safe."

Whatever your subject matter is when you speak in front of a group, whether it be 20 or 2000 people, you will gain visibility. When you are introduced, the host of the event will often mention information about your background to the audience. Make sure you always have a short paragraph or two with you to make it easy for the emcee to present the information *you* want to convey.

For example, based on information you provide, the emcee might introduce you like this: "Good evening ladies and gentlemen. Our dinner speaker today is Jeanna Jones. Some of you might know her from her weekly column 'Keeping Your Home Safe' in the *Town Times*. Some of you might know her from seeing her on patrol with the Some City Police Department. Today she will be helping you understand how to keep your children safe from child predators online. Please join me in welcoming Jeanna Jones."

As you can see, Jeanna is getting exposure that can help her gain career visibility. Jeanna may make contacts and increase her network. The important thing to remember is to use every opportunity to get what you are looking for in your career.

Tip from the Coach

If you aren't comfortable speaking in front of large groups, consider joining Toastmasters or the Dale Carnegie Institute. Both will help you gain experience in a nurturing and safe environment.

On a local level, you will generally get no fee for most of these types of presentations. The benefit of increased visibility, however, will usually be well worth it. When you are scheduled to do a presentation, make sure you send out press releases announcing your speech. If it was a noteworthy event, you might also send out a release after the event as well. Many organizations will also call the media to promote the occasion. Sometimes the media will call you for an interview before the event. Once again, take advantage of every opportunity.

It's exciting once you start getting publicity. Take advantage of this too. Keep clippings of all the stories from the print media. Make copies. If you have been interviewed on television or radio, get clips. Keep these for your portfolio. Every amount of positive exposure will help set you apart from others and help you market yourself to career success.

I can almost hear some of you saying, "Oh, no! I'm not getting up to speak in public."

Here's the deal. If you don't feel comfortable speaking in public, you don't have to. These

Words from a Pro

The media works on very tight deadlines. If they call you, get back to them immediately or you might lose out.

ideas are meant to be a springboard to get you thinking outside of the box. Use any of them to get you started and then find ways you *are* comfortable in marketing yourself.

More Strategies to Market and Promote Yourself

If you aren't comfortable speaking in public, how about writing an article on your area of expertise instead?

What about writing a weekly column for your weekly newspaper? How about writing an article for a trade journal? The idea once again is to keep your name in the public's eye in a positive manner. While it's helpful to write about something in your career area, it is not essential.

For example, you might write an article on what life is like as rookie or a day in the life of a court reporter. (Of course, you need to check with your employer first to make sure you are able to write about these things.) You might write an article on collecting coins or cookbooks. You might write articles on organizing your office, your schedule, or your life. You might write an article on stress management or laughter or humor. If you can tailor the articles in some manner to your career area, all the better. If not, that's okay as well.

If you look at similar types of articles or stories in newspapers, you will notice that if the article is not written by a staff reporter, after the article there generally is a line or two about the author. For example, "Daniel Lawson is a corporate security consultant." Or "Kathy King works at the Some County sheriff's department as a sheriff's deputy."

How do you get your articles in print? Call the editor of the publication you are interested in writing for and ask! Tell them what you want to do, and offer to send your background sheet, resume, or bio and a sample. Small or local publications might not pay very much. Don't get caught up on money. You are not doing this for cash. You are doing it to get your name and your story before the public.

Don't forget to tell media editors about your expertise. You can call them or send a short note. Ask that they put you on their list of experts for your specific area of expertise. Then when they are doing a story on something that relates to your subject area, it will be easy to get in touch with you.

Remember that if you don't make the call or write the note, no one will know what you have to offer. You have to sometimes be assertive (in a nice way) to get things moving.

Consider teaching a class, giving a workshop, or facilitating a seminar in your area of expertise. Everyone wants to learn how to do something new and you might be just the person to give them that chance. Every opportunity for you is an opportunity to become visible and move your career forward. Can you give someone the basics of writing a press release or doing publicity? Offer to teach a class at a local college or school. Can you easily explain how to understand what you see when watching a game on television? Offer to teach a workshop. Do you think you can illustrate the basics of putting together a fund-raiser? Suggest a workshop! What a great way to get your name out!

There are a plethora of possibilities. You just need to use your imagination.

What can your expertise do for you? It will get your name out there. It will give you credibility and it will give you visibility. Of course, when you're at meetings or speaking to the media, it's up to you to network. Tell people what you do. Tell people what you want to do. Give out cards. This technique works effectively no matter what area of the law enforcement you want to succeed. As a matter of fact, this technique can help you succeed in any venture.

Join professional associations and volunteer to be on committees or to chair events that they sponsor. Similarly, join civic groups and not-for-profit organizations volunteering to work on one or two of their projects.

"I don't have time," you say.

Make time. Volunteering, especially when you chair a committee or work on a project, is one of the best ways to get your name out there, obtain visibility, and network. In many cases, your volunteer activities can help you jump to the next rung on the career ladder quicker than your counterparts who do not volunteer.

The radio and television talk show circuit is yet another means to generate important visibility. Offer to be a guest on radio, cable, and television station news, variety, and information shows.

"Who would want me?" you ask.

You can never tell. If you don't ask, no one will even know you exist in many instances. Check out the programming to see where you might fit. Then send your bio, resume, or CV with a letter to the producer, indicating that you're available to speak in a specific subject area. Pitch an idea. A producer just might take you up on it.

Here's a sample pitch letter to get you started.

★ The Inside Scoop

Don't get caught up in the theory that if you help someone do something or learn how to do something, it will in some way take away opportunities from you. Help others when you can.

Gail Gilbert, Producer
WNOW Radio
Talk Tonight Show
P.O. Box 3333
Anytown, NY 44444

Dear Ms Gilbert:

As far back as I can remember, I have wanted to work as a police officer. I wanted to make a difference. I know that it is a dream many have. I got lucky. My dream is coming true.

Six years ago I graduated college and became a community police officer. The job is challenging yet rewarding.

Unfortunately, all too often, in the past few years, I've been seeing young people from our community and in the surrounding areas end up in the hospital emergency room in critical condition because they have been driving while under the influence of alcohol or drugs. Some make it…others do not.

It is now my mission to help educate young people on the seriousness of these actions.

I would love to share some of my stories with your listeners. I regularly listen to your program and believe that the subject matter fits well with your show's format.

I have included my background sheet for your review. Please let me know if you require additional information.

I look forward to hearing from you.

Sincerely,
Gina Hastings

Wait a week or so after sending the letter. If you don't hear back, call the producer and ask if he or she is interested. If there is no interest, simply thank the producer for his or her consideration and request that your background sheet be kept on file.

Remember that people talk to each other so that every person you speak in front of who reads an article about you, who hears you on radio, or sees you on television has the potential of speaking to other people, who might then speak to others.

Tip from the Top

Many people lose out because they just don't follow up. They either feel like a nuisance or feel like they are being a pain. No matter how awkward and uncomfortable you feel, call and follow up on things you are working on. Be polite, but call to see what's happening.

As we've discussed, networking is one of the best ways to get a job, get a promotion, and advance your career. Even if your expertise is in something totally unrelated to law enforcement, just getting your name out can help boost your career.

If your expertise happens to be something related to law enforcement, that's even better. Whatever your expertise, exploit it and it will help your career move forward.

More Ways to Market Yourself

Here's another idea that can get you noticed: A feature story in a newspaper or magazine. How do you get one of these? Everyone wants a story about them or their product or service, so you have to develop an angle to catch people's attention. Then contact a few editors and see if you can get one of them to bite.

Before you call anyone, however, fully think out your strategy. What is your angle? Why are *you* the person someone should talk to or do a story on? Why would the story be interesting, unique, or entertaining to the reader?

How do you develop an angle? Come up with something unique that you do or are planning to do. What is the unique part of your package? Were you the one who was so afraid to speak in high school that you skipped the class where you had to give a report, yet today you are the spokesperson for a police department? Were you the one who succeeded despite severe adversities? Do you have a human interest story?

Send a letter with your idea and a background sheet, bio, CV, or resume. Wait a week and then call the editor you sent your information to. Ask if he or she received your information. (There is always a chance it is lost, if only on the editor or reporter's desk.) If the answer is no, offer to send it again and start the process one more time. Sometimes you get lucky. Your angle might be just what an editor was looking for or they might need to fill in a space with a story.

Opening Up the Door to New Opportunities

If you keep on doing the same old thing, things might change on their own, but they probably won't. It's important when trying to create a more successful career to find ways to open up the door to new opportunities.

Start to look at events that occur as new opportunities to make other things happen. If you train yourself to think of how you can use opportunities to help you instead of hinder you, things often start looking up.

Do you want to be around negative people who think nothing is going right, people who think they are losers? Probably not. Well neither

does anyone else. Market yourself as a winner, even if you are still a winner in training.

The old adage "misery loves company" is true. One problem people often have in their career and life is that they hang around other people who are depressed or think that they're not doing well. Remember that negative energy attracts negative results, so here's your choice. You can either stay with the negative energy, help change the negative energy, or move yourself near positive energy. Which choice do you want to make?

Work on developing *new* relationships with positive, successful people. Cultivate new business relationships. When doing that, don't forget cultivating a business relationship with the media. How? Go to events where the media is present. Go to chamber of commerce meetings, not-for-profit organization events, charity functions, entertainment events, sports events, meetings, and other occasions.

Walk up, extend your hand, and introduce yourself. Give out your business cards. Engage

> ### ★ Words from the Wise
>
> Do not be negative in the workplace. It will negatively affect your career. I've seen countless cases of people in law enforcement who were negative in their day-to-day work life who consistently lost out on promotions.

in conversation. If a reporter writes an interesting story about anything, drop him or her a note saying you enjoyed it. If a newscaster does something special, drop a note telling him or her. The media are just like the rest of us. They appreciate validation. Most people don't give it to them. If you do, you will be the one they remember.

Don't just be a user. One of the best ways to develop a relationship with the media or anybody else is to be a resource. Help them when you can.

Want to close the door to opportunity? Whine, complain, and be a generally negative person who no one wants to be near. Want the doors to opportunity to fly open? Whatever level you are in, more doors will open if you're pleasant, enthusiastic, and professional.

Dreams can come true. They can either happen to you or happen to someone else. If you want it bad enough and market yourself effectively, you will be the winner.

It's essential in marketing yourself and your career to move out of your comfort zone, even if it's just a little bit. Take baby steps if you need to, but learn to move out of your comfort zone. Find new places to go, new people to meet, and new things to do.

You can be the number one factor in creating your own success. Don't let yourself down! Market yourself and reap the rewards of the great career you've been wishing for in law enforcement.

10

SUCCEEDING IN THE WORKPLACE

Learning As You Go

Congratulations! You got the job. Now what? Are you ready to succeed or are you going to just leave things to chance and hope your career goes in the direction you want?

No matter what segment of law enforcement you are pursuing, there are things you can do that can help you increase your chances of success…things you can do that can turn your job into the career of your dreams.

"Can't I worry about that later?" you ask. "I just got the job."

Lots of people have jobs. You don't just want a job. You want a great career! It doesn't matter which segment of law enforcement you are pursuing. In order to succeed and move up the career ladder, you sometimes have to do a little extra, do more than is expected of you, and put some effort into getting what you want.

No matter how it looks, there are very few overnight successes. Appearances can be very deceiving. While it may seem that some individuals might just appear to get their foot in the door one day and zoom to the top rung of the career ladder the next, it generally doesn't happen like that.

While there are exceptions, more than likely, the people you *think* are overnight suc-

cesses have been working at it and preparing for their dream career for some time. Many of them were probably in the same position you are now.

What looks like someone who just became an overnight success is generally an individual who had a well-thought-out plan, did a lot of work, had some talent, a bit of luck, and was in the right place at the right time.

Unfortunately, just getting your foot in the door is not enough. It's essential once you get in to take positive actions to climb the ladder to success. If you don't take those actions, someone else will.

Once you get your foot in the door, you want to create your perfect career. Getting a job is a job in itself. However, just because you've been hired doesn't mean your work is done. It's essential once you get in to learn as you go.

If you look at some of the most successful people, in all aspects of life and business, you'll see that they continue the learning process throughout their lives. If you want to succeed, you'll do the same.

Learning is a necessary skill for personal and career growth and advancement. Many think that your ability and willingness to learn is linked to your success in life. This doesn't necessarily mean going back to school or taking traditional classes, although in some situations you may want to. In many cases, it means life learning.

What's life learning? Basically, it's learning that occurs through life experiences. It's learning that occurs when you talk to people, watch others do things, work, experience things, go places, watch television, listen to the radio, hear others talking, or almost anything else. Every experience you have is a potential learning experience.

Not only that, but almost everyone you talk to can be a teacher. If you're open to it, you can usually learn something from almost everyone you come in contact with.

"What do you mean?" you ask.

Look for opportunities. Be interested. Everything you learn might not be fascinating, but it might be helpful, maybe not today or tomorrow but in the future. Sometimes you might learn something work related, sometimes not. It doesn't matter. Use what you can. File the rest away until needed.

How do you learn all these things? Observe what people say or do. Sometimes you might see that someone has a skill you want to master. You might, for example, see an interesting method a detective uses to investigate a crime, a different way an officer questions a suspect, or how someone develops resources in the community.

Don't be afraid to ask others how to do something. Whether it's simple or complicated, most people are flattered when someone rec-

> ### ⭐ Tip from the Top
> Career progression does not always follow traditional paths. Treat supervisors, colleagues, and subordinates all with the same respect.

ognizes they're good at something and asks for their help.

Challenge yourself to learn something new every day. Not only will it help improve your total package, but it will make you feel better about yourself. Whether it's a new word, a new skill, a new way to do something, or even a new way to deal better with people, continue to learn as you go.

How else can you continue to learn? Take advantage of internships, formal and informal education, company training programs, in-service programs, and volunteer opportunities.

Volunteer opportunities can also be helpful. What can you learn? The possibilities are endless. You might learn a new skill or a better way to get along with others. You might learn how to coordinate events, how to run organizations, or pick up some leadership skills. You might learn almost anything. And as a bonus, if you volunteer effectively, you not only will get some experience—you might obtain some important visibility, get your name known in the community, and make important contacts.

Don't discount books as a learning tool. As the saying goes, reading is fundamental. Are you a community patrol officer who wants to be a detective? A dispatcher who wants to be an officer? An administrative assistant who aspires to be a corrections officer? A probation officer who wants to move up the career ladder? Look for a book. Read more about it.

> ### ⭐ Tip from the Coach
> While success does sometimes just fly in the window, it always helps to at least open up the window.

Tip from the Coach

Don't assume that because someone is under you on the career ladder they know less than you do.

Are you working in a local law enforcement agency but dream of working in a federal agency? Look for a book. See which area you want to pursue. Are you interested in learning more about doing fundraising for your department? Find a book. Need help improving your leadership skills? Check out some books for ideas? Want to know more about the lives of FBI special agents? Look for a book! Want to know more about any aspect of the law enforcement industry? There are tons of books on all aspects of law enforcement. The more you read, the more you'll know. Books often hold the answer to many of your questions. They give you the opportunity to explore opportunities and learn about things you didn't know.

Trade journals offer numerous possibilities as well. They'll keep you up-to-date on industry trends and let you know about industry problems and solutions. What else can you find in the trades? You might discover advertisements for job openings, notices for trade events, seminars, and current news.

How do you find trade journals? You might check with your local library. If your library doesn't have the periodical you are looking for, try your local community college or university library. If you happen to live in an area with a college offering a degree in criminal justice, the bookstore may offer some periodicals.

You can also always surf the net to check out journals specific to areas of law enforcement in which you are interested.

If you are already working in some aspect of law enforcement, these trades may also be available in your workplace. If you're not currently working in the industry, you still might be able to contact a law enforcement agency and see if anyone there will let you browse through some of their trade journals.

National bookstore chains such as Borders or Barnes & Noble may also often carry some of the more popular trade publications. Be sure to check out the online versions of trade publications. While many require subscriptions to access some areas, they still often carry the latest news and job openings in the free section.

How about workshops, seminars, and other courses? In addition to learning new skills in or out of the area you are pursuing in law enforcement, there are a number of benefits to going to these. First, you'll have the opportunity to meet other people interested in the same subject area as you are. You also be able to network. Instructors, facilitators, and even other students in the class are all potential contacts who might be instrumental in your career.

"But," you say, "I'm busy enough without doing extra work. Is this really necessary? Do I have to take classes?"

No one is going to make you do anything, but you should be aware that they can help take your career to a new level. Classes, workshops, and seminars will help give you new ideas and

Tip from the Top

Seminars in the area of the industry in which you are working are so important that even if your agency, company, organization, or department won't pay for them, you should find a way to attend.

> ⭐ **Words from the Wise**
> In some situations, having additional education or training may help you get a better job, a new promotion, or even higher compensation. It will also open up more opportunities.

---

help you look at things from a different perspective. And if you are already working in the industry, they will often give you the edge over others.

If you see an industry-related seminar in which you are interested, ask your supervisor if the agency will pay for you to attend. If you are told that they can't afford it or it's not the policy of the agency to pay for seminars, don't just decide not to go. Ask whether you can be given the time off to attend if you pay the fee.

Whether you are taking workshops, seminars or classes, learning new techniques or honing skills, the results will help you in your quest to be the best at what you do. If you continue to navigate your way through formal and informal learning experiences throughout your life and career, you will be rewarded with success and satisfaction.

Workplace Politics

In order to succeed in your career in law enforcement, it is essential to learn how to deal effectively with some of the challenging situations you'll encounter. Workplace politics are a part of life. And depending on what area of law enforcement you are pursuing, the *workplace* can be almost anyplace.

The real trick to dealing with workplace politics is trying to stay out of them. No matter which side you take in a workplace dispute, you are going to be wrong. You can never tell who

the *winner* or *loser* will be, so try to stay neutral and just worry about doing your job. Is this easy? No. But for your own sake, you have to try.

Will keeping out of it work all the time? Probably not and therein lies the problem. There's an old adage that says the workplace is a jungle. Unfortunately, that's sometimes true.

If you think you're going to encounter politics only in the office, think again. As we just mentioned, in law enforcement, the *workplace* can be almost anyplace. It can be in a patrol car, an administration office, any part of a law enforcement agency, or correctional facility. It can be in a forensic lab, a courtroom, or a corporate office. It can even be in the community in which you work.

What all this means is that no matter what part of law enforcement you are working in, you often may have additional challenges. In many cases, workplace politics will now be expanded to every area of your life from your personal relationships to your family to work. With this in mind, let's learn more about them.

Why are there are politics in the workplace? Much of it comes from jealousy. Someone might think you have a better chance at a promotion that they think they deserve. Someone might think that you are better at your job than they are at theirs, or they might think that they are better, but you are getting the accolades. Someone might think you slighted them. Believe it or not, someone just might not like you.

In any business setting, there are people who vie for more recognition, feel the need to prove themselves right all the time, or who just want to get ahead. There really is nothing you can do about workplace politics except to stay out of them to the best of your ability.

In certain segments of law enforcement, feelings of jealousy sometimes escalate. There are

> ⭐ **Words from the Wise**
>
> We've all heard of someone who when others refer to them they say, "You know, he (or she) is such a nice man (or woman). He (or she) never says a bad word about anyone." These people stay out of office politics. They stay out of office squabbles and they stay out of trouble in the workplace. If you can keep this in mind and try to follow their lead, you will be ahead of the game. It may not be easy, but before you decide to speak about someone, remember that office politics and gossip can be problematic.

many reasons for this. Someone may feel they are more talented than you in their area of the industry. They may, for example, feel that they are a better investigator, detective, or officer.

Often, jealousy surfaces when someone doesn't understand why *you* got the job or the promotion and he or she did not. Some may not understand why you are a department head and they can't get a promotion. Some may not understand why you were snagged for a plumb assignment and they weren't even asked.

Sometimes people may want to protect themselves from feeling like a failure or may just be frustrated with their career (or lack of it).

In these situations, many lash out and talk about others. Real or not, these words can hurt. Worse than that, your words can come back to haunt you—big time.

Office Gossip

Gossip is a common form of office politics. Anyone who has held a job has probably seen it and perhaps even participated in it in some form. Have you? Forget the moral or ethical issues. Gossip can hurt your career.

Here's a good rule of thumb. Never, ever say anything about anyone that you wouldn't mind them hearing and knowing it came from you. If you think you can believe someone who says, "Oh, you can tell me; it's confidential," you're wrong.

"But she's my best friend," you say. "I trust her with my life."

It doesn't matter. Your friend might be perfectly trustworthy, but trust is not always the problem. Sometimes people slip and repeat things during a conversation. Other times a person might tell someone else whom they trust what you said and ask him or her to keep it confidential, but then that person tells another person and so it goes down the line. Eventually, the person telling the story doesn't even know it's supposed to be confidential and might even mention it to a good friend or colleague of the person everyone has been gossiping about.

The reason people gossip is because it makes them feel like part of a group. It can make you feel like you're smarter or know something other people don't. Most of the time, however, you don't even know if what you're gossiping about is true, yet once a gossip session gets started, it's difficult to stop.

Most people are good at heart. After gossiping about someone else, they often feel bad. It might just be a twinge of conscience, but it's there. Is it worth it? No. Worse than that, it's safe to assume that if you are gossiping about others, they are gossiping about you.

How do you rise above this? Keep your distance. People generally respect that you don't want to be involved. Don't start any gossip, and if someone starts gossiping around you, just don't get involved.

How do you handle the conversation?

Suppose someone says to you, "Did you hear that the chief got so drunk, he fell over at the convention in the city last week?"

You respond, "No, didn't hear about that. Did you see the game last night?"

Of course, some people might not let it go and might want to keep the conversation going. The person might respond, "No, I didn't catch it…and I hear he wasn't even with his wife. He was with his girlfriend."

All you have to do is either change the subject again or say, "I made a decision a long time ago not to get involved in gossip. It can only get me in trouble."

Every now and then, you hear through the grapevine that people are gossiping about you. It might be related to your job or your personal life. It's not a good feeling, but you might have to deal with it. What do you do? You have a few options.

- You can ignore it.
- You can confront the person or people who are gossiping about you.
- You can start gossiping about the person or people gossiping about you.

What's your best choice? Well, it's definitely not gossiping about the person who is gossiping about you. Ignoring the gossip might be your best choice except that suppressing your feelings of betrayal and anger can be stressful. So how about confronting the person or people who are gossiping about you? If you're certain about who has been spreading the gossip and you can do this calmly and professionally, it often resolves the situation.

Whatever you do, don't have a public confrontation and don't ever confront a group. Instead, wait until the person is alone. Calmly approach him or her and say something like this:

Tip from the Top

Use coffee breaks or meetings at the water cooler or break room to your advantage. Instead of gossiping, try using the situations as opportunities. A few pleasant words or a smile can often win over even those with conflicting opinions.

"John, I didn't want to bring this up in front of anyone else, because I didn't want to embarrass you, but I've heard that you've been talking to others here in the department about my performance and discussing my personal life. I've always had respect for you, so I really questioned the people who told me it was happening. I'd just like to know if it's true."

At this point, John probably will be embarrassed and claim that he doesn't know what you're talking about. He might ask you who mentioned it.

Words from a Pro

Do you like to be around negative people? Probably not. Well, neither does anyone else.

We all have bad days when we complain and whine that nothing is going right. The problem comes when it occurs constantly. If you want to succeed in your career, try to limit the negativity, at least around your colleagues. While they say misery loves company, in reality after a while people won't want to be around you. Eventually, they'll start to avoid you.

On the other hand, most people like to be around positive people who make them smile and laugh. If you can do this, you'll have an edge over others.

Tip from the Coach

Remember the philosophy that on the ladder to success, *real* successful people pull others up the ladder with them; the ones who try to push others down the ladder will never be real successes themselves.

"Who told you that?" he might ask. "I want to straighten them out."

Do not give out any names. It's better to let him start questioning the trust of all the people he's been talking to and gossiping with.

While he might tell a couple of people you confronted him on the gossip subject, John will probably find someone else to gossip about in the future…or at least do so with more discretion.

In many segments of law enforcement, gossip may often lead to bigger problems. Depending on your work environment, you might be privy to information about others in either your work environment or the community.

Here's the deal. Gossiping about what happens in the workplace, what you hear, or what you know (even if it is true) can seriously affect your career in a negative manner, especially if it leads to the embarrassment of powerful people or breeches confidentiality or the integrity of investigations.

It's essential to your success and your career not to spread rumors in the workplace. Don't

Tip from the Top

It is never a good idea to speak badly about your employer, your supervisors, or your colleagues, no matter what. When you do, people on the outside start doubting your loyalties.

talk about the inside information you have, whether it's good or bad. If anyone pumps you for information, learn to simply say, "Sorry, that's confidential."

Money, Money, Money

How upset would you be if you found out that a coworker who had a job similar to yours was making more money than you? I'm assuming you probably would be pretty upset. Whether it's what you're making, your coworker is making, or someone else is making, money is often a problem in the workplace. Why? Because everyone wants to earn more. Generally, no matter how much money people are paid for a job, they don't think they're getting enough. If they hear someone is getting paid better than they are, it understandably upsets them.

Here's the deal. If you know you're making more than someone else, keep it to yourself. If you're making less than someone else, keep it to yourself. No matter what your earnings are, keep it to yourself. Don't discuss your earnings with coworkers. The only people in the workplace you should discuss your earnings with are the human resources department and your supervisors.

With that said, keep in mind that if you are holding a civil service position, at least your base earnings may be public knowledge. That doesn't mean, however, that coworkers may not be jealous of your overtime pay, bonuses, and so on.

Here's the deal on earnings. Even if you've just landed a big promotion, a new job, or you got a raise, it's okay to be happy; it's okay to be ecstatic, but it probably isn't a good idea to walk around gloating, especially around colleagues who may not have the great salary you do.

Why would one person be earning more than another in a similar position? There might be a number of reasons. In some situations, compensation for many positions is negotiated, and the person might be a better negotiator. He or she might have more experience, more education, seniority, different skills, or more responsibilities. Even where salary is fixed by statute, an employer may classify two similar employees in different positions that would affect salaries. Individuals may also be working a lot of overtime. In some situations, employers may also badly need someone with certain skills or attributes. There are any number of scenarios.

"But it's frustrating," you say.

I understand, but being frustrated won't help. Worry about your own job. Don't waste time comparing yourself to your coworkers, colleagues, or others in positions you consider similar. Definitely don't whine about it in your workplace. It will get on people's nerves.

What can you do? Make sure you are visible in a positive way. Make sure you're doing a great job. If you're already doing a great job, try to do a better job. Keep notes on projects you've successfully completed, ideas you've suggested that are being used, and things you are doing to make things better in the department, agency, organization, or company. Then, when it's time for a job review and possible promotion, you'll have the ammunition to ask for the compensation you deserve.

If you're in a situation where salaries are mandated, use your experience and successes to land a promotion that will result in increased earnings.

Dealing with Colleagues

Whatever area of law enforcement you choose to work in, you're going to be dealing with others. Whether they are superiors, subordinates, or colleagues, the way you deal with people you work with will affect your opportunities, your chances of success, and your future.

Many people treat colleagues and superiors well yet treat subordinates with less respect. One of the interesting things about law enforcement is that like other industries, career progression doesn't always follow a normal pattern. What that means is that with the right set of circumstances someone might jump a number of rungs up the career ladder quicker than expected. The end result could be someone who is a subordinate might technically become either a colleague or even a superior. It's essential to treat everyone with whom you come in contact with dignity and respect.

Want to know a secret about dealing effectively with people? If you can sincerely make every person you come in contact with feel special, you will have it made. How do you do this? There are a number of ways.

When someone does or says something interesting or comes up with a good idea mention it to them. For example, "That was a great idea you had at the meeting, Eric. You always come up with interesting ways to solve problems."

Sometimes you might want to send a short note instead. For example:

★ Tip from the Coach

It's very easy to start comparing your earnings with those of others who are making more and start feeling sorry for yourself. Try not to compare yourself, your job, or your earnings to anyone else. Instead of concentrating on what "they're making," try to concentrate on how you can get "there."

Jean,

While I'm sure you're ecstatic that the press conference for the new police chief is over, I hope you know how impressed everyone was with the event. You handled the coordination like a seasoned pro. No one would ever have guessed that this was the first time you ever put together a press conference.

Everything was perfect. But the real coup was getting the story about the new chief on *20/20*. You did a great job. I'm glad we're on the same team.

Daniel

If another employee does something noteworthy, write a note. If a colleague receives an award or an honor, write a note. It doesn't make you any less talented or skilled and your words will not only make someone else's day but help you build a good relationship with a colleague.

Everyone likes a cheerleader. At home, you hopefully have your family. In your personal life, you have friends. If you can be a cheerleader to others in the workplace, it often helps to excel yourself.

Never be phony and always be sincere. Look for little things that people do or say as well. "That was a great closing argument, John." "Nice suit, Amy. You always look so put together. " "That was a great presentation you did on crime prevention, Jim. The audience loved it."

Notice that while you're complimenting others, you're not supposed to be self-deprecating. You don't want to make yourself look bad; you want others to look good. So, for example, you wouldn't say, "Nice suit, Amy. You always look so put together. I couldn't coordinate a suit and blouse if I tried." "Great job on the press conference. I never could have coordinated an event like that."

The idea is to build people up so they feel good about themselves. When you can do that,

Tip from the Coach
In an attempt to build themselves up, many try to tear others down. Unfortunately, it usually has the opposite effect.

people like to be around you, they gain self-confidence, and they pass it on to others. One of them might be you. Best of all, you will start to look like a leader. This is a very important image to be building when you're attempting to move up the career ladder.

Dealing with Your Superiors

While you are ultimately in charge of your career, superiors are often the people who can help either move it along or hold it back. While this is true in every industry, it is especially important to know in law enforcement.

Try to develop a good working relationship with your superiors. A good supervisor can help you succeed in your present job as well as in your future career.

One of the mistakes many people make in the workplace is looking at their bosses as the enemy. They get a mind-set of us against them. Worse than that is they sit around and boss-bash with other colleagues.

Want to better your chances of success at your job? Make your boss look good. How do you do that?

◎ Don't boss-bash.
◎ Speak positively about your boss to others.
◎ Do your work.
◎ Cooperate in the workplace.
◎ If you see something that needs to be done, offer to do it.

◎ Volunteer to help with projects that aren't done.

◎ Ask if he or she needs help.

"But what if my boss is a jerk?" you ask.

It's still in your best interest to make him or her look good. Believe it or not, it will make you look good.

While we're on the subject, let's discuss jerky bosses. With any luck, your boss will be a great person who loves his or her job. But every now and then, you just might run into a bad boss.

He or she might be a jerk, a fool, an idiot. But that really doesn't matter.

"I could do a better job than he does," you say.

Well you might be able to, but not if you can't learn to deal with people so you still have a job. In many cases, your supervisor has already proven him- or herself to the organization and is therefore more of a commodity than you are at this point. So just how do you deal with a bad boss and come out on top?

Let's first go over a list of don'ts.

◎ Don't be confrontational. This will usually only infuriate your boss.

◎ Don't shout or curse. Even if you're right, you will look wrong.

◎ Don't talk about your boss to coworkers. You can never tell who is whose best friend or who is telling your boss exactly what you're saying.

◎ Don't send e-mails to people from your office about things your boss does or says.

◎ Don't talk about your boss to students, teachers, parents, colleagues, clients, and so on. It's not good business and it's not really ethical.

◎ Don't and I repeat don't cry in your workplace. No matter how mad your boss or supervisor makes you, no matter what mistake you made, no matter what nasty or obnoxious thing someone says about you, keep your composure until you're alone. If you have to bite your lip, pinch yourself, or do whatever you have to do to keep the tears under control.

◎ Think twice before you complain to the union about a problem where you think you have been wronged. Is the problem you are having one you can work out? Will you win the battle but lose the war? Take some time, look at all angles, and think about repercussions before you make a move.

Now let's go over a list of dos which might help.

◎ Do a good job. It's hard to argue with someone who has done what they are supposed to do.

◎ Complete all reports, thoroughly and in a timely manner.

◎ Be at work when you are scheduled to be there and always be on time.

◎ Attend all scheduled meetings.

◎ Keep a paper trail. Keep notes when your supervisor asks you to do things and when you've done them. Keep notes regarding calls that have been made, dates, times, and so on. Keep a running list of assignments you've completed successfully. Do this as a matter of course. Keep it to yourself. Then if and when you need something to jog your memory, you can refer to it.

◎ Volunteer to help a colleague after your shift is over or on your day off. For example, ask one of the detectives if they need a hand interviewing witnesses. People will remember that you were visible when an opening comes up.

◎ Wait until there is no time constraint to finish something and there is no emergency and ask your supervisor if you can speak to him or her. Then say you'd like to clear the air. Ask what suggestions he or she can give you to do a better job.

　▫ You might say, "Mr. Anderson, I just wanted to clear the air. We're on the same team and if there is something I can be doing to do a better job or be a better probation officer, just let me know. I'll be glad to try to implement it."

◎ Think long and hard before you decide to leave. If your supervisor is as much of a jerk as you think, perhaps he or she will find a new job or be promoted.

No matter what type of boss or supervisor you have, learning to communicate with him or her is essential. Everyone has a different communicating style and it's up to you to determine what his or hers is.

Does your supervisor like to communicate through e-mail? Some organizations today communicate almost totally through e-mail. Everything from the daily "Good morning" until "See you tomorrow" and everything in between will

---

Tip from the Top

Check out your workplace's policy on private e-mail. Be aware that in many situations, private e-mails are not allowed.

---

be in your inbox. If this is the way it is at your office, get used to it. E-mail will be your communication style. The good thing about e-mail is you pretty much have a record of everything.

Some bosses communicate mainly on paper. They may give you directions, tell you what's happening, or ask for things via typed or handwritten notes. Sometimes communications may be in formal memos; other times informal or even on sticky notes.

It's important to realize that you have a choice in your career. You can sit there and hope things happen or you can make them happen. You can either be passive or pro-active. In order to succeed in your career, being pro-active is usually a better choice.

You can go to work and let your supervisor tell you what to do or you can do that little bit extra, share your dreams and aspirations, and work toward your goals. No matter what segment of the industry you are pursuing, supervisors can help you make it happen.

Words from the Wise

Do not put anything in e-mail that you wouldn't mind someone else reading. No matter what anyone tells you, e-mail is not confidential. Furthermore, be aware that in many situations your e-mails, private or business, may be classified as company property. What this means is management may have the right to access your e-mail.

Tip from the Coach

If you carry a personal cell phone, set it to vibrate mode while working. Getting constant calls from friends when you are working, even on your cell phone, is inappropriate. While we're on the subject, it is not appropriate to take calls on your personal cell phone while you are performing any work-related tasks.

Tip from the Top

Actively look for ways to assist others in your job, even if you do it on your day off. If you're a police officer, for example, you might offer to help detectives interview witnesses. You might help someone write a report. Why would you do this? Aside from being part of a team, doing a little extra keeps you visible in a positive manner. In a small department, where there is generally a lot of communication among the department, higher-ups will generally be aware of your extra efforts. In larger departments, the sergeants and lieutenants would most likely hear that you were going that extra step. Why is this important? When a new assignment, opening, or promotion comes up, you will have a good chance of someone thinking of you.

Ethics, Morals, Integrity and More

We all have our own set of ethics and morals. They help guide us on what we think is right and wrong. Ethics, morals, and integrity are essential to success in your career in law enforcement. Let's take a few moments to discuss these a bit.

We have already covered the importance of honesty. Lying is never a good idea, especially if you are looking forward to a successful career in law enforcement. If you tell the truth, you never have to remember what story you told.

In your career you may be faced with situations where a person or group of people wants you to do something you know or feel is wrong. In return for doing it, you may be promised financial gain or career advancement.

Would you do it? "Well," you might say, "that depends on what I'd have to do and what I'd get." Here's the deal. No matter what any-

one wants you to do, if you know it's wrong, even if you only think it *might* be wrong, it probably is a bad idea, especially if you are trying to build a successful career in any area of law enforcement.

"But they told me no one would know," you say. Hmm…most people are not that good at keeping secrets and if *they* get caught, you're going down too. If you're just getting started in your career, you might be looking at ending it for a few dollars. If you're already into your career, are you really prepared to lose everything you worked that hard to get.

"But they told me if I did this or did that, they'd remember me when promotions came up," you say. Hmm—how do you know someone isn't testing you to see what your morals are? And exactly what are you planning on doing after you do whatever the person asked you to do and he or she doesn't give you the promotion? Report them? Probably not.

It's important to realize that people move around. They move from job to job and location to location. It is not unheard of to hear that someone took a job on the other side of town or the other side of the country. And don't forget with a click of the mouse, you can find out almost anything about anyone.

What this means is that while every supervisor you have may not know every other supervisor, there is a chance that some of them may know other people in the industry. With this in mind, do you really want to take a chance doing something stupid or unethical? Probably not.

You are pursuing a career in law enforcement to uphold the law. Your morals and your ethics almost must be above the rest.

How do you get out of doing something you don't want to do? You might simply say something like, "My dream was to work in law enforcement. I am not about to mess it up for something like this." Or "I've worked so hard to get where I am now, I really don't want to want to lose what I have." What about, "No can do. Sorry." How about, "Sorry, I'm not comfortable with that."

But what do you do if a supervisor wants you to do something you consider unethical? How do you handle that? You can try any of the lines above, but if your job is on the line, you have a bigger problem to deal with. In cases like this, document as much as you can. Then, if you have no other choice, go to human resources, a higher supervisor, or someone else you think can help.

"What do I do if I see something going on around me?" you ask. "What if I'm not involved, but I see a supervisor or colleague doing something that I know is wrong? Then what?"

This is a tough one as well. No one likes a tattle-tale, but if something major is going on, you have a decision to make.

Do you say something? Bring it to the attention of a higher-up? Mention it to the alleged wrongdoer? Or just make sure you're not involved and say nothing?

Hopefully at the time, you'll make the right choice. It generally will depend on the position you hold, your responsibilities, and the alleged crime. It's a difficult decision. If you decide to say something, be very sure that you are absolutely positive about your information.

What else do you need to know? Do not use illegal drugs. Don't even associate with people who use illegal drugs.

It also isn't a good idea to drink alcohol excessively. Never go to work under the influence of alcohol or drugs. And finally, if you are drinking, do not drive. Don't drive drunk while

you're working or, for that matter, in your off time. A DWI will very likely end your career.

Accountability

No one is perfect. We all make mistakes. No matter how careful anyone is, things happen. Accept the fact that sometime in your career you are going to make one too. In many cases it's not the mistake itself that causes the problem, but the way we deal with it.

The best way to deal with it is to take responsibility, apologize, try to fix it, and go on. Be sincere. Simply say something like, "I'm sorry. I made a mistake. I'm going to try to fix it and will make sure it doesn't happen again." With that said, it's very difficult for anyone to argue with you.

If on the other hand you start explaining mitigating circumstances, blame your colleagues, your coworkers, your secretary, your boss, or make excuses, others generally go on the defensive.

When you're wrong, just admit it and go on. People will respect you; you'll look more professional; and you'll have a lot less turmoil in your life.

For example, "I was wrong about the report. You were right. Good thing we're a team." "I am so sorry I was late today. I know we had a meeting scheduled. I'll make sure it doesn't happen again. Thanks for covering for me."

Okay, you're taking credit for your mistakes, but what happens if someone else makes a mistake and you're blamed or you're the one who looks like you're unprepared. What do you do? Blame someone else?

The best thing to do in these types of situations is also to acknowledge the problem, apologize, and see what you can do to fix it quickly.

The result? What could have been a major faux pas is now just a minor inconvenience that no one will probably even remember a few weeks down the line.

In work as in life, many people's first thought when there is a problem is to cover themselves. So when things go wrong, most people are busy reacting or coming up with excuses.

Here's something to remember. The most successful people don't come up with excuses. Instead, when something goes wrong, their first thoughts are how to fix the problem, mitigate any damages, and get things back to normal. If you can do this, and remain cool in a crisis, it will enhance your position no matter what your segment of law enforcement.

Time, Time Management, and Organization

Here's a question for you. What is one thing every person on the planet has the same amount of? Do you know what it is?

Here's a hint. I have the same amount you have. Bill Gates has the same amount I have. Oprah Winfrey has the same amount Bill Gates has. William Shakespeare had the same amount as Oprah Winfrey does. Do you know what it is yet?

Every person in this world, no matter who they are or what they do, has the same 24 hours a day. You can't get less and you can't get more, no matter what you do. It doesn't matter who you are or what your job is. You don't get more time during the day if you're young, old, or in-between. You don't get more time if you're a millionaire or you're making minimum wage. You wouldn't even get more time if you were a Nobel Prize winner who had discovered a cure for cancer or found a method for totally eliminating crime.

With all this in mind, it's important to manage your time wisely. That way you can fit more of what you need to do into your day and get the most important things accomplished.

To start with, let's deal with your workday. Try to get to work a little earlier than you're expected. It's easier to get the day started when you're not rushing. On occasion, you might also want to stay late. Why? Because when superiors see you bolting at five (or whenever your work day ends), it looks like you are not really interested in your job.

You also want to be relaxed before dealing with your job, not stressed because you got stuck in a traffic jam and started worrying that you were going to be late getting to work.

No matter what your career choice in law enforcement, in order to be successful you will need to learn to prioritize your tasks. How do you know what's important?

If your supervisor needs it now, it's important. If it's dealing with a life-or-death situation,

---

⭐ The Inside Scoop

The time period before everyone else gets in or after everyone has left the workplace is usually less formal and less stressed. If you make it a habit to come in right before the big brass comes in and leave either when they leave or just afterwards, you will generally become visible in a more positive manner to higher-ups. More than that, however, you will often have the opportunity to ask a question, make a comment, or offer a suggestion. If someone questions you about what you're doing at work so early or so late, simply say something like, "Preparing for the day ahead." "Getting some project started before it gets busy." Or "Finishing up a few things so I can devote tomorrow to new assignments."

> ⭐ **Words from the Wise**
>
> In prioritizing, don't forget that you must fit in the things you promised others you would do. Don't get so caught up in wanting to be liked or wanting to agree or even wanting to be great at your job that you promise to do something you really don't have time to get done. Doing so will just put you under pressure.

it's important. If someone is in trouble and there is something you can do about it, it's important. If you promised to do something for someone, it's important. If something is happening today or tomorrow and you need to get a project done, it's important. If things absolutely *need* to get done now, they're important.

Generally, what you need to do is determine what is most important and do it first. Then go over your list of things that need to get done and see what takes precedence next.

The more organized you are, the easier it will be for you to manage your time. Make lists of things you need to do. You might want to keep a master list and then a daily list of things you need to do. You might also want a third list of deadlines that need to be met.

It's important to remember that just making lists won't do it. Checking them on a consistent basis to make sure the things that you needed to do actually got done is the key.

Here's an example of the beginnings of a master list. Use it to get you started on yours.

◎ Call Alex Myers to set up appointment.
◎ Finish Trebeck report.
◎ Check into dates and times of seminar.
◎ Check class schedule for certification program.

◎ Confirm in-service meeting time.
◎ Talk to Chief regarding exam times.
◎ Dinner with Tom L, Monday, 7:00 p.m.
◎ Shift change, Tuesday, March 9.

Writing things down is essential to being organized. Don't depend on your memory—or anyone else's. Whatever your job within law enforcement, it is sure to be filled with lot of details, things that need to get done, and just plain stuff in general. The more successful you get, the busier you will be and more things you'll have to remember. Don't depend on others reminding you. Depend on yourself.

If you want, you can input information into your Blackberry or another PDA device. However, always keep a back-up.

Here's an idea if you want to be really organized. Keep a notebook with you where you jot things down as they occur. Date each page so you have a reference point for later. Then make notes. Like what?

◎ The dates people called and the gist of the conversation.
◎ The dates you call people and the reason you called.
◎ Notes on meetings you attend. Then when someone says something like, "Gee, I don't remember whether we said May 9 or May 10," you have it.
◎ Names of people you meet.
◎ Things that happened during the day.

After you get used to keeping the notebook it will become a valuable resource. You might, for example, remember someone calling you six months ago. "What was his name?" you ask yourself. "I wish I knew his name." Just look in your notebook.

"It seems like a lot of trouble," I hear you saying. "I already keep a notebook for work notes."

It is a little extra effort, but I can almost guarantee you that once you keep a notebook like this for a while, you won't be able to live without it. You won't be looking for little sheets of paper on which you have jotted down important numbers and then misplaced. You won't have to remember people's names, phone numbers, or what they said. You won't have to remember if you were supposed to call at 3:00 or 4:30. You'll have everything at your fingertips.

A Few Other Things

It's important to realize that while of course you want to succeed in your career, everything you do may not be successful. You might not get every job you apply for. You might not get every promotion you want. Every idea you have may not work out. Every project you do may not turn out perfectly. And every job may not be the one you had hoped it would be.

It also is essential to remember that none of these scenarios mean that you are a failure. What they mean simply is that you need to work on them a little bit more. Things take time. Careers take time—especially great careers.

Be aware that success is often built on the back of little failures. If you ask most successful people about their road to success, many will tell you it wasn't always easy. And no matter what it looks like, most people are not overnight successes.

While some may have it easier, others may have had one or more rejections or failures before they got where they were going. What you will find, however, is those who are now successful didn't quit. After keeping at it and plugging away, they landed the jobs they aspired to, got the promotions, received good work reviews, and got where they are today.

You might not get the promotion you wanted right away. You might not have the job of our dreams—yet. That does not mean it won't happen. Keep plugging away and work at it and success will come to you.

Most successful people have a number of key traits in common. They have a willingness to take risks, a determination that cannot be undone, and usually an amazing amount of confidence in themselves and their ideas.

Can they fail? Sure. But they might also succeed and they usually do. What does this have to do with you? If you learn from the success of others, you can be successful too. If you emulate successful people, you too can be on the road to success.

Don't be so afraid of getting things right that you don't take a chance at doing it a better way, a different way, or a way that might work better. Don't get so comfortable that you're afraid to take a risk. Don't get so comfortable that you don't work toward a promotion or accept a new job or new responsibilities. Be determined that you know what you want and how to get it… and you will.

If you want to succeed in your career and your life, I urge you to be confident and be willing to take a risk. Success can surprise you at any time.

Take advantage of opportunities that present themselves, but don't stop there. Create opportunities for yourself to help launch your career to a new level by using creativity and innovative ideas.

Know that you not only can *have* success in your career in law enforcement but *deserve* success and if you work hard enough you can achieve your goals and dreams.

Whether your dream is to be a community police officer, detective, bailiff, probation officer, parole officer, corrections officer, or assistant district attorney; whether it is to be a state police officer, FBI special agent, DEA agent, or Secret Service agent; whether your dream is to be a police sketch artist, courtroom sketch artist, court clerk, or court reporter; whether your dream is a career as a police chief, police commissioner, sheriff, or warden of a federal prison; whether your dream is to be a crime scene technician, forensic chemist, private investigator, or investigator with the police department; whether your dream is be a data security specialist, information systems security specialist, gaming surveillance guard, or casino security guard; whether your dream is to be a store detective, retail director of shrinkage control, security training specialist, corporate security consultant, or private body guard; whether your career aspirations are these or you have any other dreams for your career in law enforcement, know this: The more you work toward success, the quicker it will come.

Your success is waiting. You just need to go after it!

11

SUCCEEDING AS A LAW ENFORCEMENT OFFICER OR SPECIAL AGENT

We've discussed a multitude of things throughout this book that can help you in your quest for a great career in law enforcement. We've talked about a variety of jobs and career options in various areas of the industry. We've discussed making your job into a career. We've investigated ways to get past the gatekeeper, some unique ways to obtain interviews, and interview tips.

We've covered developing resumes, cover letters, and putting together action plans. We've talked about job search strategies and tools for success. We've discussed why marketing is so important and how to market yourself.

You may have picked up this book for many reasons. I'm assuming if you're still reading that you've decided you want to work in some segment of law enforcement. We've discussed that there are a wide array of career options you might choose within the industry and talked about a number of them throughout this book. What I would like to do now is to focus a bit more on a number of career options for police officers and special agents on the local, state, and federal level.

If working as a law enforcement officer or special agent is not your career choice, you can skip over this chapter if you wish. However, even if this is not your career choice, you might find some of the information helpful in your career as well.

Many young people grow up dreaming of a career as a policeman or policewoman. Some grow up, change their dreams, and go on to careers in other fields, while others grow up and follow their original dreams. Maybe one of these scenarios was yours.

Perhaps it was one of these instead. How many times have you read a story in the newspaper about a police officer who saved someone's life and wished you were that officer? How many times have you watched the news covering the police on a high-speed chase finally catching a criminal and wished you were part of the team? How many times have you seen a story about a hostage negotiator negotiating the release of hostages and wished that were your job?

How many times have you seen a police officer, state police officer, or deputy in uniform and wished you had already gone through the training, had his or her job, and were wearing the uniform and on the job yourself? How many times have you seen FBI special agents on the news and wished you had one of their jobs? How many times have you read a story about the DEA partnering with the local police and orchestrating a major drug bust and wished you were part of that team?

How many times have you wished you could help someone feel safer, stop a crime in progress, or even solve a crime? How many times have you turned on the news and watched as a police officer made a difference in someone else's life and wished it were you on the job? How many times have you seen a law enforcement officer helping someone in need at an accident scene and wished you were the one providing the help? How many times have you read an article in the newspaper about the state police investigating a crime and wished you were the one doing the investigating?

How many times have you watched the Secret Service guarding the president or members of the first family and wished that was your job? How many times have you read stories involving the FBI and wished you were a special agent?

I'm betting if you are reading this section of the book, there's a good chance you see yourself in one if not more of these scenarios.

There certainly is nothing wrong with wishing. It definitely can't hurt…as a matter of fact, it sometimes helps you focus more clearly on what you want. But wishing alone can't make something happen. In order to succeed, it's essential to take some positive steps.

Is This the Right Area of Law Enforcement for You?

Before we take those steps, however, let's make sure that this area of law enforcement is the right career choice for you. Have you decided you want to become a law enforcement officer or agent? Has it been your life's calling for as long as

you can remember? As we just discussed, some people know from the time they are quite young that they are going to be police officers when "they grow up." Others made the decision when they were in high school or in college. There are also many who make the decision *after* they have already been in another career…but realize a career in law enforcement is their *real* dream. Some were in the military and decided that a career in law enforcement would be a good next step. Are any of these your scenarios?

Many people go into law enforcement because they have a genuine desire to help others. Some have parents or other family members who worked in law enforcement on the local, state, or federal level. Others just decide that law enforcement is a good career choice.

Whatever the reasons you have chosen this profession, know that no matter what type of law enforcement officer or special agent you become, you can have a tremendous impact on the lives of others.

And while everyone has their own reason why they decide to enter the field, if you haven't made your decision yet…read on.

I've often been asked by people making career choices if I thought law enforcement was the right choice for them; if I thought they would be good police officers (or state police officers, highway patrol officers, deputies, or federal law enforcement agents)? If you are wondering the same thing, you might want to ask yourself a few questions.

◎ Do I really *want* to become a police officer (or state police officer, highway patrol officer, deputy, or federal law enforcement agent)?

This question sounds like it should be easy to answer, but in some cases, people become police officers for the wrong reasons. Perhaps someone else told them it's a good idea or it is someone else's dream. Perhaps someone thinks a career as a police officer is a good choice because they have heard that there is a need for law enforcement officers and they think it will be easy to find a job. Maybe they want to be a police officer because they want to boss people around or be in a position of power. Maybe they want to be a police officer because they think it's *cool* to wear a uniform and have a badge. Or they might not really know what they want to do and law enforcement seems like the easiest choice. None of these are good reasons.

◎ Do I have a genuine desire to work in law enforcement? Is this what I really want to do?

◎ Am I passionate about becoming a law enforcement officer or agent?

◎ Do I want to make a positive impact on the lives of others?

◎ Do I want to make a positive difference in my community?

◎ Am I prepared to uphold the law and help prevent crime?

◎ Am I prepared to risk my life? No one likes to think about dying, but as an officer, you put your life at risk every day. While, of course, it is not something to dwell on, it's important to remember to be alert at all times and take precautions such as wearing your bulletproof vest when necessary.

◎ Can I be a role model?

◎ What are my core values? There are certain core values that good law enforcement officers have. Are you responsible? Are you honest? Are you fair? Do you have personal integrity? Do you have good judgment? Can you keep a confidence? Are you committed to doing the right thing?

Now that you've answered those questions, have you decided that a career in law enforcement is for you? Are you ready to make that commitment?

What Kind of Law Enforcement Officer Should I Be?

How do you know what type of law enforcement officer you should be? Do you want to work on the local level? What about the state level? How about a career in one of the federal law enforcement agencies? How do you know what direction you should go in?

The answer to those questions depends to a great extent on you and your passions as well as job availability. Do you want to work in a situation where you know a lot of the people in your area and on your beat? Do you want to work in a community atmosphere? Do you want to make a difference that you can see? Then you might want to work as a municipal police officer. Do you want to be a big fish in a small pond? Do you want a career with more generalized duties? Then you might enjoy working in a smaller town. If you want to have more specialized duties, you might prefer working in a department in a large city atmosphere.

Do you want to work on the county level? Sheriffs and deputy sheriffs work on a county level enforcing the law much as police do on the local level. While police chiefs are appointed, sheriffs are generally elected to their posts. The two perform similar duties.

Perhaps you are interested in a career as a state police officer, highway patrol officer, or state trooper. Individuals in this area arrest criminals on a statewide basis as well as patrolling highways to enforce motor vehicle laws. Many of us are used to seeing state police officers issuing traffic citations to motorists traveling too fast on the highway. These important officers are frequently the first at the scene of accidents, giving first aid and calling for emergency equipment. They also are often called on to assist other law enforcement agencies including those in rural areas or small towns.

There is a tremendous range of opportunities in federal law enforcement. FBI special agents are the U.S. government's principal investigators of violations in more than 200 categories of federal law. These special agents also conduct sensitive national security investigations.

What other opportunities exist? Do you want to be the one of the people who enforces the laws and regulations relating to illegal drugs? Do you want to help break up drug cartels? Can you imagine yourself conducting criminal investigations? What about infiltrating illicit drug organizations as an undercover agent? If these types of activities pique your interest, a career with the U.S. Drug Enforcement Administration, better known as the DEA, might appeal to you.

Is your interest investigating counterfeiting? What about investigating the forgery of government checks or bonds or even the fraudulent use of credit cards? What about protecting the president, vice president, and their immediate families, presidential candidates, former presidents, and foreign dignitaries visiting our country? Then you might be interested in a career with the Secret Service.

Is it your dream to protect the federal courts? Do you want a career protecting federal witnesses, transporting federal prisoners, protecting the

federal judiciary, and pursuing and arresting federal fugitives? Then you might want to be a U.S. marshal or deputy marshal.

Would you find it challenging to investigate violations of federal firearms and explosives laws? Would like you to investigate violations of alcohol and tobacco tax regulations? Then you might enjoy a career in the Bureau of Alcohol, Tobacco, Firearms and Explosives, better known as the ATF.

Do you want to be part of the team that helps battle terrorism? The U.S. Department of State's Bureau of Diplomatic Security does just that. Individuals in this area may work in this country or abroad. Some advise ambassadors oversees on security matters. Others investigate passport and visa fraud, conduct personnel security investigations, and issue security clearances. Some Bureau of Diplomatic Security special agents also train foreign civilian police.

Since the September 11th tragedy, many interested in a career in law enforcement are especially attracted to a career with the Department of Homeland Security. This department employs numerous law enforcement officers under several different agencies to protect international land and water boundaries.

One of the ways to help you determine the area you are interested in is to talk to professionals in various areas of law enforcement. You might, for example, contact any law enforcement agency on the local, state, or federal level and discuss career opportunities. Simply call up and tell the receptionist you are considering a career with (whatever the agency is) and would like to speak to someone to get some general information. You might also check out agency Web sites to read more about career options.

Try to talk to people who are working in various areas of law enforcement. Tell them about your aspirations. See if anyone you know can refer you to someone in the area in which you are interested. Just because you want a career as an FBI special agent doesn't mean that you can't talk to your local police chief to see if he or she knows someone in another agency who might be able to give you some information.

In some cases, you might also be able to observe professionals on the job. For example, if you think you might be interested in a career as a municipal police officer, state police officer, or sheriff's deputy, you might call the police chief, commander, or sheriff and tell him or her you are considering a career in law enforcement. Ask if it would be possible to do a ride along for a week or so. This will give you the opportunity to see if this is a career area you want to pursue.

You might also ask if there are any upcoming career fairs, programs, or internships available.

Internships

Internships are a wonderful way to get your foot in the door, learn more about a career, get hands-on experience, and make important contacts. Where do you find them? Almost any law enforcement agency is a possibility. Sometimes the internships are formal. In other situations, the programs may be less structured.

If you are interested in an internship with a local or state police agency, you can always just call the agency to see if such a program exists. If there isn't a formal program, ask who you can speak to who might be able to put together an internship for you. Don't be shy. Keep asking until you find someone who will help. If you are still in school or college, your advisor might be able to help coordinate an internship with an agency.

If you're interested in an internship with a federal law enforcement agency, contact them

as well. Be sure to check out agency Web sites. Many have information about internship opportunities right on their Web sites. The FBI, for example, has an annual FBI Honors Internship Program held in Washington, D.C., as well as one at regional computer forensics laboratory in various areas throughout the country.

Your Road to Becoming a Great Law Enforcement Officer

Becoming a good law enforcement office takes time, education, experience, and a great deal of commitment. Are you ready? If not, now is the time to prepare.

What do you need to do? What are the requirements? What can you do to increase your chances of success?

Specific requirements will depend, of course, on the area of law enforcement you choose to enter. However, many of the requirements may be similar. For example, generally most candidates must:

- Take and pass a written test
- Go through one or more interviews and/or oral examinations
- Go through extensive background investigations
- Take and pass polygraph tests
- Go through medical examinations including vision and hearing tests
- Go through and pass physical agility and strength exams
- Go through and pass a psychological examination
- Take and pass drug tests

What else do you need? You need to possess a clean valid driver's license. You also need to be a U.S. citizen. There are also age requirements. While you should check with the specific agency in which you aspire to work, police officers working in a local or state agency need to be at least 20 years old although in some agencies, the minimum age requirement may be 21.

Minimum ages vary for those aspiring to work as federal law enforcement agents. In certain agencies, the minimum age requirement is 21. However, to become an FBI special agent, the minimum age is 23. We'll go over some of the other requirements to become an FBI special agent in a moment in case that is your choice.

What else? You need to have a minimum of a high school diploma if you are pursuing a career in a local agency. A college background, associate's degree, or bachelor's degree would be better. If you are pursuing a career in a state or federal law enforcement agency, you will generally be required to hold a minimum of a bachelor's degrees. Get the best education you can. It will give you an edge over others.

What's the best major? Successful people in law enforcement have degrees in a variety of areas. Some study criminal justice. Others get degrees in business, accounting, or law. Still others have broad liberal arts degrees. Some feel a degree in psychology, sociology, or English is helpful. The important thing is to make sure you get a degree. It will be important not only in getting your job, but in climbing the career ladder to success as well.

What can stop your career in law enforcement in its tracks? You cannot have a felony conviction and you cannot have been dishonorably discharged from the military.

"Working in local law enforcement is probably a good job, but my dream is to be an FBI special agent," you say. "What do I need to do?"

> ### ⭐ Tip from the Top
>
> If you are considering a career as an FBI special agent, remember that one of the requirements is that you must be available to be assigned anywhere in the FBI's jurisdiction. If you *cannot* or *do not* want to leave your home base for an extended period of time for any reason, this might not be the area of law enforcement for you.

Let's take a few minutes to go over some of the basic requirements you must fulfill if you are interested in becoming an FBI special agent.

- ◎ You must be a U.S. citizen (or a citizen of the Northern Mariana Islands).
- ◎ You must be at least 23 years old, but younger than 37 at the time of your appointment as a special agent.
- ◎ You must possess a minimum of a four-year degree from an accredited college or university.
- ◎ You must have at least three years of professional work experience.
- ◎ You must possess a valid driver's license.
- ◎ You must be available to be assigned anywhere in the FBI's jurisdiction.

Police Exam

Whether you aspire to work in local, state, or federal law enforcement, you most likely will have to take a written exam prior to being hired.

If you want to work on the local or state level, you will need to take some version of a police exam. Depending on the specific situation, these may be administered by the local municipality or by a state agency. (Federal agencies give their own version of the police exam to those seeking to become special agents.)

The exam helps establish an eligibility list from which police officer vacancies can be filled as well as demonstrating the knowledge and understanding of police work.

Doing well on the police exam is essential to getting the job. Do not take this important exam lightly. Don't just leave this important test to chance. Potential applicants are normally chosen from the highest scorers. Your goal, therefore is to ace this exam.

How can you increase your score? Prepare ahead of time. Get one or more police test review book and *read* them. Take the practice tests. There are also seminars and classes that are very helpful in giving you tips to taking the test and assisting you in knowing what you need to learn to increase your score.

What is the exam like? While no two are exactly the same, written exams will cover areas such as:

- ◎ Reading comprehension
  - ▫ Can you understand what is written and then follow instructions?
- ◎ Memory retention
  - ▫ Can you remember things you have seen, heard, and read? Can you remember faces, facts, etc.?
- ◎ Geographic orientation
  - ▫ Can you find your way around? It's essential to know how to get to an address quickly in case of emergency. This portion of the exam may be tested in various ways from determining how to get from one point to another to identifying landmarks.
- ◎ Forms and reports
  - ▫ Can you fill in forms and reports completely? As a police officer it is essential to fill in forms accurately,

thoroughly, and in a timely manner. The police report will also often be presented as evidence in court. This portion of the exam will give you specific scenarios and then test your knowledge of filling out reports based on that information. It may also test your ability of properly extracting information from existing reports.

- ◎ Writing skills
  - ▫ Writing skills are important in every career and police work is no exception. As a police officer you may be required to write police reports, field reports, memos, e-mails, letters and more. This portion of the exam will test your knowledge of written communication skills. These may include areas such as spelling, word usage, grammar, punctuation, and sentence structure to name a few. Questions will generally be in multiple-choice format.

In some areas the exam may be separated into components such as:

- ◎ The Written Ability Test (WAT)
  - ▫ This measures the cognitive abilities which are essential when performing the duties of a police officer. The section includes verbal expression, verbal comprehension, deductive and inductive reasoning, information ordering, and problem sensitivity.
- ◎ The Work Styles Questionnaire (WSQ)
  - ▫ This component assesses the characteristics related to motivation, values, and attitudes relevant to becoming a successful police officer.

Words from the Wise

One of the most common reasons people don't do well on the police exam is that they don't carefully read the questions. Take your time reading questions. Make sure you understand exactly what the question is asking. For example, a question may ask you to choose the option that is "not the right answer." If you don't fully read and comprehend the questions, you might choose the incorrect options.

◎ The Life Experiences Survey (LES)
   ▫ This component consists of multiple-choice questions related to an individual's history and experience that may be relevant to the success of a police officer.

Here are some tips that may help you score higher on the police exam.

◎ Most test questions are multiple choice. Read the questions and the answers thoroughly *before* answering them.

◎ Read the instructions thoroughly. Exactly what is the question asking you to do?

◎ Read the essays and scenarios provided carefully. Get the facts. Some people find it helpful to take notes. Then base your answers on information provided in those essays.

Tip from the Top

Whether taking an exam, filling in applications, writing reports, letters, memos, or e-mails, always proofread your work, then proofread again. You will often see an error you can fix quickly.

◎ Proofread your answers.
◎ Relax. Being stressed will not help your score.

Military Service and Law Enforcement

Military service can be a big plus to you if you are pursuing a career as a law enforcement officer. While each state and agency has its own set of rules regarding military service, you should be aware that in some situations the presence of military service in your background may give you benefits ranging from giving you an edge over other applicants to adding a certain number of points to your score on the civil service or police exam.

In some situations, instead of going through normal channels to become a police officer, you may also have the ability to do so by becoming an officer through something called military reciprocity. To do this, you generally need to have served a specific number of years in the military police in addition to receiving an honorable discharge. In situations such as this, you probably will also have to take and pass some sort of reciprocity exam.

Military experience will also prove useful if you are pursuing a career in federal law enforcement.

Generally, as we just discussed, if you want to become a police officer on the local or state level, you will be taking a police exam. Candidates are chosen from the top scorers. In some situations, if you have military service in your background, you may have a number of points added to your score.

Oral Interviews

Earlier in the book, we discussed the interview process. Let's take a few more moments to discuss this important step of the process. Once you are invited to come in for an interview for a job as a law enforcement officer, prepare ahead of time. Get your ducks in a row.

Go over your resume. Is it up-to-date? Do you have clean copies to bring to the interview? Do you know the information on your resume? Can you quickly discuss your accomplishments without saying, "Uh, well, I have done a lot—let me think." Can you easily provide examples?

Can you show that you are a leader? Can you show that you are a team player? Can you show that you would be a good addition to the team?

Can you intelligently discuss your career goals? Can you answer the questions you are sure to be asked? Why do you want to become a police officer? Where do want to be in five years? What about 10 years? What do you want to accomplish?

Can you rattle off some of your previous jobs and find a way that your experience is related to police work? Have you practiced answering that probable question, "So tell us a little about yourself?"

Interviews for police positions are like other interviews. Depending on the situation,

Tip from the Coach

While it is never a good idea to lie, fabricate, or stretch the truth in any manner during your interview, it is an especially bad idea in law enforcement. You will be going through an extensive background investigation and the truth will most likely come out.

they may be one-on-one with the police chief, a hiring officer, or a human resources director. In some situations, you will be asked to go to a structured or panel interview. Instead of being one-on-one, this type of interview will be done in front of a group of people that might include the chief as well as other officers and supervisors of the department.

During this type of interview, members of the panel have the opportunity to ask you questions. Look at each person as he or she asks questions and then try to glance at each member of the panel as you are providing your answer.

Don't forget to prepare questions ahead of time that you can ask the interviewer or the panel. That way, when you are asked if you *have* any questions, you will be prepared.

While, of course, it is normal to be nervous during your interview, try to relax. You want to project a strong and confident image.

Tip from the Top

In some situations, your interview may be recorded or videotaped. The taping may be done for a variety of reasons. Sometimes the powers that be may want to review the interviews before making a choice. In other situations, the taping serves to assure that there were no biases during the interview. If you are placed in a situation where you are being interviewed on tape, don't focus on the microphone or the camera. Just try to ignore that they are there and relax as much as you can.

The Inside Scoop

In small departments, you most likely will be interviewed by the police chief, who is generally also the final decision maker in choosing candidates. In larger departments there will often be a panel and perhaps even a hiring board who will do the interviewing.

Police Academy

What is the police academy? Basically, it is where you go to get the training needed to be a good police officer. At the police academy you go through classroom training as well as practical training.

You may be taught about things like the best ways to take notes and the proper way to write reports. You'll learn about various constitutional, family, criminal, and traffic areas of law. You'll be taught how to act in a courtroom, and about cultural diversity and legal ethics. You'll learn investigative skills, forensics, and arrest techniques. You will receive DUI and DWI training as well as being trained in first-aid methods.

You will be performing physical agility tests and increasing your physical stamina. You will also be learning about firearms and be practicing your firearm skills. Additionally, you will be taught about other police practices and procedures.

The police academy training course may run from 11 to 26 weeks or more depending on the specific academy. Upon completion of the basic police training program, officers receive what is known as a POST (Peace Officer Standard and Training) certificate. This is a required certification that all police officers must possess.

You Got the Job: Now What?

Let's move ahead a bit. Let's say you got the job. Now what? As a rookie or new police officer, you will generally have to go through a probationary period that may last between one and two years, depending on the specific department. During this time you most likely will first be assigned to patrol duty and working under the supervision of a field training officer.

Learn as much as you can during this time. Don't take the easy way out. Ask questions. Do that little bit extra that no one asked you to do. As a matter of fact, ask other officers and your supervisor if there is anything you can do to help. Offer to interview witnesses. Offer to help write reports. Offer to do the things no one else really wants to do.

Why do all these things? Because it will make you a better officer; because it will help you begin to stand out as a team player; because it will help higher-ups in the organization, notice that you are willing to do more; and because it will help your career.

What else can you do? Continue taking classes, seminars, and workshops. Go to conferences. Actively seek out these opportunities. They not only will help you learn new skills and help you make new contacts—they often help you see things from a different perspective. This is essential in law enforcement.

Develop resources and contacts in the community as well as in law enforcement. How do you do this? There are various ways. To begin with, get involved in the community. Volunteer to be on hand for community events. Volunteer to speak at civic groups. Volunteer to talk to kids about crime prevention, drug abuse, or gangs.

Successful police officers also develop resources "on the street." Over time, you will need to find ways to build your network of resources as well. These people will prove useful in your job.

What else? When you are in a position where you can meet other officers, detectives, or special agents, meet them. Let's say you are on the scene of an automobile accident. So are the state police. When you are done doing what you need to do, walk over and introduce yourself to the other officers.

Let's say you are one of the officers on a team conducting a drug bust. After you've done your job, walk over and introduce yourself to DEA agents, the state police officers, etc. Why are you doing this? Because resources and contacts are key to success in your job. You can never tell when one of your contacts can be instrumental in you doing your job better or a supervisor may need a resource that you just happen to have and you can say, "I know him. I'll give him a call for you."

What else? No matter what area of law enforcement you are pursuing, become the best officer or special agent you can be. What does that mean? Basically, it means always do your best, always have highest integrity, and always remain above the law.

Moving Up: Success in Law Enforcement

How do you move up the career ladder? There are a number of ways depending on your career aspirations. Some individuals start out in smaller departments, go through their probationary period, get some experience, and then make lateral moves to larger departments.

"What about promotions?" you ask. "How does that work?"

The promotion process depends to a great extent on the specific department. In some departments, many promotions are determined by civil service exams. What that means is that applicants interested in being promoted to a higher position take a civil service examination and the promotions are given to the highest scorers.

In many departments this is the way individuals are promoted to sergeant and lieutenant. In some departments, promotion to the position of detective is also determined by civil service exams.

If your department bases promotions on civil service testing, it is important that you find out when the exams are being given. It also is important to prepare for exam, much the same way you did for the police test. There are similar seminars and books that can help you improve your score and nab the promotion.

In some departments the promotion process may not be based on civil service rankings at all. Sometimes it may be based purely on an individual's experience, skills, and talent. Sometimes the promotion process is also political.

Let's say you have taken the detective exam and done well. What then? Once you receive the promotion, you often go back to the police academy for some addition training.

What then? Depending on the situation, you might want to specialize in a specific area of law enforcement. You might, for example, want to specialize in forensics, criminal scene investigation, burglary, or homicide among other areas.

What else can you do? After some experience on the job, some individuals working in local law enforcement decide that they want to go into a career in federal law enforcement. If this is your scenario, you might want to speak to your supervisor. He or she can often help you get your foot in the door.

Those working in federal law enforcement may advance their careers by getting better assignments or being promoted to supervisory positions.

You should be aware that some individuals don't seek success in administrative promotions at all. Instead they want to continue working hands-on in law enforcement. Success to these individuals may mean making a difference in the lives of people in the community, helping people feel safer, or simply going to a job every day that they love.

Tip from the Coach

Technology is such a useful tool in law enforcement today that it is essential for law enforcement officers and special agents to be computer literate, familiar with various software programs, and know how to research. If you are not already totally comfortable with computer technology, take classes and get comfortable. It is crucial to your career success.

Tip from the Coach

The ability to speak and understand more than one language will be extremely useful in your career. Consider taking an immersion course to pick up another language and make yourself more marketable and valuable.

Only you can decide what success means to you and go after it. It is your decision and your decision alone.

Being the Best You Can Be

I'm assuming that now that you are a police officer or special agent, you want to be the very best you can be. I'm assuming you want to be a respected member of the law enforcement community. And I'm assuming you want to be successful. What can you do to increase your chances?

In order to succeed you need to act in a professional manner…all the time and in every situation. That means on the job, off the job, and in the community in which you work.

How can you be professional? Present yourself professionally. Be reliable and responsible. If you say you're going to be someplace, be there. If you say you're going to call someone, call them. If someone calls you and leaves a message, call them back in a timely basis. If you say you're going to do something, do it.

It goes without saying that you should be at work on time. But it goes much further. If you have a meeting scheduled, be there on time not 10 minutes late. If you have an appointment with a supervisor, colleague, witness, etc., whether in person or on the phone, be where you say you're going to be at the time you say you're going to be there.

If you have a report due on Monday morning, make sure it is handed in Monday morning, not Monday afternoon or some time on Tuesday.

In case I'm not making myself clear enough, be on time for everything. There is nothing worse for your career than being known as the officer who is habitually late.

It is totally unprofessional to drink when you are on duty. It is also against the law to use illegal drugs at any time. You might *think* that you are doing a better job, but no matter what you have heard, you will not do a better job if you are under the influence.

In that same vein, it's important to remember that police officers are often role models for young people. What does that mean? Youngsters often look up to police officers. They admire them. In many cases they may try to emulate them. Right or wrong, that's the way it is.

What does that have to do with you? Like it or not, your life as a police officer will often be scrutinized more closely than others. Using illegal drugs or drinking to excess at any time may not only send a negative message to people in the community, it also sends a message to the department and your supervisors who may use this as a reason not to give you a promotion.

"It's not fair," you say.

Here's the deal. To begin with, everything isn't fair. When you decide to be a police officer, especially if you are living in a smaller, rural area where everyone knows everyone, you need to realize that like it or not, your life will probably be scrutinized more closely than others.

Here's something else you should know. It doesn't matter what level you're at in your career. If you're just starting your career, people in authority will use any negative thing you do as a reason why you shouldn't move up the career ladder. If you are at the top, people will say you

should know better; you're a professional. The lesson here is to remember that if you want a career as a successful law enforcement professional and want to take advantage of everything the career affords, act professionally.

Here's something else for you to think about. Every successful police officer and special agent, no matter what their area of specialization, no matter who they are, no matter where they are in their career at this moment, had to start somewhere. While of course everyone has a slightly different set of circumstances, most officers and special agents have been where you are today. They've had to take the step from trainee or rookie to full-fledged officer; they've had to find their first job; and they've had to go through that exciting, but perhaps scary, first day.

As they climb the ladder of the success, most officers and special agents face similar challenges as well. They have to face the challenges of higher crime rates, a changing society, more drugs and guns, and a lack of funding. They face the challenges of leaving their families every day not knowing if they will return safe at night.

They have to worry about doing a good job, keeping people safe, and making a difference. They have to worry about being burned out and being stressed. And…they still love their jobs.

You want everything about you to stand out from others in a positive manner. You want to be well informed and keep up on changes and current trends in law enforcement. To give yourself the best chances at success, learn as much as possible about all aspects of law enforcement and the process.

Read as much as you can about every aspect of law enforcement you can find. Go to the library and the bookstore and find books. Read

> ### ★ Tip from the Top
> Make it part of your daily routine to learn at least one new thing every day. Learn something new every opportunity you get.

> ### ★ Tip from the Coach
> There are hundreds of opportunities in between the point where you might currently be in your career and where you want to be. Becoming a successful police officer or special agent is a journey. Some people get there faster than others. Whatever your final destination, you can have a successful career getting there. The important thing to remember is to look at every opportunity as a way to get where you want to go.

trade publications. Find other magazines and periodicals with articles on various areas of law enforcement. Scour the Web for information.

If you just find one piece of information in a book, or magazine, or on the Internet that you can use to do something in a better way, or one thing that you can relate to your career, it will be worth it. And don't stop there. Share the information with your colleagues. Don't keep it to yourself.

As mentioned earlier, look for workshops, seminars, and classes that may be of value. You will gain valuable information, learn new skills, and have the opportunity to network and make important contacts.

> ### ★ The Inside Scoop
> Openings for law enforcement officers and agents may occur anytime during the year. People may leave, municipalities may get grant money, and new programs may begin. In addition to checking out the classifieds, if you are looking for a job as a police officer or special agent, keep your eye out for recruiting seminars. Find out where and when civil service openings are posted or listed and routinely check to see what is available. Don't forget to look online. Check out traditional jobs sites such as monster.com and hotjobs.com. Then check out law enforcement-oriented career Web sites. Law enforcement agency Web sites also may offer possibilities.

How do you succeed in the workplace? Great law enforcement officers don't just appear one day. They develop over time. Basic law enforcement skills are just the beginning. You need to develop a variety of other skills in order to develop yourself as an officer.

You need to develop your people skills. You need to develop your "law enforcement personality." You need to know you are going to be great and begin to have confidence in yourself.

Here are some other tips that will help you succeed as a law enforcement officer no matter which agency you choose to work.

◎ Be a team player. Step in and help other colleagues and superiors when needed.
   ▫ Not only will this help you become a team player; it will help you hone skills, learn new things, and bring you to the attention of those in the upper echelon of the agency.
◎ Set goals for yourself. Where do you want to be at the end of the year? What do you want to be doing in five years? What are your priorities?
◎ Project a positive, neat image. Keep up with your appearance. Just because you

got the job, does not mean you should come to work looking sloppy or poorly groomed.

◎ Stay in shape. You don't want to miss out on a promotion because you are 30 pounds overweight. More importantly, you don't want to be out of breath when running after a perpetrator.

◎ Make sure you have good people skills.

◎ Be fair and respectful to everyone you come in contact with.

◎ Keep your sense of humor. It will help in every situation.

◎ Believe in yourself. No one will believe in you, unless you do so first.

 Tip from the Coach
You might be able to get another opportunity, but you can never get back the opportunity you missed.

No matter what type of law enforcement officer you become—whether you choose to work on the local, state, or federal level—you can have a long and successful career. Work toward your goals. No matter what specific career you choose, be the best you can be. You will be rewarded with an exciting and fulfilling career.

12

SUCCESS IS YOURS FOR THE TAKING

Do You Have What It Takes?

Imagine living in a society where there are no rules, there are no laws, and everyone can do what they want. While as children, many may have wished there were no rules and that we could do whatever we wanted with no repercussions, as adults we realize why this wouldn't work.

Our society is dependent on a system that governs with laws that we all are expected to follow. Within that system, we are also dependent upon people to enforce those laws.

Whether in this country or in countries on the other side of the world, the enforcement of laws makes a big difference in the way people live and exist. On the most basic level, law enforcement provides a safer environment. There are a myriad of people in a wide array of careers involved in various areas of law enforcement. One of them can be you.

Imagine knowing that the job you have can help others have better lives. Imagine knowing that the job you have can save someone's life. Imagine knowing that the job you have can make others safer.

Imagine working in an industry that really makes a difference. Imagine knowing you are not only living your dream, you are succeeding.

If you are reading this book, you don't have to imagine one more second. You are closer than ever to your dream career in law enforcement.

This book was written for every single person who aspires to work and succeed in law enforcement in any capacity. If this is you, and you know who you are, I need to ask you a very important question.

Do you have what it takes?

"What do you mean, do I have what it takes?" you ask.

Do you have what it takes to be successful in this industry?

"Well, I think so," you say.

You think so? That's not good enough. You have to know so! Why? Because if you don't believe in yourself, no one else will.

"Okay," you say. "I get it. I *know* I can be successful."

That's good. That's the attitude you need to succeed!

With that out of the way, let's go over a couple of other facts that can help you in your quest for success in law enforcement. You have to remember that no matter what comes your way, you can't give up. Whatever you have to deal with, when you achieve your goals, you most likely will feel it was worth it. There may be stumbling blocks. You may have to take detours. There may even be times you have to choose a fork in the road. But if you give up, it's over.

Here's another fact you should know. When you share your dreams and goals with others about working in any aspect of law enforcement, there will always be some people who insist on telling you their version of the statistics of the industry.

They may try to tell you the dangers of working in law enforcement. "Do you know how many cops are shot every year?" someone might ask. "Do you know how many are killed?"

They may tell you how dangerous it is working as an FBI agent or a CIA or a corrections officer, parole officer, or even a court reporter. As a matter of fact, no matter what job you choose, someone will probably share some story they heard about a problem someone else head.

"Watch the news," someone may say. "You'll see what happens. You're never going to be safe."

"A lot of people just don't *like* cops," someone might say to you. "Why do you want to be involved in a job like that?"

They may tell you that they heard that most people don't do well on the police test or rattle off some statistics on how many people who take the civil service test are not the top scorers. They might even tell you how difficult it is to climb the career ladder in your chosen field.

There might be people who quote statistics on everything from burnout to high stress levels of those working in law enforcement, and the list will go on. It probably doesn't matter what area of law enforcement (or any other industry for that matter) in which you are trying to create a career—there will be people who will try

to make you feel like if you go for your dreams, statistically you will stand absolutely *no* chance of success at all.

If you listen to those people and start believing them, you probably will become one of their statistics. If you pay attention to them, a career in any aspect of law enforcement, probably isn't for you. I'm willing to bet that no matter what career you choose and in what industry, they will probably have something negative to say about it.

However, if you have gotten to the section of the book, I'm guessing you aren't going to let anyone negatively influence you. I am also betting that you are still going to go after your dream.

Here's something to think about. Let's look at a few analogies. Statistically, it's difficult for most people to lose weight, yet there are many people who do. Statistically, most people who play the lottery don't win, yet there are always winners. Statistically, the chances of winning the Publishers Clearing House Sweepstakes aren't great, yet someone always wins. Will it be you? Not if you don't enter.

With those analogies in mind, I stand behind what I have said throughout this book. No matter what the statistics are, someone has to succeed. Why shouldn't it be you? Someone has to be at the top. Why shouldn't it be you? If you give up your dream, someone else will be there. You will be standing on the outside looking in and watching someone doing what you want. I don't think that's your dream.

Will it be easy? Not always. But, the industry is full of police officers, state police officers, sheriffs, and deputies. It's filled with prosecutors, criminal attorneys, court reporters, bailiffs, parole officers, probation officers, and corrections officers. It's filled federal agents who work in the FBI, IRS, CIA, DEA, Secret Service, border patrol, and homeland security.

It's full of people who work in private security, corporate security, and Internet security. It's full of people who do corporate security training in a wide array of industries.

It's full of forensic scientists and polygraph examiners. It's full of fire inspectors and animal control officers. It's full of forest rangers, special agents who protect the land and people who protect our national parks.

The industry is full of people working in the business and administration segments of law enforcement. It's full of people working in various trade associations and organizations in all aspects of law enforcement. It's full of crime reporters, journalists, writers, columnists, and authors. It is full of people doing research, developing programs, writing grants, and more. The industry is huge. It is jam packed with wonderful and fulfilling opportunities. Why shouldn't you live your dream and be part it?

Many are concerned about their chances for success. Often they are concerned that there are too many variables. Will there be jobs? Will you have to move to a different geographic location? Will you be good enough? Will you get burned out? Will you be able to actually make a difference? And the list goes on.

Many are concerned that in certain parts of the industry, success (or failure) is too dependent on others. What you need to know is that while it is true that others can affect your career, they can't stop it—unless you let it happen. You are in the driver's seat. You can make it happen! Make the decision to keep on working toward your goal is yours.

You have the power. Are you going to quit?

Here's what I want you to remember. Whether you are dreaming of success as a small town police officer, large city police officer, country sheriff's deputy, highway patrol officers, or state police officer; whether you are dreaming of success as an FBI agent, CIA agent, DEA agent, or any other federal law enforcement official; whether you are dreaming of working as a border patrol guard or in another area of homeland security; whether you are hoping for a career as a corrections officer, warden or in another segment of the prison system; whether you are dreaming of success in the business or administration area of law enforcement;

Whether you are dreaming of protecting the president and first family or the family of a major Hollywood star; whether you are dreaming of success as a parole officer, probation officer, bail bondsman, or a bounty hunter. Whether you are dreaming of success training police officers, federal agents, security guards, or corporate Internet security directors; whether you are dreaming of success as a police detective, private detective, or investigator.

Whether you are dreaming of success as a crime reporter, journalist, reporter, or author; the editor of some sort of law enforcement Web site, one of the writers or even the owner or the writer or developer of educational materials, police exams, or civil service exams.

Whether you want to be in the forefront of the industry, behind the scenes, or somewhere in between, know this: You *can* do it and do it successfully as long as you don't give up.

Throughout your journey, always keep your eye on the prize: the great career you are working toward in law enforcement.

Sometimes your dream may change. That's okay. As long as you are following *your* dreams, not those of others, you usually are on the right road.

Whatever segment of law enforcement in which you are interested, your choices are huge. What is going to be your contribution to this important industry?

What path do you want to follow? Where do you envision yourself? What do you see yourself doing? Seize your opportunity. It's there for you. Grab onto your dream to start the ball rolling.

Over the years, I've talked to many people who are extremely successful in a variety of careers and an array of industries. One of the most interesting things about them is that most were *not* surprised at all that they were successful. As a matter of fact, they expected it.

While researching this area, I found that while some decided as young adults what their career path would be, many people knew from the time they were children what their career choice was. Not only that; they also knew they would be great at their job. Those working in law enforcement were no different.

I want to share a story with you. While it isn't about someone in law enforcement, it does help illustrate the point of just how important a positive focus can be in your career. This focus can help drive you toward success.

One night I was on the road with one of the acts I represented and we were sitting backstage before the concert. I was talking to one of the singers and we were discussing some of the other hot artists in the industry. The singer was telling me a story of another artist who was on the charts.

"We knew he was going to be a star," he said about the other artist. "When he was still in school, he told everyone he was going to be a star, and that's all he talked about."

"Doesn't everyone say that?" I asked.

"Sometimes they do," he continued, "But what made him different was he was specific about what he was going to do and when. He told everyone he was going to have a hit record before he graduated. (At the time, the man hadn't even recorded anything yet.) He started acting like a star and then dressing the part of a star. He went on and on about it so much that he almost had to become a star to save face. Funny thing was, he did have a hit before he graduated and he did turn into a huge star."

This is not an isolated story. There are probably hundreds like it in every industry. Stories like this do help prove the point of just how important not only a positive focus can be in your career but believing in yourself as well. What's really interesting is that in many cases, way before successful people even plan their success, they expect it.

Is it the planning and the work that creates the reality or is it the dream that puts them on the road to success? I think it's a combination.

And in case you're thinking that you're only supposed to expect success in law enforcement if your career aspirations are to be a police or law enforcement officer in the local, state, or federal level, think again. You are supposed to expect success in whatever area of the industry you pursue. Every job is important. Every job can make a difference to someone.

Are you ready for success? Are you really ready?

Do you know what you're going to say when you're being interviewed by the television news as Police Officer of the Year? Can you imagine the feeling you will have as you accept the award?

Can you imagine how proud you will feel as a police chief when the mayor gives you a commendation for crime going down 50 percent since you've been on the job?

Can you imagine how you will feel as a DEA special agent when you and your team break up a major drug cartel? Can you almost feel the excitement you experience when you find a kidnapped child? Can you imagine the feeling you will have when you negotiate a hostage release?

Can you imagine how proud you will be when you become the director of the county probation department? Can you imagine the feeling you will have when you are elected district attorney? Can you see the headline in the newspaper? Do you have your speech prepared for the night you are elected sheriff?

Can you imagine the feeling you will have when a child comes up to you and tells you he or she is lost and wants their mom? Can you imagine how you will feel when a young woman tells you she is becoming a police officer because you made such an important impact on her life?

Have you chosen the perfect suit you're going to wear to the meeting when you are named Commissioner of the State Commission of Corrections? Can you see the press release in the newspaper when you are named for this important position?

Can you hear the introduction you are given when you are presenting a paper at a major law enforcement conference?

Can you almost see what you will be wearing when you sign an employment contract with a major corporation as the IT security director? Can you picture what your office will look like?

Can you picture yourself in your uniform for the first time? Can you see yourself driving down the road in your patrol car?

If not, you should—at least in your mind. Why? Because if you claim something, you're often closer to making it happen.

Over the years, I have heard many similar stories from people who are very successful in their careers of choice. Was it that they knew what they wanted to do and focused on it more than others? Was it that they had a premonition and things just worked out? Were they just lucky? Were they more talented than others? Was it visualization? Or was it that a positive

⭐ The Inside Scoop

Before writing my first book, I mentioned to a number of people that I wanted to write a book and was looking for a publisher. Their response was always the same. "It is very difficult to get a publisher. It's very hard to write a book. Don't get your hopes up."

While my book wasn't yet written, I had already seen it in my mind. I knew what it would look like; I knew what it was going to say.

I had a plan and told everyone the same story. I was going to send out queries to publishers whose names started with A and go through the alphabet until I reached Z and knew I would find a publisher. The book would be a reality no matter what anyone thought.

By the time I got to the Fs, I had sold my book idea. I wasn't surprised, because I not only knew it would happen, I expected it. That first book, *Career Opportunities in the Music Industry*, is now in its fifth edition. Shortly after that, I sold other book ideas. The rest is history. Over 25 books later, my dream turned into reality.

attitude helped create a positive situation? No one really knows. The only thing that seems evident is that those who expect to be successful usually have a better chance of achieving it. Those who have a positive attitude usually have a better chance of positive things happening.

We've covered visualization earlier in the book. Whether you believe this theory or not, one thing is for sure: it can't hurt. So start planning your acceptance speech for becoming Police Officer of the Year. Start planning the party you are going to have when your book on crime prevention is published.

Plan on what you will say when you win the Pulitzer Prize for writing a book on finding a way to stop children abuse. Plan your own celebration for your promotion or for the career of which you've been dreaming. Plan for your own success, and then get ready for it to happen.

Creating a Career You Love

While working toward your perfect career, it's important to combine your goals with your life objectives. The trick to success in any industry is not only following your interests but following your heart. If you're working toward your dream, going that extra mile and doing that extra task won't be a chore.

And when you run into obstacles along the way, they won't be problems, just stepping-stones to get you where you're going.

By now, you have read some (if not all) of this book. You've learned that there are certain things you need to do to stack the deck in your favor no matter what segment of the law enforcement industry in which you aspire to work.

You know how to develop your resume and/or CV, captivating cover letters, career portfolios, business cards, and other tools. You know how to get past the gatekeeper. You know what to do in interviews…and what not to do.

You know how important it is to help develop a plan and you know how essential it is to have a good attitude.

You know that it is crucial to read everything before you sign it so you can protect yourself and you know how important good communications skills are no matter what segment of law enforcement you are pursuing.

You know about taking police exams, civil service exams, and other tests. You know a bit about what it's going to be like working in law enforcement and how you can increase your chances of success.

You've learned how to network and how to market yourself. You've learned some neat little tips and tricks to get your foot in the door. You've learned that you need to find ways to stand out from the crowd.

Most of all, you've learned that it's essential to create a career you love. You've learned that you don't ever want to settle and wonder "what if?"

Creating the career you want and love is not always the easiest thing in the world to accomplish, but it is definitely worth it. In order to help you focus in on what you want, you might find it helpful to create a personal mission statement.

Your Personal Mission Statement

There are many people who want a career in various areas of law enforcement. Some will make it and some will not. I want you to be the one who makes it. I want you to be the one who succeeds.

Throughout this book, I've tried to give you tips, tricks, and techniques that can help. I've tried to give you the inspiration and motivation to know you can do it. Here's one more thing which might make your journey easier.

Create your personal mission statement. Why? Because your mission statement can help you define your visions clearly. It will give you a path, a purpose, and something to follow. Most importantly, putting your mission statement in writing can help you bring your mission to fruition.

What's a mission statement? It's a statement declaring what your mission is in your life and your career. How do you do it? As with all the other exercises you've done, sit down, get comfortable, take out a pen and a piece of paper, and start writing. What is your mission? What do *you* want to accomplish in your career?

Remember that your mission statement is for *you*. You're not writing it for your family, your friends, or your employer. It can be changed or modified at any time.

Think about it for a moment. What do you want to do? Where do you want be? What's the path you want to take? What are your dreams? What is your mission?

There is no one right way to write your mission statement. Some people like to write it in paragraph form. Others like to use bullets or numbers. It really doesn't matter as long as you get it down in writing. The main thing to remember is to make your statement a clear and concise declaration of your long-term mission.

Your mission statement might be one sentence, one paragraph, or even fill two or three pages. It's totally up to you. As long as your mission statement is clear, you're okay.

Here are some examples of simple mission statements.

◎ Police officer
  ▫ My mission is to use my education, skills, training, and talent to become a police officer in my hometown.

I want to make a difference to the residents of my community and make it a safer place to live for everyone.

◎ DEA agent
  ▫ My mission is to use my education, training, skills, and talent to be a federal DEA agent. I want to be instrumental in helping stop the sale of illegal drugs. My ultimate goal is to help break up major drug cartel.

◎ Prosecutor
  ▫ My mission is to complete law school, pass the bar exam and become a successful prosecutor. One of my goals is to run for district attorney in my county and win becoming the youngest DA in the state.

◎ Prison warden
  ▫ It is my mission to become the warden of a federal penitentiary. I want to administer the facility creating a safe environment for both the convicted offenders and my staff. I also want to create programs that help decrease the recidivism of inmates. I eventually want to develop the program so that other prison facilities can use it as well. After I retire, I want to become a consultant to correctional facilities.

◎ Corrections officer
  ▫ My mission is to have a career as a corrections officer in a federal facility. I want to use my skills and training to provide a safe, secure, and humane environment for criminal offenders. I eventually want to move into a supervisory position within the facility.

◎ Forensic scientist
  ⊡ My mission is to become one of the most sought-out forensic scientists in the world. I want to be one everyone looks to when they have a big crime. I also want to write a book on my experiences which will be so interesting, it will become a best-seller.
◎ Court TV reporter
  ⊡ My mission is to use my education, skills, action, and passion to become a Court TV reporter. After obtaining some experience, I really want my own show! I also want to write a book—a best-seller on courtroom stories.

What do you do with your mission statement? Use it! Review it to remember what you're working toward. Use it as motivation. Use it to help you move in the right direction.

You would be surprised how many successful people have their personal mission statement hanging on their wall, taped to their computer, or in their pocket. I know individuals who keep a copy of their mission statement in their wallet; taped to their bathroom mirror; stuck on their computer monitor and placed in the inside of a desk drawer or in another location where they can regularly glance at it.

Wherever you decide to place your mission statement, be sure to look at it daily so you can always keep your mission in mind. It makes it easier to keep focused on your ultimate goal.

Success Strategies

We have discussed marketing, promotion, and publicity. Used effectively, they can help your career tremendously. Here's what you have to remember: Don't wait for someone else to recognize your skills, accomplishments, and talents; promote yourself. There are many keys to success. Self-promotion is an important one.

Don't toot your own horn in an annoying or obnoxious manner, but make sure people notice you. You want to stand out in a positive way. Don't keep your accomplishments a secret. Instead claim them proudly.

We've all been taught to be modest. "Don't boast," your mother might have said as you were growing up. But if your goal is success in your career, sometimes you can just be too quiet for your own good.

Your ultimate challenge is to create buzz. You need to create spin. You need others to know what you've done and what you're doing in the future. Some people aren't willing or able to do what it takes. If you want to succeed, it's imperative that you get started. Buzz doesn't usually happen overnight, but every day you wait is another day you're behind in the job.

Begin to think like a publicist. Whatever segment of law enforcement you're working in (unless you are an undercover officer or something similar), you need to constantly promote yourself or no one will know you exist. While others may help, the responsibility really is on *you* to make your career work and make your career successful.

No matter what segment of the industry you are in, or what level you are at, continue to look for opportunities of all kinds. Search out

---

⭐ **Tip from the Coach**
Put your personal mission statement on post-it notes and stick them up all around to help keep you focused.

The Inside Scoop

Don't procrastinate when an opportunity presents itself. Someone else is always on the lookout just like you and you don't want to miss your chance.

opportunities to move ahead in your career and then grab hold of them.

You need to be aware that in your life and career, on occasion, there may be doors that close. The trick here is not to let a door close without looking for the window of opportunity that is always there. If you see an opportunity, jump on it immediately. It is usually there just waiting for you!

Throughout the book we've discussed the importance of networking. Once you become successful, it's important to continue to network. Just because you landed a new job as a police officer doesn't mean you don't want to meet other law enforcement officers, police chiefs, federal agents, etc. Just because you just landed a job as a probation officer doesn't mean you don't want to meet other people in the industry. Just because you got a job in the business area of law enforcement doesn't mean you don't want to meet other executives in the industry. Just because you got a job as a crime reporter doesn't mean you shouldn't know other reporters, writers, editors, and publishers.

Once you've landed a new job, keep networking. Continue meeting people. Continue getting your name out there. You can never tell who knows who and what someone might need. There are always new opportunities ahead and if you don't keep networking, you might miss some of them. Keep nurturing your network and developing contacts. This is also true

as your career progresses. Keep on networking, meeting people, and making contacts. It is essential to the success of your career.

Don't be afraid to ask for help. If you know someone who can help you in your career, ask. The worst they can say is no. The best that can happen is you might get some assistance. Of course, if you can help someone else, do that as well.

Always be prepared for success. It might be just around the corner. Whatever segment of the industry you are pursuing, continue honing your skills. Keep taking classes, attending seminars, and going to workshops. If you want to move up the ladder and there are exams, prepare for them and then take them.

Law enforcement has changed over the years and continues to change and evolve. Keep up with the trends, read the trades, and make sure you know what is happening today.

Don't get caught into the thought pattern of "that's not how they did it in the old days." Get used to the idea that in our ever-changing world, there will be change. Instead of pushing it away or making believe it doesn't exist, embrace it. You might just come up with a better or more effective way to do things.

Stay as fit and healthy as you can. Try to eat right, get sleep, exercise, and take care of yourself. After all your hard work, you don't want to finally succeed and be too sick or tired to enjoy it.

Stay away from illegal drugs. Don't take them and don't hang around with people who take them. In the same vein, stay away from anyone who might be considered an unsavory character. You don't want anyone or anything hurting your career.

Whatever facet of the industry you are involved with, you are going to be selling yourself. You might be selling yourself to a hiring committee at a police department, or federal law enforcement agency or a human resources manager in a prison or other facility. You might be selling yourself to partners in a criminal law firm or the district attorney.

What else? You might be selling or *pitching* your story for publicity or a variety of other situations. Take a lesson from others who have made it to the top and prepare ahead of time. That way when you're in a situation where you need to say something, you'll be ready.

Sales skills are essential. Know that you are the best and know how to sell yourself the best way possible. Come up with a pitch and practice it until you're comfortable.

Always be positive. A good attitude is essential to your life and your professional success.

Tip from the Coach

They say it takes approximately 21 days to break one habit and form a new one. With that in mind, if there is any habit you have that bothers you, is detrimental to your career or any part of your life for that matter, know that you can not only change it, but do so fairly quickly. If for example, you find yourself speaking over others when they are talking, begin today by consciously making an effort to listen, then speak. You will find that if you continue to do that on a daily basis, soon it will become a habit.

Similarly, if you are told that you are negative at work, start today by consciously making an effort to be positive. Before you make a comment about something, stop, think about what you are saying, and try to put a positive spin on it. Continue doing this and a few weeks later, you will find that not only will your attitude be perceived more positively, it will be more positive.

Words from the Wise

Keep all professional conversations professional and positive. Don't complain. Don't whine. Don't be negative.

Here's the deal. We've discussed this before. People want to be around other people who are positive. If there is a choice between two people with similar talents and skills and you have a better outlook than anyone else, a more positive type of personality and passion, you're going to be chosen. You're going to get the job. You're going to succeed.

Change the way you look at situations and the situations you look at will change. What's that mean? If you look at a situation as a problem, it will be a problem. If, on the other hand, you look at a situation as an opportunity, it becomes one.

If all you see are the trials and tribulations of trying to succeed in your career in law enforcement, all you will have are trials and tribulations. If, on the other hand, you look at the road to success in this industry as a wonderful and exciting journey, it will be.

Keep Things Confidential

Privacy and confidentiality are crucial when working in most segments of law enforcement. What this means is that it is your responsibility to keep people's names and issues private and confidential when required.

Climbing the Career Ladder

Generally, whatever you want to do in life, you most likely are going to have to pay your dues. Whatever segment of law enforcement you've chosen to pursue, most likely you're going to have to *pay your dues* as well. Now that we've accepted that fact, the question is, how do you climb the career ladder? How do you succeed?

How do you go, for example, from a job as a rookie police officer to a seasoned detective? How do you move up to become a supervisor? How do you become a sergeant, a lieutenant, or even the chief of police?

How do you go from a position as a new special agent to the position of director of the department at an agency? How do you go from a job as an assistant director to the full-fledged director of a department?

How do you go from crime reporter for a local weekly paper to becoming a successful crime reporter for a major publication? How do you go from a position as a new forensic scientist to one who is sought out?

There are many things you're going to have to do to climb the career ladder, but it can be done. We've covered a lot of them. Work hard, keep a positive attitude, and act professionally at all times. Stay abreast of the business, network, and hone your skills and talents so you can backup your claims of accomplishments.

Look for a mentor who can help you move your career in the right direction and propel you to the top of your field. Join trade associations and the unions. Read the trades; attend seminars, classes and workshops; and take part in other learning opportunities. Continue your education when you can. Be the best at what you do. Keep your goal in mind.

Look at every opportunity with an open mind. When you're offered something, ask yourself:

◎ Is this what I want to be doing?
◎ Is this part of my dream?
◎ Is this part of my plan for success?

◎ Is this opportunity a stepping-stone to advancing my career?
◎ Will this experience be valuable to me?

Fortunately or unfortunately, job progression doesn't always follow the normal career path. A police officer who is newer on the job than another may get the promotion because he or she has done better on an exam, or even because of politics. An unknown author may get a mention on *Oprah* about his book on some aspect of crime prevention and be catapulted to a best-seller and tremendous success. A special agent may crack a big case and get a promotion before someone else who has seniority. It all depends. If success can happen to someone else, it might happen to you. That is one of the greatest things about your career. You just never know what tomorrow might bring.

You never know when a chance meeting is going to land you a great job or someone passing through town might see read about one of your accomplishments in a local newspaper and recruit you for a position in a larger or more prestigious school or situation. You never know who will tell a headhunter, recruiter, or human resources director about you and you will get a call. You really never know when success will come your way. It can happen at any time.

It should be noted that success means different things to different people. There are many people who work in law enforcement who work in a local town department; a small public defenders office, or as a crime reporter for a local weekly. There are many people in law enforcement who never become sergeants or lieutenants, or the chief of police. They never become the sheriff or the district attorney. There are many who never become the director of the department. Yet these people are all still successful. They are earning a living, doing what they love, living their dream and helping others live theirs as well.

And it's like that in all segments of law enforcement. There are thousands of individuals working in law enforcement and the peripheral fields who may not be the ones you hear of, might not be the ones winning the awards, but they are successful just the same. That doesn't preclude them from having a successful career. To the contrary, one of the best things about working in law enforcement is that almost every job has some sort of an impact on others. Every job can make a difference, even if it's just a little one. And that little difference can make a big difference in the lives of others.

Risk Taking—Overcoming Your Fears

Everyone has a comfort zone from which they operate. What's a comfort zone? It's the area where you feel comfortable both physically and psychologically. Most of the time, you try to stay within this zone. It's predictable, it's safe, and you generally know what's coming.

Many people get jobs, stay in them for years, and then retire. They know what's expected of them. They know what they're going to be doing. They know what they're going to be getting. The problem is that it can get boring, there's little challenge, and your creativity can suffer.

> **Tip from the Top**
> Try to treat everyone from subordinates to superiors to colleagues to other people you run into in the course of your workday the way you want to be treated—with respect and dignity.

> **Tip from the Coach**
> If you're starting to feel comfortable in your career or starting to feel bored, it's time to step out of your comfort zone and look for new challenges.

Stepping out of your comfort zone is especially important to your career. Wanting to step out of your comfort zone is often easier said than done, but every now and then you're going to have to push yourself.

The key to career success in the law enforcement as well as your own personal growth is the willingness to step outside of your comfort zone. Throughout your career you're going to be faced with decisions. Each decision can impact your career. Be willing to take risks. Be willing to step out of your comfort zone.

Is it scary? Of course, but if you don't take risks you stand the chance of your career stagnating. You take the chance of missing wonderful opportunities.

Should you take a promotion? Should you stay at the same job? Should you go to a different department? Should you move from a local agency to a federal law enforcement agency? Should you go back to school? Should you move? Should you take a chance?

How do you make the right decision? Try to think about the pros and cons of your choices. Get the facts, think about them, and make your decision.

"What if I'm wrong?" you ask.

Here's the good news. Usually, you *will* make the right decision. If by chance you don't, it's generally not a life-and-death situation. If you stay at the same job and find you should have left, for example, all you need to do is look for a new job. If you change jobs and you're not happy, you can usually find a new job as well. Most things ultimately work out. Do the best you can and then go on.

If your career is stagnant, do something. Don't just stay where you are because of the fear of leaving your comfort zone and the fear of the unknown.

Some Final Thoughts

No matter where you are in your career, don't get stagnant. Always keep your career moving. Once you reach one of your goals, your journey isn't over. You have to set new goals and move on to reach them.

Keep working toward your goal. It can happen. Don't settle for less than what you want. Every goal you meet is another stepping-stone toward an even better career, no matter what segment of the industry you are pursuing.

While I would love to promise you that after reading this book you will become police officer of the year, your state's commissioner of corrections, the head of the probation department, a partner in a prestigious criminal law firm, a sought-after forensic scientist, the director of your department, or win the Nobel Peace Prize for discovering an effective way to stop illegal drug use, unfortunately I can't.

What I can tell you is that the advice in this book can help you move ahead and stack the deck in your favor in this industry. I've given you the information. You have to put it into action.

There are numerous factors that are essential to your success. You need to be prepared. There's no question that preparation is neces-

> **Words from the Wise**
>
> Persevere. The reason most people fail is because they gave up one day too soon.
> —Shelly Field

sary. Talent in your field is critical as well. Being in the right place at the right time is essential, and good luck doesn't hurt. Perseverance is vital to success, no matter what you want to do, what area of the industry you want to enter, and what career level you want to achieve.

Do you want to know why most people don't find their perfect job? It's because they gave up looking *before* they found it. Do you want to know why some people are on the brink of success yet never really get there? It's because they gave up.

Do you want to know what single factor can increase your chances of success? It's perseverance! Don't give up.

Have fun reading this book. Use it to jumpstart your career and inspire you to greater success and accomplishments. Draw on it to achieve your goals so you can have the career of your dreams. Use it so you don't have to look back and say, "I wish I had." Use it instead so you can say, "I'm glad I did."

I can't wait to hear about your success stories. Be sure to let us know how this book has helped your career by logging on to http://www.shellyfield.com. I would also love to hear about any of your own tips or techniques for succeeding in any aspect of law enforcement. You can never tell. Your successes might be part of our next edition.

APPENDIX I

PROFESSIONAL ASSOCIATIONS, UNIONS, AND OTHER ORGANIZATIONS

Professional associations, unions, and other organizations can be valuable resources for career guidance as well as professional support. This listing includes many of the organizations related to law enforcement. Names, addresses, phone numbers, fax numbers, e-mail addresses, and Web sites (when available) have been included to make it easier for you to obtain information. Check out the Web sites to learn more about organizations and what they offer.

Airborne Law Enforcement Association (ALEA)

411 Aviation Way
Frederick, MD 21701
(301) 631-2406
(301) 631-2466 (fax)
singley@alea.org
http://www.alea.org

American Academy of Forensic Sciences (AAFS)

410 North 21st Street
Colorado Springs, CO 80904
(719) 636-1100
(719) 636-1993

awarren@aafs.org
http://www.aafs.org

American Association For Correctional and Forensic Psychology (AACFP)

c/o Terre Marshall, Treasurer
PO Box 7642
Wilmington, NC 28403
(805) 489-0665
pres@eaacp.org
http://www.aa4cfp.org

American Association of Police Polygraphists (AAPP)

PO Box 657
Waynesville, OH 45068
(888) 743-5479
(937) 488-1046 (fax)
nom@policepolygraph.org
http://www.policepolygraph.org

American Association of State Troopers (AAST)

1949 Raymond Diehl Road
Tallahassee, FL 32308
(850) 385-7904

(850) 385-8697 (fax)
alpasini@statetroopers.org
http://www.statetroppers.org

American Bar Association (ABA)

321 North Clark Street
Chicago, IL 60610
(312)988-5000
(312)988-5177 (fax)
service@abanet.org
http://www.abanet.org

American Correctional Association (ACA)

206 North Washington Street
Alexandria, VA 22314
(703) 224-0000
http://www.aca.org

American Deputy Sheriffs' Association (ADSA)

3001 Armand Street
Monroe, LA 71201
(800) 937-7940
(318) 398-9980 (fax)
adsa@deputysheriff.org
http://www.deputysheriff.org

American Federation of Government Employees AFL-CIO

80 F Street NW
Washington, DC 20001
(202) 737-8700
(202) 639-6441 (fax)
comments@afge.org
http://www.afge.org

American Federation of Police and Concerned Citizens

6350 Horizon Drive
Titusville, FL 32780
(321) 264-0911

(321) 264-0033 (fax)
dshepherd@aphf.org
http://www.aphf.org

American Federation of Security Officers

4311 Wilshire Boulevard
Los Angeles, CA 90028
(323) 461-3441
(323) 462-8340 (fax)
helpdesk@visualnet.com
http://americanfederationofsecurityofficers.
visualnet.com

American Jail Association (AJA)

1135 Professional Court
Hagerstown, MD 21740
(301) 790-3930
(301) 790-2941 (fax)
stevei@aja.org
http://www.aja.org

American Judges Association (AJA)

300 Newport Avenue
Williamsburg, VA 23185
(757) 259-1841
(757) 259-1520 (fax)
aja@ncsc.dni.us
http://aja.ncsc.dni.us

American Polygraph Association (APA)

PO Box 8037
Chattanooga, TN 37414
(423) 892-3992
(423)894-5435 (fax)
manager@polygraph.org
http://www.polygraph.org

American Probation and Parole Association (APPA)

2760 Research Park Drive
Lexington, KY 40511

(859) 244-8203
(859) 244-8001 (fax)
appa@csg.org
http://www.appa-net.org

American Society of Criminology (ASC)

1314 Kinnear Road
Columbus, OH 43212
(614) 292-9207
(614) 292-6767 (fax)
asc41@infinet.com
http;//www.asc41.com

American Society of Law Enforcement Training (ASLET)

7611-B Willow Road
Frederick, MD 21702
(301) 668-9466
(301) 668-9482 (fax)
info@aslet.org
http://aslet.org

ASIS International

1625 Prince Street
Alexandria, VA 22314
(703) 519-6200
(703) 519-6299 (fax)
asis@asisonline.org
http://www.asisonline.org

Association for Crime Scene Reconstruction (ACSR)

PO Box 51376
Phoenix, AZ 85076
(602) 534-9280
brucemwiley@yahoo.com
http://www.acsr.org

Association of Certified Fraud Examiners (ACFE)

The Gregor Building
716 West Avenue

Austin, TX 78701
(512)478-9000
(512) 478-9297 (fax)
info@cfenet.com
http://www.acfe.com/home.asp

Association of Former Agents of the U.S. Secret Service (AFAUSSS)

525 SW 5th Street
Des Moines, IA 50309
(515) 282-8192
(515) 282-9117 (fax)
afausss@assoc-mgmt.com
http://www.oldstar.org

Association of National Park Rangers

PO Box 108
Larned, KS 67550
(316) 285-2107
anprbusiness@anpr.org
http://www.anpr.org

Computer Security Institute (CSI)

600 Harrison Street
San Francisco, CA 94107
(415) 947-6320
(818) 487-4550 (fax)
csi@cmp.com
http://www.gocsi.com

Federal Administrative Law Judges Conference (FALJC)

2000 Pennsylvania Avenue NW
Washington, DC 20006
(202) 675-3065
wood.pamela@dol.gov
http://www.faljc.org

Federal Bureau of Investigation Agents Association (FBIAA)

PO Box 250
New Rochelle, NY 10801

(914) 235-7580
(914) 235-8235 (fax)
fbiaa@fbiaa.org
http://www.fbiaa.org

Federal Criminal Investigators Association (FCIA)

PO Box 23400
Washington, DC 20026
(703) 426-8100
(800) 528-3492 (fax)
info@fedcia.org
http://www.fedcia.org

Federal Law Enforcement Officers Association (FLEOA)

PO Box 326
Lewisberry, PA 17339
(717) 938-2300
(717) 932-2262 (fax)
fleoa@fleoa.org
http://www.fleoa.org

Fraternal Order of Police (FOP)

1410 Donelson Pike
Nashville, TN 37217
(615) 399-0900
(615) 399-0400 (fax)
nationalsecretary@grandlodgefop.org
http://www.grandlodgefop.org

High Technology Crime Investigation Association (HTCIA)

4021 Woodcreek Oaks Boulevard
PMB 209
Roseville, CA 95747
(916) 408-1751
(916) 408-7543 (fax)
exec_secty@htcia.org
http://www.htcia.org

Information Systems Security Association (ISSA)

7044 S 13th Street
Oak Creek, WI 53154
(414) 908-4949
(414) 768-8001 (fax)
customercare@issa.org
http://www.issa.org

International Association of Airport and Seaport Police (IAASP)

c/o Mike Toddington, Executive Director
111, B3-1410 Parkway Boulevard
Coquitlam, BC, Canada V3E 3J7
(604) 782-6386
(604) 945-6134 (fax)
derik@toddington.com
http://www.iaasp.net

International Association of Arson Investigators (IAAI)

12770 Boenker Road
Bridgeton, MO 63044
(314) 739-4224
(314) 739-4219 (fax)
wlemire@foleymansfield.com
http://www.firearson.com

International Association of Bomb Technician and Investigators (IABTI)

PO Box 160
Goldvein, VA 22720
(540) 752-4533
(540) 752-2796 (fax)
admin@iabti.org
http://www.iabti.org

International Association of Chiefs of Police

515 N Washington Street
Alexandria, VA 22314
(703) 836-6767

(703) 836-4543 (fax)

http://www.theiacp.org

International Association of Crime Analysts (IACA)

9218 Metcalf Avenue

Overland Park, KS 66212

(800) 609-3419

iaca@iaca.net

http://www.iaca.net

International Association of Financial Crimes Investigators (IAFCI)

873 Embarcadero Drive

El Dorado Hills, CA 95762

(916) 939-5000

(916) 939-0395 (fax)

admin@iafci.org

http://www.iefci.org

International Association of Professional Security Consultants (IAPSC)

c/o Norma S. Fox, Executive Director

525 SW 5th Street

Des Moines, IA 50309

(515) 282-8192

(515) 282-9117 (fax)

iapsc@iapsc.org

http://www.iapsc.org

International Association of Undercover Officers (IAUO)

142 Banks Drive

Brunswick, GA 31523

(800) 876-5943

(800) 876-5912 (fax)

http://www.undercover.org

International Association of Women Police

c/o Terrie S Swann

PO Box 1762

Tulsa, OK 74101

(918) 581-7738

(918) 357-4297 (fax)

terrieswann@aol.com

International Brotherhood of Police Officers (IBPO)

159 Burgin Parkway

Quincy, MA 02169

(617) 376-0220

(617) 376-0285 (fax)

jflynn@nage.org

http://www.ibpo.org

International Conference of Police Chaplains (ICPC)

PO Box 5590

Destin, FL 32540

(850) 654-9736

(850) 654-9742 (fax)

icpc@icpc.gccoxmail.com

http://www.icpc4cops.org

International Guards Union of America (IGUA)

Route 8, Box 32-14

Amarillo, TX 79118

(806) 622-2424

(806) 622-3500 (fax)

igua@amaonline.com

http://www.amaonline.com/igua

International Homicide Investigators Association (IHIA)

10711 Spotsylvania Avenue

Fredericksburg, VA 22408

(877) 843-4442

(540) 898-5594 (fax)

ihia@adelphia.net

http://www.ihia.org

International Union of Police Associations (IUPA)

1549 Ringling Boulevard

Sarasota, FL 34236

(941) 487-2560

(941) 487-2570 (fax)

iupa@iupa.org

http://www.iupa.org

International Union of Security Officers (IUSO)

2201 Broadway Street

Oakland, CA 94612

(510) 625-9913

(510) 625-0998 (fax)

seiulocal247@hotmail.com

http://www.seiu247.org

Law Enforcement Alliance of America (LEAA)

5538 Port Royal Road

Springfield, VA 22151

(703) 847-2677

(703) 556-6485 (fax)

membership@leaa.org

http://www.leaa.org

National Alliance of Gang Investigators Associations (NAGIA)

c/o Sergeant Larry Rael, Sacramento County Sheriff's Department

9250 Bond Road

Elk Grove, CA 95624

(916) 875-0443

(916) 875-0407 (fax)

lrael@sacsheriff.com

http://www.nagia.org

National Alliance of Police, Security and Corrections Organizations (NAPSCO)

25510 Kelly Road

Roseville, MI 48066

http://www.napsco.org

National Association of Chiefs of Police (NACOP)

6350 Horizon Drive

Titusville, FL 32780

(321) 264-0911

(321) 264-0033 (fax)

policeinfo@aphf.org

http://www.aphf.org

National Association of Crime Commissions (NACC)

c/o Mr. Bobby Stout, Treas.

Wichita Crime Commission

125 N Market

Wichita, KS 67202

(316) 267-1235

(316) 263-0011 (fax)

bs@wichitacrimecommission.org

http://www.crimecom.org/naccc

National Association of Drug Diversion Investigators (NADDI)

PO Box 611

Manchester, MD 21102

(443) 398-6257 (fax)

ccichon@naddi.org

http://www.naddi.org

National Association of Medical Examiners (NAME)

430 Pryor Street SW

Atlanta, GA 30312

(404) 730-4781

(404) 730-4420 (fax)

denise.mcnally@thename.org

http://www.thename.org

National Association of Police Athletic Leagues

618 N US Highway 1

North Palm Beach, FL 33408

(561) 844-1823

(561) 863-6120 (fax)

copnkid@nationalpal.org

http://www.nationalpal.org

National Association of Police Organizations (NAPO)

750 1st Street NW

Washington, DC 20002

(202) 842-4420

(202) 842-4396 (fax)

info@napo.org

http://www.napo.org

National Association of School Resource Officers (NASRO)

1951 Woodlane Drive

St. Paul, MN 55125

(651) 209-3153

(651) 457-5665 (fax)

kevin.campana@nasro.org

http://www.nasro.org

National Association of Special Police and Security Officers (NASPSO)

1101 30th Street NW

Washington, DC 20007

(202) 625-8306

(202) 582-6006 (fax)

naspso@aol.com

National Association of Women Law Enforcement Executives (NAWLEE)

3 Dunham Street

Carver, MA 02330

(781) 789-9500

(508) 866-8707 (fax)

info@nawlee.com

http://www.nawlee.com

National Black Police Association (NBPA)

3251 Mt. Pleasant Street NW

Washington, DC 20010

(202) 986-2070

(202) 986-0410 (fax)

nbpanatofc@worldnet.att.net

http://www.blackpolice.org

National Black State Troopers Coalition (NBSTC)

c/o Kim Hoffman-Davis, Treasurer

PO Box 2661

Joliet, IL 60434

National Border Patrol Council (NBPC)

PO Box 678

Campo, CA 91906

(619) 478-5145

nbpc-info@nbpc.net

http://www.nbpc.net

National Center for Women and Policing (NCWP)

433 S Beverly Drive

Beverly Hills, CA 90212

(310) 556-2526

(310) 556-2509 (fax)

womencops@feminist.org

http://www.womenandpolicing.org

National Council of Juvenile and Family Court Judges (NCJFCJ)

PO Box 8970

Reno, NV 89507

(775) 784-6012

(775) 784-6628 (fax)
staff@ncjfcj.org
http://www.ncjfcj.org

National Council on Crime and Delinquency (NCCD)

1970 Broadway
Oakland, CA 94612
(510) 208-0500
(510) 208-0511 (fax)
aboldon@mw.nccd-crc.org
http://www.nccd-crc.org

National Crime Prevention Council (NCPC)

1000 Connecticut Avenue NW
Washington, DC 20036
(202) 466-6272
(202) 296-1356 (fax)
webmaster@ncpc.org
http://www.ncpc.org

National Defender Investigator Association (NDIA)

460 Smith Street
Middletown, CT 06457
(860) 635-5533
(860) 613-1650 (fax)
ndia@cox.net
http://www.ndia.net

National Drug Enforcement Officers Association (NDEOA)

Office of Training/TRDS
FBI Academy
PO Box 1475
Quantico, VA 22134
(202) 298-9653
paul.stevens@state.mn.us
http://www.ndeoa.org

National Fire Protection Association (NFPA)

1 Batterymarch Pike
Quincy, MA 02169
(617) 770-3000
(617) 770-0700 (fax)
nfpajournal@nfpa.org
http://www.nfpa.org

National Latino Peace Officers Association (NLPOA)

PO Box 1717
Las Vegas, NV 89125
(702) 355-8704
(702) 388-6082 (fax)
nlpoanv@yahoo.com
http://www.nlpoa.org

National Law Enforcement Council (NLEC)

1620 Eye Street NW
Washington, DC 20006
(202) 331-1275
(202) 785-8949 (fax)

National Narcotic Detector Dog Association (NNDDA)

379 CR 105
Carthage, TX 75633
(888) 289-0070
thenndda@yahoo.com
http://www.nndda.org

National Native American Law Enforcement Association (NNLEA)

PO Box 171
Washington, DC 20044
(800) 948-3863
info@nnalea.org
http://www.nnalea.org

National Organization of Black Law Enforcement Executives (NOBLE)

4609 Pinecrest Office Park Drive
Alexandria, VA 22312
(703) 658-1529
(703) 658-9479 (fax)
jlee@noblenational.net
http://www.noblenational.org

National Police Officers Association of America (NPOAA)

c/o National Police and Security Officers Association of America
PO Box 663
South Plainfield, NJ 07080
(908) 226-8715
(908) 226-8715 (fax)
npsoaa@aol.com
http://npoaa.tripod.com

National Sheriffs' Association (NSA)

1450 Duke Street
Alexandria, VA 22314
(703) 836-7827
(703) 838-5349 (fax)
nsamail@sheriffs.org
http://www.sheriffs.org

National Tactical Officers Association (NTOA)

PO Box 797
Doylestown, PA 18901
(800) 279-9127
(646) 485-1182 (fax)
membership@ntoa.org
http://www.ntoa.org

National Treasury Employees Union

1750 H Street, NW
Washington, DC 20006
(202) 572-5500

(202) 572-5641 (fax)
nteu-pr@nteu.org
http://www.nteu.org

North American Police Work Dog Association (NAPWDA)

c/o Jim Watson, National Secretary
4222 Manchester Avenue
Perry, OH 44081
(440) 259-3169
(440) 259-3170 (fax)
napwda@napwda.com
http://www.napwda.com

North American Wildlife Enforcement Officers Association (NAWEOA)

c/o Steve Kleiner, Secretary/Treasurer
PO Box 22
Hollidaysburg, PA 16648
(801) 942-9432
(206) 201-6953 (fax)
naweoa@ureach.com
http://www.naweoa.org

Park Law Enforcement Association (PLEA)

c/o Steve Newsom, President
Hamilton County Park District
10245 Winton Road
Cincinnati, OH 45231
(513) 521-3980
snewsom@greatparks.org
http://www.parkranger.com

Police Association for College Education (PACE)

63 Lake Forest Drive
Mineral, VA 23117
(540) 894-8781
(540) 894-8782 (fax)

loumayo@police-association.org
http://www.police-association.org

Police Foundation
1201 Connecticut Avenue NW
Washington, DC 20036
(202) 833-1460
(202) 659-9149 (fax)
pfinfo@policefoundation.org
http://www.policefoundation.org

Police Officer Standards and Training Council
Law Enforcement Resource Center
285 Preston Avenue
Meriden, CT 06450
(203) 238-6531
(203) 238-6643 (fax)
Gerald.Seagrave@po.state.ct.us
http://www.post.state.ct.us

Society of Former Special Agents of the Federal Bureau of Investigation (SFSAFBI)
PO Box 1027
Quantico, VA 22134
(703) 640-6469
(703) 640-6537
socxfbi@socxfbi.org
http://www.socxfbi.org

Society of Professional Investigators (SPI)
PO Box 1128
Bellmore, NY 11710
(516) 781-5100
(516) 783-0000 (fax)
info@spionline.org
http://www.spionline.org

United Armed Guards of America
c/o John Keeley
305 Milburn Avenue
Lyndhurst, NJ 07071
(201) 531-9157

United States Police Canine Association (USPCA)
c/o Russell Hess, National Executive Director
PO Box 80
Springboro, OH 45066
(800) 531-1614
uspcadir@aol.com
http://www.uspcak9.com

Women Peace Officers Association (WPOA)
7355 Dayton Avenue
Hesperia, CA 92345
(760) 947-6005
info@wpoaca.com
http://www.wpoaca.com

APPENDIX II

CAREER WEB SITES

The Internet is a premier resource for information, no matter what you need. Surfing the net can help you locate almost anything you want, from information to services and everything in between.

Throughout the appendices of this book, whenever possible, Web site addresses have been included to help you find information quicker. This listing contains an assortment of Web sites related to law enforcement. Use this list as a start. More sites are emerging every day. This listing is for your information. The author is not responsible for any site content. Inclusion or exclusion in this listing does not imply that any one site is endorsed or recommended over another by the author.

American Bar Association
http://www.abanet.org/careercounsel/jobs.html

American Bar Association Career Council
http://www.abanet.org/careercounsel/archive.
html#pracarea

American Correctional Association
http://www.aca.org/jobs/results.asp?union=AND
&viewby=50&startrec=1

Americas Job Bank
http://www.americasjobbank.com

Bureau of Alcohol, Tobacco, Firearms and Explosives
http://www.atf.gov/jobs/index.htm

Careerbuilder.com
http://www.careerbuilder.com

Career One Stop
http://www.jobbankinfo.org

Central Intelligence Agency (CIA)
https://www.cia.gov/careers/index.html

Copcareer.com
http://www.copcareer.com

Correction Connection Network
http://www.corrections.com/networks/careers

Corrections Corporation of America
http://www.correctionscorp.com/careers.html

Drug Enforcement Administration
http://www.usdoj.gov/dea/index.htm

Drug Enforcement Administration Jobs
http://www.usdoj.gov/dea/resources/job_
applicants.html

Federal Bureau of Investigation
http://www.fbi.gov

Federal Bureau of Investigation Careers
http://www.fbijobs.gov

Federal Bureau of Prisons
http://www.bop.gov/jobs/index.jsp

HotJobs.com
http://www.hotjobs.com

International Bodyguard Network
http://www.samurai-warrior.com

JobCop.com
http://www.jobcop.com

Lawenforcementjobs.com
http://www.lawenforcementjobs.com

Loss Prevention World
http://www.hotlpjobs.com

Monster.com
http://www.monster.com

National Park Service Employment Information
http://www.nps.gov/personnel

911hotjob.com
http://www.911hotjobs.com

Paralegaljobs.com
http://www.paralegaljobs.com/plj/jobseekers_
hp.shtml

PoliceEmployment.com
http://www.policeemployment.com

Policejobs.com
http://www.policejobs.com

Policejobsinfo.com
http://www.policejobsinfo.com

Policeone.com
http://www.policeone.com/careers

Los Angeles County Sheriff's Department
http://www.lasd.org

Loss Prevention World
http://www.hotlpjobs.com/lpworld/loss-
prevention-jobs

New York State Trooper Recruitment
http://www.nytrooper.com

Officer.com
http://www.officer.com

PoliceOne.com
http://www.policeone.com/careers

Professionalprotectiongroup.com
http://www.professionalprotection.com

USA Jobs
http://jobsearch.usajobs.opm.gov/dhscareers

U.S. Department of Justice
http://www.usdoj.gov

U.S. Department of Justice Jobs
http://www.usdoj.gov/06employment/06_1.html

U.S. Immigration and Customs

http://www.uscis.gov/portal/site/uscis

U.S. Internal Revenue Service

http://www.irs.ustreas.gov

U.S. Internal Revenue Service Careers

http://jobs.irs.gov/home.html

U.S. Marshals Service

http://www.usmarshals.gov/careers/index.html

U.S. Secret Service

http://www.ustreas.gov/usss

U.S. Secret Service Employment Opportunities

http://www.ustreas.gov/usss/opportunities.shtml

BIBLIOGRAPHY

A. Books

There are thousands of books on all aspects of law enforcement. Sometimes just reading about someone else's success, inspires you, motivates you, or just helps you to come up with ideas to help you attain your own dreams.

Books can be a treasure trove of information if you want to learn about a particular aspect of a career or gain more knowledge about how something in the industry works.

The books listed below are separated into general categories. Subjects often overlap. Use this listing as a beginning. Check out your local library, bookstore, or online retailer for other books that might interest you about the industry.

Bail Bondsman

Verrochi, Richard. How *to Start a Bail Bond Business and Become a Bail Bondsman.* Amherst, NH: Richard Verrochi, 2006.

Bounty Hunting

Chapman, Duane. You *Can Run but You Can't Hide: The Life and Times of Dog the Bounty Hunter.* New York: Hyperion Press, 2007.

BodyGuard

Thompson, Leroy. *Bodyguard Manual.* London: Greenhill Books/Lionel Leventhal, Limited, 2006.

Weaver, Alf. *Alf Weaver: First Rock 'n' Roll Bodyguard.* Sanctuary Publishing, London: Limited, 2003.

Wilson, Leah. *Perfectly Plum: On the Life, Loves and Other Disasters of Stephanie Plum, Trenton Bounty Hunter.* Dallas, TX: BenBella Books, 2007.

CIA

Central Intelligence Agency. *CIA Factbook 2006.* Charleston, SC: BiblioBazaar, 2006.

Tenet, George. *At the Center of the Storm: My Years at the CIA.* New York: Harper Collins, 2007.

Waters, T. J. *Class 11: My Story Inside the CIA's First Post-9/11 Spy Class.* New York: Penguin Group (USA) Incorporated, 2007.

Zegart, A. *Spying Blind: The CIA, the FBI, and the Origins of 9/11.* Princeton: Princeton University Press, 2007.

Community Police

Hess, Karen M. *Community Policing: Partnerships for Problem Solving.* Belmont, CA: Thomson Wadsworth, 2007.

Williamson, Tom. *The Handbook of Knowledge Based Policing: Current Conceptions and Future Directions.* Hoboken, NJ: John Wiley & Sons, Incorporated, 2008.

Computer/Data Security

Petkovic, Milan. *Security, Privacy and Trust in Modern Data Management.* New York: Springer, 2007.

Salomon, David. *Foundations of Computer Security.* New York: Springer, 2005.

Waldo, James. *Engaging Privacy and Information Technology in a Digital Age.* Washington, DC: National Academies Press, 2007.

Corporate Security

Halibozek, Edward P. *The Corporate Security Professional's Handbook on Terrorism.* San Diego, CA: Butterworth-Heinemann, 2007.

Courtroom

Edelin, Kenneth C. Broken Justice: A *True Story of Race, Sex and Revenge in a Boston Courtroom.* Sarasota, FL: PondView Press, 2007.

Gianna, Dominic J. *Reel Justice!: Power Passion and Persuasion in the Modern Courtroom.* Minnetonka, MN: Professional Education Group, Incorporated, 2002.

Goode, Steven. *Courtroom Evidence Handbook, 2007-2008.* Student Edition. Eagan, MN: Thomson West, 2007.

Detectives

Jackall, Robert. *Street Stories: The World of Police Detectives.* Cambridge, Mass: Harvard University Press, 2005.

Pinkerton, Allan. *Thirty Years a Detective.* Warwick, NY: 1500 Books, 2007.

District Attorney

Train, Arthur. *True Stories of Crime from the District Attorney's Office.* Cambridge, MA: IndyPublish.com, 2007.

Exam Help

Connor, Paul. *Blackstone's Police Sergeant's Mock Exam.* New York: Oxford University Press, Incorporated, 2006.

Holtz, Larry E. and Paprota, David. *Promotional Exam Preparation for Law Enforcement.* Miamisburg, OH: LexisNexis, 2006.

Learning Express Staff. *Police Officer Exam: The Complete Preparation Guide.* New York: Learning Express, 2007.

Learning Express Staff. *Probation Officer/Parole Officer Exam.* New York: Learning Express, 2007.

Learning Express Staff. *State Trooper Exam.* New York: Learning Express, 2007.

Schroeder, Donald J. *Police Officer Exam.* Hauppauge, NY: Barron's Educational Series, Incorporated, 2005.

Schroeder, Donald J. *Court Officer Exam: Including Bailiff, Sheriff, Marshall, Courtroom Attendant, and Courtroom Deputy.* Hauppauge, NY: Barron's Educational Series, 2004.

Thomson/Arco Staff. *Mastering the Probation Officer/Parole Officer Exam.* Lawrenceville, NJ: Peterson's, 2006.

FBI

Batvinis, Raymond J. *The Origins of FBI Counterintelligence.* Lawrence, KS: University Press of Kansas, 2007.

Burrough, Bryan. *Public Enemies: America's Greatest Crime Wave and the Birth of the FBI, 1933-34.* Darby, PA: Dianne Publishing Company, 2007.

Charles, Douglas M. *Edgar Hoover and the Anti-Interventionists: FBI Political Surveillance and the Rise of the Domestic Security State, 1939–1945.* Columbus, OH: Ohio State University Press, 2007.

Freeh, Louis J. *My FBI: Bringing Down the Mafia, Investigating Bill Clinton, and Fighting the War on Terror.* New York: Saint Martin's Press, 2006.

Hack, Richard. *Puppetmaster: The Secret Life of J. Edgar Hoover.* Beverly Hills, CA: Phoenix Books, 2007.

Herzberg, Bob. *The FBI and the Movies: A History of the Bureau on Screen and Behind the Scenes in Hollywood*. Jefferson, NC: McFarland & Company, 2006.

Jeffreys-Jones, Rhodri. *The FBI: A Short History*. New Haven, CT: Yale University Press, 2007.

Kennedy, Weldon L. *On-Scene Commander: From Street Agent to Deputy Director of the FBI*. Dulles, VA: Potomac Books, Incorporated, 2007.

Theoharis, Athan G. *The FBI: A Comprehensive Reference Guide*. Darby, PA: Diane Publishing Company, 2006.

Turchie, Terry, and Kathleen Pucket. *Hunting the American Terrorist: The FBI's War on Homegrown Terror*. Palisades, NY: History Publishing Company, LLC, 2007.

Van Zandt, Clinton. *Facing Down Evil: Life on the Edge As an FBI Hostage Negotiator*. East Rutherford, NJ: Penguin Group (USA) Incorporated, 2007.

Forensics

Martin, Tom. *Crime Scene Forensics Handbook: Police Officer Patrol Edition*. Fresh Meadows, NY: Looseleaf Law Publications, Incorporated, 2007.

Gangs

Schmidt, Linda M. and O'Reilly, James, T. *Gangs and Law Enforcement: A Guide for Dealing with Gang-Related Violence*. Springfield, IL: Charles C. Thomas Publisher, Limited, 2007.

Investigations

Angell, M L. *The Muscle Car Mystery: From the Case Files of Private Investigator James Mitchell*. Frederick, MD: PublishAmerica, Incorporated, 2007.

Askew, Mike. *Secrets of Top Private Eyes: Professional Investigator's Course*. Murphy, ORE, 1993.

Guerin, Lisa. *The Essential Guide to Workplace Investigations*. Berkeley, CA: NOLO, 2007.

Jetmore, Larry F. *Path of the Hunter: Entering and Excelling in the Field of Criminal Investigation*. Flushing, NY: Looseleaf Law Publications, Incorporated, 2007.

MacDonald, Ross. *The Archer Files: The Complete Short Stories of Lew Archer, Private Investigator, Including Newly Discovered Case Notes*. Norfolk, VA: Crippen & Landru, Publishers, 2007.

Sampson, Fraser and Hutton, Glenn. *Blackstone's Police Investigators' Manual*. New York: Oxford University Press, Incorporated, 2006.

Parole/Probation

Champion, Dean J. *Probation, Parole and Community Corrections*. East Rutherford, NJ: Prentice Hall PTR, 2007.

Cromwell, Paul F. *Community Based Corrections*. Belmont, CA: Thomson Wadsworth, 2007.

Padfield, Nicola. *Who to Release? Parole, Fairness and Criminal Justice*. Devon, UK: Willan Publishing, 2007.

Police/Law Enforcement

Adams, Blakeney. *A Cop's Life: Stories of a Police Officer's Law Enforcement Career* Book I. Frederick, MD: PublishAmerica, Incorporated, 2007.

Aitchison, Will. *The Rights of Law Enforcement Officers*. Portland, ORE: Labor Relations Information System, 2005.

Brockman, Elizabeth. *The Blue Guide: Written Communication for Leaders in Law Enforcement*. Boston: Allyn & Bacon, Incorporated, 2007.

Brown, Robert P., and Olson, Steven, P. *Some Gave All: A History of Baltimore Police Officers Killed in the Line of Duty 1808-2007*. Baltimore: Chesapeake Book Company, 2007.

Cain, Michael J. *The Tangled Web: The Life and Death of Richard Cain—Chicago Cop and Mafia Hitman.* New York: Skyhorse Publishing Company, Incorporated, 2007.

DeSario, Frankie. *Badge #1: True Stories from a Boston Cop.* Charleston, SC: The History Press, 2007.

Gilmartin, Kevin M. *Emotional Survival for Law Enforcement: A Guide for Officer and Their Families.* Tucson, AZ: E-S Press, 2002.

Hassine, Victor. *Life Without Parole: Living in Prison Today.* Cary, NC: Oxford University Press, 2007.

Hicks, Wendy L. *Police Vehicular Pursuits: Constitutionality, Liability and Negligence.* Springfield, IL: Charles C. Thomas Publisher, Limited, 2007.

Lewis, Wendy. *Dumbest Criminals.* Chatswood, Australia: New Holland Publishers Pty., Limited, 2007.

Lofland, Lee. *Howdunit Police Procedure and Investigation.* Cincinnati: F & W Publications, Incorporated, 2007.

Lyman Michael D Staff. *Practical Drug Enforcement.* Boca Raton, FL: C R C Press LLC, 2006.

Miraglia, Greg. *Coming Out from Behind the Badge: Stories of Success and Advice from Police Officers Out on the Job.* Bloomington, IN: AuthorHouse, 2007.

National Public Safety Information Bureau. *National Directory of Law Enforcement Administrators, Correctional Institutions, and Related Agencies.* 2008 edition. Stevens Point, WI: National Public Safety Information Bureau, 2008.

Steverson, Leonard A. *Policing in America: A Reference Handbook.* Santa Barbara, CA: ABC-CLIO, Incorporated, 2007.

Sutton, Randy. *A Cop's Life.* New York: Saint Martin's Paperbacks, 2006.

Trautman, Neal E. *How to Be a Great Cop.* East Rutherford, NJ: Prentice Hall PTR, 2001.

Retail Security

Hayes, Read. *Retail Security and Loss Prevention.* New York: Palgrave Macmillan, 2007.

Secret Service

Holden, Henry. *To Be a U.S. Secret Service Agent.* St. Paul, MN: MBI Publishing Company LLC, 2006.

Melanson, Philip H. *The Secret Service: The Hidden History of an Engimatic Agency.* New York: Basic Books, 2005.

Petro, Joseph. *Standing Next to History: An Agent's Life Inside the Secret Service.* New York: Saint Martin's Press, 2006.

State Police

Glatt, John. *One Deadly Night: A State Trooper, Triple Homicide, and a Search for Justice.* New York: Saint Martin's Press, 2005.

Hogan, John I. *Turnpike Trooper.* Philadelphia: Xlibris Corporation, 2006.

Toland, Harry G. *Gentleman Trooper: How John C. Groome Shaped America's First State Police Force.* Westminster, MD: Heritage Books, 2007.

Technology

Snow, Robert L. *Technology and Law Enforcement: From Gumshoe to Gamma Rays.* Cary, NC: Greenwood Publishing Group, Incorporated, 2007.

Undercover Work

Richardson, Alex H. *Lines Crossed: The True Story of an Undercover Cop.* Lincoln, NE: iUniverse, Incorporated, 2007.

Rosenthal, Richard. *Rookie Cop: Deep Undercover in the Jewish Defense League.* Wellfleet, MA: Leapfrog Press, 2000.

B. Periodicals

Magazines, newspapers, membership bulletins, and newsletters may be helpful for finding information about a specific job category, finding a job in a specific field, or giving you insight into what certain jobs entail.

This list should serve as a beginning. There are many periodicals that are not listed because of space limitations. The subject matter of some periodicals may overlap with others. Periodicals also tend to come and go. Look in your local library or in the newspaper/magazine shop for other periodicals that might interest you.

Names, addresses, phone numbers, Web sites, and e-mail addresses have been included when available.

CAMPUS POLICE

Campus Law Enforcement Journal
International Association of Campus Law Enforcement Administrators
342 N Main Street
West Hartford, CT 06117
(860) 586-7517
(860) 586-7550 (fax)
E-mail: kbreseman@iaclea.org
http://www.lace

Campus Safety Magazine
3520 Challenger Street
Torrance, CA 90503
(310) 533-2400
(310) 533-2500 (fax)
order@bobit.com
http://www.bobit.com

CANINE UNIT

Canine Courier
United States Police Canine

c/o Russ Hess
PO Box 80
Springboro, OH 45066
(800) 531-1614
uspcadir@aol.com
http://www.uspcak9.com

CORRECTIONS

American Jails
1135 Professional Court
Hagerstown, MD 21740
(301) 790-3930
(301) 790-2941 (fax)
jails@worldnet.att.net
http://www.aja.org

Corrections Today
206 N Washington Street
Alexandria, VA 22314
(703) 224-0000
(703) 224-0179 (fax)
gdaley@aca.org
http://www.aca.org

CRIME/CRIMINOLOGY

Crime Beat
10 East 39th Street
New York, NY 10016
(212) 681-1017
(212) 532-4428 (fax)

Crime Control Digest
529 14th Street NW
Washington, DC 20045
(202) 662-7035
(703) 352-2323 (fax)

Criminology
Blackwell Publishing, Inc.
Commerce Place

350 Main Street
Malden, MA 02148
(781) 388-8206
(781) 388-8232 (fax)
http://www.blackwellpublishing.com

Criminology, Corrections and Police Science

Newark Public Library
5 Washington Street
Newark, NJ 07101

CRIMINAL JUSTICE

Criminal Justice Ethics

Institute for Criminal Justice Ethics
John Jay College/CUNY
555 West 57th Street
New York, NY 10019
(212) 237-8033
(212) 237-8030 (fax)
cjethics@jjay.cuny.edu
http://www.lib.jjay.cuny.edu

FBI

FBI Law Enforcement

U.S. Federal Bureau of Investigation
935 Pennsylvania Avenue NW
Washington, DC 20535
(202) 324-3000
http://www.fbi.gov

FORENSIC SCIENCE

Forensic Science and Medicine

Humana Press, Inc.
999 Riverview Drive
Totowa, NJ 07512
(973) 256-1699
(973) 256-8341 (fax)

humana@humanapr.com
http://humanapress.com

LAW ENFORCEMENT

Aele Law Enforcement Legal Center Monthly Law Summaries

841 West Touhy Avenue
Park Ridge, IL 60068
(847) 685-0700
(847) 685-9700 (fax)
aele@aol.com
http://www.aele.org

American Cop

Publishers Development Corp.
12345 World Trade Drive
San Diego, CA 92128
(858) 605-0253
(858) 605-0247 (fax)

American Police Beat

One Brattle Square
Cambridge, MA 02138
(617) 491-8878
(617) 354-6515 (fax)

Chief of Police

National Association of Chiefs of Police, Inc.
6350 Horizon Drive
Titusville, FL 32780
(321) 264-0911
(321) 321-264-0911 (fax)
policeinfo@aphf.org
http://www.aphf.org/nacop.html

Community Policing Exchange

1726 M Street NW
Washington, DC 20036
(800) 833-3085
(202) 833-9295 (fax)

cpc@communitypolicing.org
http://www.communitypolicing.org

Law and Order Magazine
130 North Waukegan Road
Deerfield, IL 60015
(847) 444-3300
(847) 444-3333 (fax)
info@hendonpub.com

Law Officer
International Conference of Police Associations
60 East 42nd Street
New York, NY 10017
(888) 456-5367
http://www.lawofficermagazine.com

National Police Journal
3033 Excelsior Boulevard
Minneapolis, MN 55416
http://www.policemag.com

Police Magazine
3520 Challenger Street
Torrence, CA 90503
(310) 533-2400
http://www.policemag.com

Police and Security News
Lomond Publications, Inc.
PO Box 88
Mt. Airy, MD 21771
(301) 829-1496
http://www.policeandsecuritynews.com

LAW ENFORCEMENT EMPLOYMENT/ PERSONNEL

Law Enforcement Employment Bulletin
Quinlan Publishing Group
610 Opperman Drive

Eagan, MN 55123
(617) 542-0048
(800) 227-7097 (fax)
info@quinlan.com
http://west.thomson.com/quinlan

Management and Supervision of Law Enforcement Personnel
1333 North US Highway 17-92
Longwood, FL 32750
(407) 695-9500
info@gouldlaw.com
http://www.gouldlaw.com

Police Career Digest
PO Box 7772
Winter Haven, FL 33883
(239) 293-1159

LAW ENFORCEMENT TECHNOLOGY

Law Enforcement Technology
Cygnus Business Media, Inc.
1233 Janesville Avenue
Fort Atkinson, WI 53538
(920) 568-8307
(920) 563-1699 (fax)

POLICE NEGOTIATION

International Journal of Police Negotiations and Crisis Management
Society of Police and Criminal Psychology
Texas State University
Hines Academic Center
San Marcos, TX 78666
(512) 245-2174
(512) 245-8063 (fax)

PRIVATE INVESTIGATION

PI Magazine

4400 Route 9 South
PO Box 7198
Freehold, NJ 07728
(732) 308-3800
(732) 308-3314 (fax)
http://www.pimagazine.com

PROBATION

Federal Probation

U.S. Administrative Office of the United States
Courts
Federal Corrections and Supervision Division
1 Columbus Circle, NE
Washington, DC 20544
(202) 502-1600
(202) 502-2250 (fax)
http://www.access.gpo.gov

RESEARCH

Center for Law Enforcement Research

International Association of Chiefs of Police, Inc.
13 Firstfield Road
PO Box 61650
Gaithersburg, MD 20878
information@theiacp.org

INDEX